CLOSED SYSTEMS AND OPEN MINDS:

THE LIMITS OF NAÏVETY IN SOCIAL ANTHROPOLOGY

CLOSED SYSTEMS
AND OPEN MINDS:
THE LIMITS OF NAÏVETY
IN
SOCIAL ANTHROPOLOGY

Edited by
MAX GLUCKMAN

ALDINE PUBLISHING COMPANY

CHICAGO

Copyright © 1964, Max Gluckman, Ely Devons,
V. W. Turner, F. G. Bailey, A. L. Epstein, Tom
Lupton, Shiela Cunnison, William Watson

First Published 1964 by Aldine Publishing Company
64 East Van Buren Street, Chicago, Illinois 60605
Published in Great Britain by Oliver & Boyd Ltd.
Edinburgh and London

Library of Congress Catalog Card Number 64-21372

Printed in Great Britain

PREFACE

This book consists of essays written during the years 1957-58 by members at various times of the Department of Social Anthropology and Sociology at the University of Manchester. The Department had agreed to present a series of papers on a common theme to a meeting of the Association of Social Anthropologists in Edinburgh in September 1957. The Association was at that time hoping to publish Memoirs covering its proceedings, and it planned that groups of members would prepare each Memoir. Research at Manchester had covered the study of African tribes and Indian villages in the traditional field of anthropology, but members of the Department had also studied factories, villages, and other fields of social relationship in Britain. Working in these diverse fields we became interested in the question of what was common in our methods and analyses, and how they were distinguished from and related to those of other social and human sciences. This question had been discussed with colleagues in other subjects in the Faculty of Economic and Social Studies, particularly with Professors Ely Devons in Economics, Dorothy Emmet in Philosophy, and W. J. M. Mackenzie in Government.

One of the issues which recurred in these discussions and was raised frequently by Devons was, what basic assumptions were implied by social anthropologists in their work? Another issue, related to this, was by what criteria social anthropologists decided how to limit the field of their studies? Naturally this led to argument about the effect of these assumptions and limitations on the significance of social anthropological analysis. The Department therefore decided to read papers to the Association meeting at Edinburgh dealing with these twin themes. The arguments were not in general or theoretically methodological terms, save for a brief introduction by Gluckman, but each contributing member of the Department analysed a recent piece of his research with these two issues in mind. At an early stage of the discussions, Gluckman suggested that social anthropologists were justified in making "naïve" assumptions outside their own field of study: indeed they had a duty to be naïve, but this naïvety would limit the conclusions that could be drawn from their analyses. It was decided, therefore, to make "the limits of naïvety in social research" the common theme of the Manchester contribution to the Edinburgh meeting.

The papers by Lupton and Cunnison, by Epstein, and by Watson, published here, were given at Edinburgh in 1957. We stress the date because Epstein's theory predicts later developments; and Watson puts forward a theory which has been independently put forward, at least in part, by later publications, such as Whyte's *The Organization Man* (1957). Turner's paper was presented at the following meeting of the Association of Social Anthropologists at University College, London, in March 1958.

The Association found it impossible to undertake the financial obligation of publishing Memoirs, and we decided to try to collect further papers around the main theme from present and former members of the Department and independently to publish these in a book. Bailey read his paper to a seminar late in 1958, but others who hoped to write articles on aspects of the problem which we wished to cover, were in the end not able to do so.

All the papers were discussed at seminars in Manchester, and Devons, who had been closely associated with the Department of Social Anthropology since its foundation at Manchester, attended most of these seminars. He agreed, though not an anthropologist, to join with Gluckman in writing a commentary on the essays and the problems in general. It became clear in discussion that the issues involved were important in other social sciences, and Devons, as an economist, stressed particularly the manner in which they affected economics. This accounts for the references to economics in the introductory and concluding chapters. But these chapters are concerned primarily with the problems which face social anthropologists, and the references to economics (like those to psycho-analysis) are included to emphasise that the issues discussed throughout the book are important in all social and behavioural sciences. In order to anticipate criticism we here state that the references to economics are included merely for this purpose: a full discussion of these problems in economics would require another book.

Writing the introductory and concluding chapters jointly raised a few difficulties. We have agreed throughout on the central methodological issues: indeed, it was this general agreement about problems of studying society, and about the nature of knowledge itself, which helped stimulate our interest in each other's subjects at Manchester. We have worked out our own contribution to this book through long discussion and several written versions. Despite the fact that we brought to our task different expertise and experience, we never disagreed on methodological issues. We had to strive for clarity, not for accommodation. We did differ on a few occasions in our evaluation of specific hypotheses, and in our judgment on what material from outside the essays in this book we should use to illustrate our argument. Though we both believe that the problem arises in all sciences, we repeat that the book is about social anthropology; hence Gluckman selected for discussion the work that he considered had raised major problems for anthropologists. It would have been tedious for the reader had we tried to denote any difference in emphasis that Devons would have placed on these problems, and we have therefore throughout used the phrasing, "We . . . ."

The general issues have been discussed by other writers, but mainly in theoretical terms and with a different emphasis from ours. We have not had space to do more than indicate by reference some of these other discussions, and here we pay our tribute of thanks to those writers.

Publication of the book was delayed while we waited for the other hoped-for essays, so that we could discuss them in our general commentary; and then the writing of this commentary was further delayed by Devon's move from Manchester to London, and by vicissitudes which afflicted us—unfortunately for our joint task—at different times. We are grateful to our colleagues for their patience in waiting for us to complete our own part of the book while their essays lay unpublished; and we are above all grateful to them for the stimulus their work has given us, and for allowing us to discuss critically their presentation of the issues, which their essays helped to clarify. We have printed the date when each of the essays was written to make clear that the writers are not responsible for failures to refer to work published after that date. We note here too that, as the symposium grew, later contributors had available the texts of those essays already completed and were able to deal at greater length with problems raised in these. All the contributors have read our conclusions in draft, but of course we take sole responsibility for the argument and interpretation we have put forward. Drs Lupton and Cunnison do not accept some of our comments on their essay, and Dr Cunnison has at the last moment rewritten the section on Dee Garment Company to clarify the basis of her argument.

We thank also the members of the Association of Social Anthropologists who discussed four of the papers published here, and particularly Professor I. Schapera, who was at the time Chairman of the Association. Gluckman had stimulating comments from anthropologists at the Australian National University in 1960. Professors Dorothy Emmet and W. J. M. Mackenzie, and Dr R. J. Frankenberg of Manchester University, as well as Mr A. B. Cherns, Professor M. Fortes, Mrs M. Gluckman, Professor Harry Johnson, Mrs Lorraine Baric, Professor M. G. Marwick, Dr Robin Mackenzie and Dr Richard Skemp have criticised our draft constructively.

Gluckman thanks also the Behavioural Sciences Division of the Ford Foundation for a generous grant to him for his personal research: through this grant we were able to secure the help of Mr Norman Long, a research student at Manchester with a training in philosophy as well as social anthropology. He worked through many books to trace how they treated our problems, and he commented pertinently on our argument. The Ford Foundation's grant also eased the burden of editorial work. Dr Moses Tyson was generous with library facilities.

Our colleagues have asked us to make acknowledgement to the sponsors of their field research, on which the essays were based:

Dr F. G. Bailey to the Treasury Committee for Studentships in Foreign Languages and Cultures;

Dr A. L. Epstein to the Rhodes-Livingstone Institute and the Colonial Social Science Research Council;

Dr T. Lupton and Dr Sheila Cunnison to the Human Sciences Committee of the Department of Scientific and Industrial Research;

Dr V. W. Turner to the Rhodes-Livingstone Institute;

Dr W. Watson to the Medical Research Council.

ELY DEVONS
MAX GLUCKMAN

July 1962

CONTENTS

PREFACE

*The aim of science is to seek the simplest explanation of complex facts. We are apt to fall into the error of thinking that the facts are simple because simplicity is the goal of our quest. The guiding motto in the life of every natural philosopher should be, Seek simplicity and distrust it.—*WHITEHEAD.

*The Attorney-General has asked us where we are to draw the line. The answer is that it is not necessary to draw it at any precise point. It is enough for us to say that the present case is on the right side of any reasonable line that could be drawn.—*LORD COLERIDGE, C. J.

I

Ely Devons & Max Gluckman

INTRODUCTION

Social anthropology, defined operationally in terms of what social anthropologists have done during the last fifty years, is the study and comparison of tribal societies and of small fields of social life with emphasis on the role of custom. Initially, anthropologists studied island and other small tribal communities in India, Australia, the South Seas, and North America, but even when they moved to the larger tribes and nations of Africa they were still dealing with relatively isolated, and in a sense complete, societies. Later, they began to study rural communities and villages in Europe, America, and Asia, and factories and sets of relations such as those of peer-groups of adolescents in cities: here they were clearly dealing with sub-systems or domains which are contained in larger social systems. During these years, political and economic developments also began to reduce the isolation of tribal communities, particularly as their members were drawn into towns and industrial employment, where anthropologists followed them. The task of isolating a field of study became increasingly difficult.

In analysing the data they collected, anthropologists separated into several distinct disciplines out of the former general subject called "anthropology," which studied not only the social life, customs, and tools of tribes but also the physical constitution of man. From this general anthropology have emerged physical anthropology, cultural anthropology, psychological anthropology,[1] and social anthropology, each increasingly associating itself with those biological, behavioural, and

[1] We thus refer to the cross-cultural study of personality.

social sciences, whose problems and modes of interpretation are most akin to its own. We shall in future refer to social anthropologists among these as "anthropologists" only, unless the context requires us to distinguish them from other anthropologists.

Social anthropologists have found that their interpretations have much in common with the interpretations of sociologists, many of whom derive from a different tradition, so that Firth has defined social anthropology as "micro-sociology,"[2] the "concentrated observation of small-unit behaviour. . . ." Yet the analysis of a social anthropologist is different from that of a sociometrician, or a sociologist or social psychologist studying a small group. Firth gives the distinguishing characteristics of social anthropology as its intensive, detailed, and systematic observation of people in group relations, its attempt to look at all aspects of the group's life, and its comparative emphasis. For the time being, we state baldly that we think an interest in *custom* is the attribute, derived from its tradition, which social anthropology distinctively applies to the study of small social fields; we shall refine this definition in our conclusion.[3] Here we have said enough to stress that not only does the social anthropologist have to isolate his field out of the complex reality he observes, as any scientist has to do, but he also has to determine what he can do with his techniques and modes of analysis as against what can be done with those of other kinds of anthropologists, and of sociologists, political scientists, economists, psychologists, physiologists, ecologists, and other scholars who are studying the same material.

Here, specifically, are the sort of questions which the social anthropologist must consider. The most striking objects in a social field are the actions, the thoughts, and the feelings of individuals, within a cultural and historical tradition in a physical environment on which they operate through material objects. Clearly the biological endowment of individuals and their personalities, both in general and in their particular variations, have important effects within the social field: and the anthropologist has to study these effects. Need he concern

---

[2] R. Firth, *Elements of Social Organization* [1951], pp. 17 ff.; and "The Future of Social Anthropology," in *Man*, [1944], No. 8.

[3] See below, pp. 254-9.

himself with the complex interdependencies which produce these effects, or with the theories that have been advanced to explain these interdependencies? In analysing a social field[4] one has to write about the thoughts, the feelings, the purposes, and the motives of individuals; and all social anthropologists speak of incumbents of social roles loving, hating, pursuing ambitions. Presumably they know that many learned studies have been concerned to define these emotions, and to discuss their relation to one another. Should the anthropologist become involved in these studies? How sophisticated does his knowledge of psychological and psycho-analytical theories have to be, if his anthropological analysis is not to go astray? Can he afford to be "naïve"—"artless"—about what he knows to be complex, and treat it as simple, crude, or gross, while he gets on with his own job?

Problems for decision thus arise when the anthropologist's work touches on individuals, clearly the subject of psychological analysis. Similar problems arise when we consider the wider physical and biological environment within which men live: geographical position, topography, climate, soil and other resources, flora and fauna, endemic and epidemic diseases, all have important effects on social life. Must the anthropologist delineate accurately the interrelations between these phenomena, and study climatological and ecological and other systems? Or can he again take these phenomena, for his purposes, as simple, though he knows them to be complex?

The anthropologist may want to study a particular group, or set of relationships, or domain of activities, which is only part of a larger or more complex social field. How far is it possible to isolate these areas of the field for significant study? In this situation, the incumbents of roles in the social relations studied may occupy other roles in a whole series of other relations. Must all be studied, to understand one? Since wider social systems and smaller areas of relations have long histories, far longer than the period which an anthropological study investigates, how do we decide when to cut short our explora-

---

[4] The concept of a field of social relations has been most clearly stated by M. Fortes in *The Dynamics of Clanship among the Tallensi* [1945], Ch. xiii, and pp. 103, 137, 233, 245. See also Firth, *Elements of Social Organization*, pp. 10-28. Cf. in psychology K. Lewin, *Field Theory in Social Science* [1952].

tion of the past? The culture of a group studied may be part of a far wider culture, as an Indian village is of Hinduism, or a Bedouin tribe of Islam, or a factory and a school of England: can we fruitfully study the small group, in isolation from the whole? And what does the study of a small group tell us about the larger system of which it is part?

These are some of the problems which the anthropologist may meet in trying to isolate one aspect of reality for his own analysis from the aspects of reality studied by other disciplines, or in trying to close off his own field of analysis from the rest of reality. In this book we are trying to clarify the problems which inevitably arise because it is possible to study only a limited number of events, in a limited way, at one time.

We considered that it would not be fruitful to expound this discussion in abstract terms, since abstract exposition of many methodological problems either has made them appear more intractable than they are in practice, or has concealed diffi- culties within general formulae. It seemed more fruitful for a number of social anthropologists, dealing with specific pro- blems, to set out explicitly what they thought and did when they came to the limits of their competence—*i.e.*, how and why they decided they must follow or need not follow the facts, and pursue or not pursue their analyses, beyond a certain point; what difference they considered it would make to their own work if events outside their area of observation were different from the view they take on these events; how relevant it would be to their own analyses if different and possibly contradictory interpretations of those other events were made by scholars in other disciplines; and what limits their competence and assumptions placed on their analyses. Not every author dis- cusses these issues explicitly. But the problems are present in all the essays.

In our first planning of this book we treated the various issues as coming under one general head: the problem of whether we had to be sophisticated or could afford to be naïve, about both the events and the aspects of interrelationship which bordered our field and method of study. We called this "the limits of naïvety." But early in our discussions we realised that we were dealing with several closely interrelated issues. First, any social scientist has to confine what he studies within certain limits: he cannot include the whole of complex reality. This limitation is vital if his study is to be manageable. The limitation can be of various kinds—a limitation in time, in space, or in the aspect of phenomena which is studied. With the limitation goes simplification, which also seems necessary in order to isolate what appear to be the essential features of the problem under examination. Within the field thus de-limited and isolated the social scientist assumes that there is a system of interrelations which can be considered separately from the rest of reality. Such systems are, so to speak, "closed." Whether closure in a particular way is fruitful or not must always be open to question, and the issue will usually be affected by the particular problems and questions that are being investigated. As well as using a "closed system," the social scientist has to make assumptions about aspects of the phenomena which are studied by other specialists. These assumptions are often, and, we argue, advisedly, "naïve."

These two issues—limiting the field of study and making naïve assumptions outside one's specialist field—are closely interrelated, and not all the contributors kept them separate, while each of the contributors has come across each issue to a varying degree in considering his own problems. In addition, as a group we were not clear about the issues when the essays were first prepared. Hence different contributors use the con-cepts of "naïvety" and of "closure" in different ways.

These problems also gave us a choice of titles for the book. In the end we decided on *Closed Systems and Open Minds*, which reflects our view on the first set of issues, but with the sub-title *The Limits of Naïvety in Social Anthropology*, which refers mainly to the second set.

As we worked out these two sets of issues, five distinct pro-cedures emerged: circumscribing a field; incorporating complex facts without analysis; abridging the conclusions of other sciences; making naïve assumptions about aspects of reality other than those under investigation; and simplifying events within the field under investigation. We shall analyse these procedures in our concluding commentary: to do so here might obscure the arguments of our colleagues' essays, each of which stands in its own right.

We are sure that these essays, in which our colleagues explain

B

how they decided that they had reached the appropriate limits of their own field and how they could, or could not, fruitfully stop their analyses at these limits, will be helpful to both practitioners and students of social science. We hope that our own attempt to examine the methodological problems involved, in which we were guided by the essays, will clarify the general issues. More specifically, the book may indicate what the field of "social anthropology" is.

We hope too—though, we fear, vainly—that the book may help to avoid some of the sterile dispute that is engendered when a critic complains that an author has not dealt with the critic's problems, instead of his own, or when a critic complains that the author has made statements that are naïve in terms of some other specialism. For example, some psychologists criticise economics because of its simple and crude assumptions about human motivation; and some psychologists criticise social anthropology because it neglects the complexity of the structure of the personality. But the economist or anthropologist may be making these neglectful assumptions knowingly and deliberately. We argue that the issue is not whether the assumptions are crude, but rather whether they materially affect the analysis and conclusions of economist and anthropologist. Conversely, when one asks whether an anthropologist or economist is justified in criticising the work of a pyschologist because it ignores the complexity of culture and social structure, or of the economic system, the issue is similar: it is not whether the psychologist is making "silly" sociological or economic assumptions or is ignoring important social and economic aspects of reality, but whether the limitations of his study and the naïve assumptions he makes do, or do not, invalidate his analysis of the particular problem with which he is concerned. We argue to the opposite effect, that it is highly dangerous to trespass beyond the limits of one's competence, and that to exercise this competence one must abstain from becoming involved in the problems of others.

If the aim of research is to analyse the several aspects of a complex situation, scientists from several disciplines may have to collaborate: this does not dispose of the necessity for each to delimit his own field of study, and to work with techniques, data, and concepts appropriate to analysis of that field. The process of combining the results of these several studies raises another complicated series of problems.

Experience of research and teaching has persuaded us to favour specialisation and keeping to one's own last in the social sciences in order to develop theoretical understanding. We are not in this book concerned with the question of how to apply the understanding thus gained to the practical problems of dealing with social issues and policies. Whether specialisation. and its procedures of limiting a field of study and making naïve assumptions, are also appropriate in applying the social sciences is a different, and in our view probably an even more complex, issue than the one with which we attempt to deal.

2

V. W. Turner

SYMBOLS IN NDEMBU RITUAL

[written in 1957]

SOME PRELIMINARY DEFINITIONS

Among the Ndembu of Northern Rhodesia, the importance of ritual in the lives of the villagers is striking. Hardly a week passes, in a small neighbourhood, without a ritual drum being heard in one or other of its villages.

By "ritual" I mean prescribed formal behaviour for occasions not given over to technological routine, having reference to beliefs in mystical beings or powers. The symbol is the smallest unit of ritual which still retains the specific properties of ritual behaviour; it is the ultimate unit of specific structure in a ritual context. Since this essay is in the main a description and analysis of the structure and properties of symbols, it will be enough to state here, following the *Concise Oxford Dictionary*, that a "symbol" is a thing regarded by general consent as naturally typifying or representing or recalling something by possession of analogous qualities or by association in fact or thought. The symbols I observed in the field were, empirically, objects, activities, relationships, events, gestures, and spatial units in a ritual situation.

Following the advice and example of Professor Monica Wilson, I asked Ndembu specialists as well as laymen to interpret the symbols of their ritual. As a result, I obtained much exegetic material. I felt that it was methodologically important to keep observational and interpretative material distinct from one another. The reason for this will soon become apparent.

I found that I could not analyse ritual symbols without

studying them in a time-series in relation to other "events." For symbols are essentially involved in social process. I came to see performances of ritual as distinct phases in the social processes whereby groups became adjusted to internal changes and adapted to their external environment. From this stand-point the ritual symbol becomes a factor in social action, a positive force in an activity-field. The symbol becomes associated with human interests, purposes, ends, and means, whether these are explicitly formulated or have to be inferred from the observed behaviour. The structure and properties of a symbol become those of a dynamic entity, at least within its appropriate context of action.

STRUCTURE AND PROPERTIES OF RITUAL SYMBOLS

The structure and properties of ritual symbols may be inferred from three classes of data:

(*a*) External form and observable characteristics.

(*b*) Interpretations offered
(1) by specialists
(2) by laymen.

(*c*) Significant contexts largely worked out by the anthropologist.

Here is an example. At Nkang'a, the girl's puberty ritual, a novice is wrapped in a blanket and laid at the foot of a *mudyi* sapling. The *mudyi* tree (*Diplorrhyncus mossambicensis*) is conspicuous for its white latex, which exudes in milky beads if the thin bark is scratched. For Ndembu this is its most important observable characteristic. I therefore propose to call it "the milk-tree" henceforward. Most Ndembu women can attribute several meanings to this tree. In the first place, they say that the milk-tree is the "senior (*mukulumpi*)" tree of the ritual. Each kind of ritual has this "senior" or, as I will call it, "dominant" symbol. Such symbols fall into a special class which I will discuss more fully later. Here it is enough to state that dominant symbols are regarded not merely as means to the fulfilment of the avowed purposes of a given ritual but also and more importantly refer to values which are regarded as ends in themselves, *i.e.*, to axiomatic values. Secondly, the women say with reference to its observable characteristics that the milk-tree stands for human breast-milk and also for the breasts which supply it. They relate this meaning to the fact that Nkang'a is performed when a girl's breasts begin to ripen, not after her first menstruation, which is the subject of another and less elaborate ritual. The main theme of Nkang'a is indeed the tie of nurturance between mother and child, not the bond of birth. This theme of nurturance is expressed at Nkang'a in a number of supplementary symbols indicative of the act of feeding and of foodstuffs. In the third place, the women describe the milk-tree as "the tree of a mother and her child." Here the reference has shifted from description of a biological act, breast-feeding, to a social tie of profound significance both in domestic relations and in the structure of the widest Ndembu community. This latter meaning is brought out most clearly in a text I recorded from a male ritual specialist. I translate literally.

The milk-tree is the place of all mothers of the lineage (*ivumu*, literally "womb" or "stomach"). It represents the ancestress of women and men. The milk-tree is where our ancestress slept when she was initiated. "To initiate" here means the dancing of women round and round the milk-tree where the novice sleeps. One ancestress after another slept there down to our grandmother and our mother and ourselves the children. That is the place of our tribal custom (*muchidi*),[1] where we began, even men just the same, for men are circumcised under a milk-tree.

This text brings out clearly those meanings of the milk-tree which refer to principles and values of social organisation. At one level of abstraction the milk-tree stands for matriliny, the principle on which the continuity of Ndembu society depends. Matriliny governs succession to office and inheritance of property, and it vests dominant rights of residence in local units. More than any other principle of social organisation it confers order and structure on Ndembu social life. But beyond this, "*mudyi*" means more than matriliny, both according to this text and according to many other statements I have collected. It stands for tribal custom (*muchidi wetu*) itself. The principle of matriliny, vertebral in Ndembu social organisation, as an element in the semantic structure of the milk-tree, itself sym-

---

[1] *Muchidi* also means "category," "kind," "species," and "tribe" itself.

bolises the total system of interrelations between groups and persons which makes up Ndembu society. Some of the meanings of important symbols may themselves be symbols, each with its own system of meanings. At its highest level of abstraction, therefore, the milk-tree stands for the unity and continuity of Ndembu society. Both men and women are components of that spatio-temporal continuum. Perhaps that is why one educated Ndembu, trying to cross the gap between our cultures, explained to me that the milk-tree was like the British flag above the administrative headquarters: *"Mudyi* is our flag," he said.

When discussing the milk-tree symbolism in the context of the girl's puberty ritual, informants tend to stress the harmonising, cohesive aspects of the milk-tree symbolism. They also stress the aspect of dependence. The child depends on its mother for nutriment: similarly, say the Ndembu, the tribesman drinks from the breasts of tribal custom. Thus nourishment and learning are equated in the meaning content of the milk-tree. I have often heard the milk-tree compared to "going to school"; the child is said to swallow instruction as a baby swallows milk and *kapudyi*, the thin cassava gruel which Ndembu liken to milk. And do we not ourselves speak of "a thirst for knowledge"? Here the milk-tree is a shorthand for the process of instruction in tribal matters which follows the critical episode in both boys' and girls' initiation—circumcision in the case of the boys and the long trial of lying motionless in that of the girls. The mother's role is the archetype of protector, nourisher, and teacher. For example, a chief is often referred to as the "mother of his people," while the hunter-doctor who initiates a novice into a hunting cult is called "the mother of huntsmanship *(mama dawuyang'a)."* An apprentice circumciser is referred to as "child of the circumcision medicine" and his instructor as "mother of the circumcision medicine." In all the senses hitherto described the milk-tree represents harmonious, benevolent aspects of domestic and tribal life.

But when the third mode of interpretation, contextual analysis, is applied, the interpretations of informants are contradicted by the way people actually behave with reference to the milk-tree. It becomes clear that the milk-tree represents aspects of social differentiation, and even opposition between the components of a society which ideally it is supposed to sym-

bolise as a harmonious whole. The first relevant context we
shall examine is the role of the milk-tree in a series of action
situations within the framework of the girl's puberty ritual.
Symbols, as I have said, produce action, and dominant symbols
tend to become focuses of interaction. Groups mobilise around
them, worship before them, perform other symbolic activities
near them, and add other symbolic objects to them, often to
make composite shrines. Usually these groups of participants
themselves stand for important components of the secular social
system, whether these components consist of corporate groups,
such as families and lineages, or of mere categories of persons
possessing similar characteristics such as old men, women,
children, hunters, or widows. In each kind of Ndembu ritual
a different group or category becomes the focal social element.
In Nkang'a this focal element is the unity of Ndembu women.
It is the women who dance around the milk-tree and initiate
the recumbent novice by making her the hub of their whirling
circle. Not only is the milk-tree the "flag of the Ndembu";
more specifically, in the early phases of Nkang'a, it is the "flag"
of Ndembu women. In this situation it does more than focus
the exclusiveness of women; it mobilises them in opposition to
the men. For the women sing songs taunting the men, and for
a time will not let men dance in their circle. Therefore, if we
are to take account of the operational aspect of the milk-tree
symbol, including not only what Ndembu say about it but
also what they do with it in its "meaning," we must allow that
it distinguishes women as a social category and indicates their
solidarity.

But the milk-tree makes further discriminations. For example, in certain action contexts it stands for the novice
herself. One such context is the initial sacralisation of a specific
milk-tree sapling. Here the natural property of the tree's im-
maturity is significant. Informants say that a young tree is
chosen because the novice is young. The girl's particular tree
symbolises her new social personality as a mature woman. In
the past, and occasionally today, the girl's puberty ritual was
part of her marriage ritual, and marriage marked her transition
from girlhood to womanhood. Much of the training and most
of the symbolism of Nkang'a are concerned with making the
girl a sexually-accomplished spouse, a fruitful woman, and a

mother able to produce a generous supply of milk. For each girl this is a unique process. She is initiated alone and is the centre of public attention and care. From her point of view it is *her* Nkang'a, the most thrilling and self-gratifying phase of her life. Society recognises and encourages these sentiments, even though it also prescribes certain trials and hardships for the novice, who must suffer before she is glorified on the last day of the ritual. The milk-tree then, celebrates the coming-of-age of a new social personality, and distinguishes her from all other women at this one moment in her life. But, in terms of its action context, the milk-tree here also expresses the conflict between the girl and the moral community of adult women she is entering. Not without reason is the milk-tree site known as "the place of death" or "the place of suffering," terms also applied to the site where boys are circumcised, for the girl novice must not move a muscle throughout a whole hot and clamant day.

In other contexts the milk-tree site is the scene of opposition between the novice's own mother and the group of adult women. The mother is debarred from attending the ring of dancers. She is losing her child, although later she recovers her as an adult co-member of her lineage. Here we see the conflict between the matricentric family and the wider society which, as I have said, is dominantly articulated by the principle of matriliny. The relationship between mother and daughter persists throughout the ritual, but its content is changed. It is worth pointing out that, at one phase in Nkang'a, mother and daughter interchange portions of clothing. This may perhaps be related to the Ndembu custom whereby mourners wear small portions of a dead relative's clothing. Whatever the interchange of clothing may mean to a psycho-analyst—and here we arrive at one of the limits of our present anthropological competence—it seems not unlikely that Ndembu intend to symbolise the termination for both mother and daughter of an important aspect of their relationship. This is one of the symbolic actions—one of very few—about which I found it impossible to elicit any interpretation in the puberty ritual. Hence it is legitimate to infer, in my opinion, that powerful unconscious wishes, of a kind considered illicit by Ndembu, are expressed in it.

Opposition between the tribeswomen and the novice's mother is mimetically represented at the milk-tree towards the end of the first day of the puberty ritual. The girl's mother cooks a huge meal of cassava and beans—both kinds of food are symbols in Nkang'a with many meanings—for the women visitors, who eat in village groups and not at random. Before eating, the women return to the milk-tree from their eating-place a few yards away and circle the tree in pcocession. The mother brings up the rear holding up a large spoon full of cassava and beans. Suddenly she shouts: "Who wants the cassava of *chipwampwilu?*" All the women rush to be first to seize the spoon and eat from it. *"Chipwampwilu"* appears to be an archaic word and no one knows its meaning. Informants say that the spoon represents the novice herself in her role of married woman, while the food stands both for her repro-ductive power (*lusemu*) and her role as cultivator and cook. One woman told my wife: "It is lucky if the person snatching the spoon comes from the novice's own village. Otherwise the mother believes that her child will go far away from her to a distant village and die there. The mother wants her child to stay near her." Implicit in this statement is a deeper conflict than that between the matricentric family and mature female society. It refers to another dominant articulating principle of Ndembu society, namely virilocal marriage according to which women live at their husbands' villages after marriage. Its effect is sometimes to separate mothers from daughters by consider-able distances. In the episode described the women symbolise the matrilineal cores of villages. Each village wishes to gain control through marriage over the novice's capacity to work. Its members also hope that her children will be raised in it, thus adding to its size and prestige. Later in Nkang'a there is a symbolic struggle between the novice's matrilineal kin and those of her bridegroom, which makes explicit the conflict between virilocality and matriliny.

Lastly, in the context of action situations the milk-tree is sometimes described by informants as representing the novice's own matrilineage. Indeed, it has this significance in the com-petition for the spoon just discussed. For women of her own village try to snatch the spoon before members of other villages. Even if such women do not belong to her matrilineage but are married to its male members they are thought to be acting on its behalf. Thus, the milk-tree in one of its action-aspects represents the unity and exclusiveness of a single matrilineage with a local focus in a village against other such corporate groups. The conflict between yet another sub-system and the total system is given dramatic and symbolic form.

By this time it will have become clear that considerable discrepancy exists between the interpretations of the milk-tree offered by informants and the behaviour exhibited by Ndembu in situations dominated by the milk-tree symbolism. Thus we are told that the milk-tree represents the close tie between mother and daughter. Yet the milk-tree separates a daughter from her mother. We are also told that the milk-tree stands for the unity of Ndembu society. Yet we find that in practice it separates women from men, and some categories and groups of women from others. How are these contradictions between principle and practice to be explained?

SOME PROBLEMS OF INTERPRETATION

I am convinced that my informants genuinely believed that the milk-tree represented only the linking and unifying aspects of Ndembu social organisation. I am equally convinced that the role of the milk-tree in action situations, where it represents a focus of specified groups in opposition to other groups, forms an equally important component of its total meaning. Here the important question must be asked, "meaning for whom?" For if Ndembu do not recognise the discrepancy between their interpretation of the milk-tree symbolism and their behaviour in connexion with it, does this mean that the discrepancy has no relevance for the social anthropologist? Indeed, some anthropologists claim, with Nadel, that "uncomprehended symbols have no part in social enquiry; their social effectiveness lies in their capacity to indicate, and if they indicate nothing to the actors, they are, from our point of view, irrelevant, and indeed no longer symbols (whatever their significance for the psychologist or psycho-analyst)."[2] Professor Monica Wilson holds a similar point of view. She writes that she stresses "Nyakyusa interpretations of their own rituals, for anthropo-

[2] S. F. Nadel, *Nupe Religion* [1954], p. 108.

logical literature is bespattered with symbolic guessing, the ethnographer's interpretations of the rituals of other people".[3] Indeed, she goes so far as to base her whole analysis of Nyakyusa ritual on "the Nyakyusa translation or interpretation of the symbolism." In my view, these investigators go beyond the limits of salutary caution and impose serious, and even arbitrary, limitations on themselves. To some extent their difficulties derive from their failure to distinguish the concept of *symbol* from that of a mere *sign*. Although I am in complete disagreement with his fundamental postulate that the collective unconscious is the main formative principle in ritual symbolism, I consider that Carl Jung has cleared the way for further investigation by making just this distinction. "A sign," he says, "is an analogous or abbreviated expression of a *known* thing. But a symbol is always the best possible expression of a relatively *unknown* fact, a fact, however, which is none the less recognised or postulated as existing."[4] Nadel and Wilson, in treating most ritual symbols as signs, must ignore or regard as irrelevant some of the crucial properties of such symbols.

FIELD SETTING AND STRUCTURAL PERSPECTIVE

How, then, can a social anthropologist justify his claim to be able to interpret a society's ritual symbols more deeply and comprehensively than the actors themselves? In the first place the anthropologist, by the use of his special techniques and concepts, is able to view the performance of a given kind of ritual as "occurring in, and being interpenetrated by, a totality of coexisting social entities such as various kinds of groups, subgroups, categories, or personalities, and also barriers between them, and modes of interconnexion."[5] In other words, he can place this ritual in its significant field setting, and describe the structure and properties of that field. On the other hand, each participant in the ritual views it from his own particular corner of observation. He has what Lupton has called his own "structural perspective." His vision is circumscribed by his occupancy of a particular position, or even of a set of situationally con-

---

[3] M. Wilson, *Rituals of Kinship among the Nyakyusa* [1957], p. 6.
[4] C. G. Jung, *Psychological Types* [1949], p. 601.
[5] Lewin, *Field Theory in Social Science*, p. 200.

flicting positions, both in the persisting structure of his society, and also in the rôle structure of the given ritual. Moreover, the participant is likely to be governed in his actions by a number of interests, purposes, and sentiments, dependent upon his specific position, which impair his understanding of the total situation. An even more serious obstacle against his achieving objectivity is the fact that he tends to regard as axiomatic and primary the ideals, values and norms which are overtly expressed or symbolised in the ritual. Thus, in the Nkang'a ritual, each person or group in successive contexts of action, sees the milk-tree only as representing her or their own specific interests and values at those times. But the anthropologist who has previously made a structural analysis of Ndembu society, isolating its organisational principles, and distinguishing its groups and relationships, has no particular bias, and can observe the real interconnexions and conflicts between groups and persons, in so far as these receive ritual representation. What is meaningless for an actor playing a specific role, may well be highly significant for an observer and analyst of the total system.

On these grounds, therefore, I consider it legitimate to include within the total meaning of a dominant ritual symbol, aspects of behaviour associated with it which the actors themselves are unable to interpret, and indeed of which they may be unaware, if they are asked to interpret the symbol outside its activity-context. But there still remains for us the problem of the contradiction between the expressed meanings of the milk-tree symbol and the meaning of the stereotyped forms of behaviour closely associated with it. Indigenous interpretations of the milk-tree symbolism in the abstract appear to indicate that there is no incompatibility or conflict between the persons and groups to which it refers. Yet, as we have seen, it is between just such groups that conflict is mimed at the milk-tree site.

THREE PROPERTIES OF RITUAL SYMBOLS

But before we can interpret, we must further classify our descriptive data, collected by the methods described above. Such a classification will enable us to state some of the properties of ritual symbols. The simplest property is that of *condensation.* Many things and actions, etc., are represented in a single formation. Secondly, a dominant symbol is a *unification of disparate significata.* The disparate *significata* are interconnected by virtue of their common possession of analogous qualities or by association in fact or thought. Such qualities or links of association may in themselves be quite trivial, or random, or widely distributed over a range of phenomena. Their very generality enables them to bracket together the most diverse ideas and phenomena. Thus, as we have seen, the milk-tree stands for, *inter alia,* women's breasts, motherhood, a novice at Nkang'a, the principle of matriliny, a specific matrilineage, learning, and the unity and persistence of Ndembu society. The themes of nourishment and dependence run through all these diverse *significata.*

The third important property of dominant ritual symbols is *polarisation of meaning.* Not only the milk-tree, but all other dominant Ndembu symbols, possess two clearly distinguishable poles of meaning. At one pole is found a cluster of *significata* which refer to components of the moral and social orders of Ndembu society, to principles of social organisation, to kinds of corporate grouping, and to the norms and values inherent in structural relationships. At the other pole, the *significata* are usually natural and physiological phenomena and processes. Let us call the first of these the "ideological pole," and the second the "sensory pole." At the sensory pole, the meaning content is closely related to the outward form of the symbol. Thus one meaning of the milk-tree—breast milk—is closely related to the exudation of milky latex from the tree. One sensory meaning of another dominant symbol, the *mukula* tree, is blood; and this tree secretes a dusky red gum.

At the sensory pole are concentrated those *significata* that may be expected to arouse desires and feelings; at the ideological pole one finds an arrangement of norms and values which guide and control persons as members of social groups and categories. The sensory, emotional *significata* tend to be "gross" in a double sense. In the first place they are gross in a general way, taking no account of detail, or the precise qualities of emotion. For it cannot be sufficiently stressed that such symbols are social facts, "collective representations," even though their appeal is to the lowest common denominator of human feeling. The

second sense of "gross" is "frankly, even flagrantly, physiological." Thus the milk-tree has the gross meanings of breast-
milk, breasts, and the process of breast-feeding. These are also
gross in the sense that they represent items of universal Ndembu
experience. Other Ndembu symbols, at their sensory poles of
meaning, represent such themes as blood, male and female
genitalia, semen, urine, and faeces. The *same* symbols, at their
ideological poles of meaning, represent the unity and continuity of social groups, primary and associational, domestic,
and political.

REFERENCE AND CONDENSATION

It has long been recognised in anthropological literature
that ritual symbols are stimuli of emotion. Perhaps the most
striking statement of this position is that made by Edward Sapir
in the *Encyclopaedia of the Social Sciences* (xiv. 492-3). Sapir
distinguishes, in a way which recalls Jung's distinction, between
two principal classes of symbols. The first he calls *referential*
symbols. These include such forms as oral speech, writing,
national flags, flag signalling, and other organisations of
symbols which are agreed upon as economical devices for
purposes of reference. Like Jung's "sign," the referential symbol
is predominantly cognitive and refers to known facts. The
second class, which includes most ritual symbols, consists of
condensation symbols, which Sapir defines as "highly condensed
forms of substitutive behaviour for direct expression, allowing
for the ready release of emotional tension in conscious or
unconscious form." The condensation symbol is "saturated
with emotional quality." The chief difference in development
between these types of symbolism, in Sapir's view, is that
"while referential symbolism grows with formal elaboration in
the conscious, condensation symbolism strikes deeper and
deeper roots in the unconscious, and diffuses its emotional
quality to types of behaviour and situations apparently far
removed from the original meaning of the symbol."

Sapir's formulation is most illuminating. He lays explicit
stress on four main attributes of ritual symbols: (1) the condensation of many meanings in a single form; (2) economy of
reference; (3) predominance of emotional or orectic quality;

(4) associational linkages with regions of the unconscious. But he tends to underestimate the importance of what I have called the ideological (or, I would add, normative) pole of meaning. Ritual symbols are at one and the same time referential and condensation symbols, though each symbol is multi-referential rather than uni-referential. Their essential quality consists in their juxtaposition of the grossly physical and the structurally normative, of the organic and the social. Such symbols are coincidences of opposite qualities, unions of "high" and "low." We do not need a detailed acquaintance with any of the current depth-psychologies to suspect that this juxtaposition, and even interpenetration, of opposites in the symbol is connected with its social function. Durkheim was fascinated by the problem of why many social norms and imperatives were felt to be at the same time "obligatory" and "desirable." Ritual, scholars are coming to see, is precisely a mechanism which periodically converts the obligatory into the desirable. The basic unit of ritual, the dominant symbol, encapsulates the major properties of the total ritual process which brings about this transmutation. Within its framework of meanings, the dominant symbol brings the ethical and jural norms of society into close contact with strong emotional stimuli. In the action situation of ritual, with its social excitement and directly physiological stimuli, such as music, singing, dancing, alcohol, incense, and bizarre modes of dress, the ritual symbol, we may perhaps say, effects an interchange of qualities between its poles of meaning. Norms and values, on the one hand, become saturated with emotion, while the gross and basic emotions become ennobled through contact with social values. The irksomeness of moral constraint is transformed into the "love of virtue."

Before proceeding any further with our analysis, it might be as well to restate the major empirical properties of dominant symbols derived from our classification of the relevant descriptive data: (1) condensation; (2) unification of disparate meanings in a single symbolic formation; (3) polarisation of meaning.

DOMINANT AND INSTRUMENTAL SYMBOLS

Certain ritual symbols, as I have said, are regarded by

Ndembu as "dominant." In rituals performed to propitiate ancestor spirits who are believed to have afflicted their living kin with reproductive disorders, illness, or bad luck at hunting, there are two main classes of dominant symbols. The first class is represented by the first tree or plant in a series of trees or plants from which portions of leaves, bark, or roots are collected by practitioners or adepts in the curative cult. The subjects of ritual are marked with these portions mixed with water, or given them, mixed in a potion, to drink. The first tree so treated is called the "place of greeting *(ishikenu),*" or the "elder *(mukulumpi).*" The adepts encircle it several times to sacralise it. Then the senior practitioner prays at its base, which he sprinkles with powdered white clay. Prayer is made either to the named spirit, believed to be afflicting the principal subject of ritual, or to the tree itself, which is in some way identified with the afflicting spirit. Each *ishikenu* can be allotted several meanings by adepts. The second class of dominant symbols in curative rituals consists of shrines where the subjects of such rituals sit while the practitioners wash them with vegetable substances mixed with water and perform actions on their behalf of a symbolic or ritualistic nature. Such shrines are often composite, consisting of several objects in configuration. Both classes of dominant symbols are closely associated with non-empirical beings. Some are regarded as their repositories; others, as being identified with them; others again, as representing them. In life-crisis rituals, on the other hand, dominant symbols seem to represent not beings but non-empirical powers or kinds of efficacy. For example, in the boys' circumcision ritual, the dominant symbol for the whole ritual is a "medicine *(vitumbu),*" called "*nfunda,*" which is compounded from many ingredients *e.g.,* the ash of the burnt lodge which means "death," and the urine of an apprentice circumciser which means "virility." Each of these and other ingredients has many other meanings. The dominant symbol at the camp where the novices' parents assemble and prepare food for the boys is the *chikoli* tree, which represents, among other things, an erect phallus, adult masculinity, strength, hunting prowess, and health continuing into old age. The dominant symbol during the process of circumcision is the milk-tree, beneath which novices are circumcised. The dominant symbol in the

C

immediate post-circumcision phase is the red *mukula* tree, on which the novices sit until their wounds stop bleeding. Other symbols are dominant at various phases of seclusion. Each of these symbols is described as "*mukulumpi* (elder, senior)." Dominant symbols appear in many different ritual contexts, sometimes presiding over the whole procedure, sometimes over particular phases. The meaning-content of certain dominant symbols possesses a high degree of constancy and consistency throughout the total symbolic system, exemplifying Radcliffe-Brown's proposition that a symbol recurring in a cycle of rituals is likely to have the same significance in each. Such symbols also possess considerable autonomy with regard to the aims of the rituals in which they appear. Precisely because of these properties, dominant symbols are readily analysable in a cultural framework of reference. They may be regarded for this purpose as what Whitehead would have called "eternal objects."[6] They are the relatively fixed points in both the social and cultural structures, and indeed constitute points of junction between these two kinds of structure. They may be regarded irrespective of their order of appearance in a given ritual, as ends in themselves, as representative of the axiomatic values of the widest Ndembu society. This does not mean that they cannot also be studied, as we have indeed studied them, as factors of social action, in an action frame of reference. But their social properties make them more appropriate objects of morphological study than the class of symbols we will now consider.

These symbols may be termed "instrumental symbols." An instrumental symbol must be seen in terms of its wider context, *i.e.* in terms of the total system of symbols which makes up a given kind of ritual. Each kind of ritual has its specific mode of interrelating symbols. This mode is often dependent upon the ostensible purposes of that kind of ritual. In other words, each ritual has its own teleology. It has its explicitly expressed goals, and instrumental symbols may be regarded as means of attaining those goals. For example, in rituals performed for the overt purpose of making women fruitful, among the instrumental symbols used are portions of fruit-bearing trees, or of trees which

---

[6] *I.e.*, objects not of indefinite duration but to which the category of time is not applicable.

possess innumerable rootlets. These fruits and rootlets are said by Ndembu to represent children. They are also thought of as having efficacy to make the woman fruitful. They are means to the main end of the ritual. Perhaps such symbols could be regarded as mere signs or referential symbols, were it not for the fact that the meanings of each are associated with powerful conscious and unconscious emotions and wishes. At the psychological level of analysis, I suspect that these symbols too would approximate to the condition of condensation symbols. But here we touch upon the present limits of competence of anthropological explanation, a problem which we will shortly discuss more fully.

THE LIMITS OF ANTHROPOLOGICAL INTERPRETATION

We now come to the most difficult aspect of the scientific study of ritual symbolism: analysis. How far can we interpret these enigmatic formations by the use of anthropological concepts? At what points do we reach the frontiers of our explanatory competence? Let us first consider the case of dominant symbols. I have suggested that these have two poles of meaning, a sensory and an ideological pole. I have also suggested that dominant symbols have the property of unifying disparate *significata*. I would go so far as to say that at *both* poles of meaning are clustered disparate and even contradictory *significata*. In the course of its historical development, anthropology has acquired techniques and concepts which enable it to handle fairly adequately the kind of data which we have classified as falling around the ideological pole. Such data, as we have seen, include components of social structure, and cultural phenomena, both ideological and technological. I believe that study of these data in terms of the concepts of three major subdivisions of anthropology, cultural anthropology, structuralist theory, and social dynamics, would be extremely rewarding. I shall shortly outline how I think such analyses might be done, and how the three frameworks might be interrelated. But first we must ask, how far and in what respects is it relevant to submit the sensory pole of meaning to intensive analysis, and, more importantly, how far are we, as anthropologists, qualified to do so? For it is evident, as Sapir has stated, that ritual symbols, like all condensation symbols, "strike deeper and deeper roots in the unconscious." Even ¦a brief acquaintance with depth-psychology is enough to show the investigator that ritual symbols, with regard to their outward form, to their behavioural context, and to several of the indigenous interpretations set upon them, are partially shaped under the influence of unconscious motivations and ideas. The interchange of clothes between mother and daughter at the Nkang's ritual; the belief that a novice would go mad if she saw the milk-tree on the day of her separation ritual; the belief that if a novice lifts up the blanket with which she is covered during seclusion, and sees her village, her mother would die: all these are items of symbolic behaviour for which the Ndembu themselves can give no satisfactory interpretation. For these beliefs suggest an element of mutual hostility in the mother-daughter relationship which runs clean counter to orthodox interpretations of the milk-tree symbolism, in so far as it refers to the mother-daughter relationship. One of the main characteristics of ideological interpretations is that they tend to stress the harmonious and cohesive aspect of social relationships. The exegetic idiom feigns that persons and groups always act in accordance with the ideal norms of Ndembu society.

DEPTH PSYCHOLOGY AND RITUAL SYMBOLISM

When psycho-analysts like Theodore Reik, Ernest Jones, or Bruno Bettelheim analyse the ritual symbolism of primitive and ancient society, they tend to regard as irrelevant the ideological pole of meaning, and to focus their attention on the outward form and sensory meanings of the symbols. They regard most indigenous interpretations of symbols, which form the main component of the ideological pole, almost as though they were identical with the rationalisations by which neurotics explain and justify their aberrant behaviour. Furthermore, they tend to look upon ritual symbols as identical with neurotic and psychotic symptoms or as though they had the same properties as the dream symbols of Western European individuals. In effect, their procedure is the exact reverse of that of the social anthropologists who share the views of Nadel and Wilson. This school of anthropologists, it will be remembered, considers that *only* conscious, verbalised, indigenous interpretations of symbols are sociologically relevant. The method of the psycho-analysts, on the other hand, is to examine the form, content and mode of interconnexion of the symbolic acts and objects described by ethnographers, and to interpret these by means of concepts formulated in Western European clinical practice. Such psycho-analysts claim to recognise, in the structure and action-context of ritual symbols material derived from what they consider to be the universal experiences of human infancy in the family situation. For example, Fenichel states that two contrary psychic tendencies exist universally in the father-son relationship, *i.e.*' submission and rebellion, and that both derive from the Oedipus complex. He then goes on to argue that

> since most patriarchal religions also veer between submission to a paternal figure, and rebellion (both submission and rebellion being sexualised), and every god, like a compulsive super-ego, promises protection on condition of submission, there are many similarities in the manifest picture of compulsive ceremonials and religious rituals, due to the similarity of the underlying conflicts.[7]

As against this point of view, we have already shown how the successive symbolic acts of many Ndembu rituals are given order and structure by the explicitly stated purposes of those rituals. We do not need to invoke the notion of underlying conflicts to account for their conspicuous regularity. Psycho-analysts might argue that in patriarchal societies ritual might exhibit a greater rigidity and compulsive quality than among the Ndembu, who are matrilineal. In other words, the formal pattern might be "over-determined" by the unconscious father-son conflict. But ethnographic comparison would seem to refute this view, for the most rigid formalism known to students of comparative religion is found among the Pueblo Indians, who are more strongly matrilineal than the Ndembu, while the Nigerian Nupe, a strongly patrilineal society, possess rituals with a "fluid" and "not over-strict" form.[8]

Other psycho-analysts profess to find in symbolic forms traces of "orally aggressive," "orally dependent," "anal-

---

[7] O. Fenichel, *The Psychoanalytic Theory of Neuroses* [1946], p. 302.

[8] Nadel, *Nupe Religion* [1954], p. 101. Nadel writes: "We might call the very fluidity of the formalism part of the typical form of Nupe ritual."

sadistic," and "masochistic" ideas and drives. Indeed, several anthropologists, after reading psycho-analytical literature, have been tempted to "explain" ritual phenomena in this way.

Perhaps the most spectacular recent attempt to make a comprehensive interpretation of ritual symbolism by using psycho-analytical concepts is Bruno Bettelheim's book *Symbolic Wounds*. Bettelheim, after observing the behaviour of four schizoid adolescent children, who formed a secret society, considered that in this behaviour lay the clue to an understanding of many features of primitive initiation ritual. From his schizoids, he inferred that one of the (unconscious) purposes of male initiation rites may be to assert that men too can bear children, and that "through such operations as subincision men may try to acquire sexual apparatus and functions equal to women's."[9] Womb-envy, and an unconscious infantile identification with the mother, in Bettelheim's opinion, were powerful formative factors, both in the *ad hoc* ritual of his four schizoids, and in male circumcision rituals all over the world.

Bettelheim's viewpoint is in important respects opposed to that of many orthodox Freudians, who hold that the symbolic events comprising these rituals result principally from the fathers' jealousy of their sons, and that their purpose is to create sexual (castration) anxiety and to make the incest taboo secure. Where psycho-analysts disagree, by what criterion can the hapless social anthropologist judge between their interpretations, in a field of enquiry in which he has neither received systematic training nor obtained thorough practical experience?

PROVINCES OF EXPLANATION

I consider that if we conceptualise a dominant symbol as having two poles of meaning, we can more exactly demarcate the limits within which anthropological analysis may be fruitfully applied. Psycho-analysts, in treating most indigenous interpretations of symbols as irrelevant, are guilty of a naïve and one-sided approach. For those interpretations which show how a dominant symbol expresses important components of the social and moral orders are by no means equivalent to the

---

[9] B. Bettelheim, *Symbolic Wounds: Puberty Rites and the Envious Male* [1954], pp. 105-23.

"rationalisations," and the "secondary elaborations" of material deriving from endopsychic conflicts. They refer to social facts which have an empirical reality exterior to the psyches of individuals. On the other hand, those anthropologists who regard only indigenous interpretations as relevant, are being equally one-sided. This is because they tend to examine symbols within two analytical frameworks only, the cultural and the structural. This approach is essentially a static one, and it does not deal with processes involving temporal changes in social relations.

But the crucial properties of a ritual symbol involve these dynamic developments. Symbols instigate social action. In a field context they may even be described as "forces" in that they are determinable influences inclining persons and groups to action. It is in a field context, moreover, that the properties we have described, namely, polarisation of meanings, transference of affectual quality, discrepancy between meanings, and condensation of meanings, become most significant. The symbol as a unit of action, possessing these properties, becomes an object of study both for anthropology and for psychology. Both disciplines, in so far as they are concerned with human actions must conceptualise the ritual symbol in the same way.

The techniques and concepts of the anthropologist enable him to analyse competently the interrelations between the data associated with the ideological pole of meaning. They also enable him to analyse the social behaviour directed upon the total dominant symbol. But he cannot, with his present skills, discriminate between the *precise sources* of unconscious feeling and wishing, which shape much of the outward form of the symbol; select some natural objects rather than others to serve as symbols; and account for certain aspects of the behaviour associated with symbols. For him, it is enough that the symbol should evoke "emotion." He is interested in the fact that emotion is evoked and not in the specific qualities of its constituents. He may indeed find it situationally relevant for his analysis to distinguish whether the emotion evoked by a specific symbol possesses the gross character, say, of aggression, fear, friendliness, anxiety, or sexual pleasure. But he need go no further than this. For him the ritual symbol is primarily a factor in *group* dynamics, and as such its references to the groups, relationships, values, norms, and beliefs of a society are his principal items of study. In other words, the anthropologist treats the sensory pole of meaning as a constant, and the social and ideological aspects as variables whose interdependencies he seeks to explain.

The psycho-analyst, on the other hand, must, I think, attach greater significance than he now does to social factors in the analysis of ritual symbolism. He must cease to regard interpretations, beliefs, and dogmas as mere rationalisations when, often enough, these refer to social and natural realities. For, as Durkheim wrote, "primitive religions hold to reality and express it. One must learn to go underneath the symbol to the reality which it represents and which gives it its meaning. No religions are false, all answer, though in different ways, to the given conditions of human existence."[10] Among those given conditions, the arrangement of society into structured group- ings, discrepancies between the principles which organise these groupings, economic collaboration and competition, schism within groups and opposition between groups—in short, all those things with which the social aspect of ritual symbolism is concerned, are surely of at least equal importance with biopsychical drives and early conditioning in the elementary family. After all, the ritual symbol has, in common with the dream symbol, the characteristic, discovered by Freud, of being a compromise-formation between two main opposing tend- encies. It is a compromise between the need for social control, and certain innate and universal human drives whose complete gratification would result in a breakdown of that control. Ritual symbols refer to what is normative, general and char- acteristic of unique individuals. Thus Ndembu symbols refer among other things, to the basic needs of social existence (hunting, agriculture, female fertility, favourable climatic conditions, and so forth), and to shared values on which communal life depends (generosity, comradeship, respect for elders, the importance of kinship, hospitality, and the like). In distinguishing between ritual symbols and individual psychic symbols, we may perhaps say that while ritual symbols are gross means of handling social and natural reality, psychic symbols are dominantly fashioned under the influence of inner

[10] E. Durkheim, *Elementary Forms of Religious Life* [1954], pp. 2-3.

drives. In analysing the former, attention must mainly be paid to relations between data external to the psyche; in analysing the latter, to endopsychic data.

For this reason, the study of ritual symbolism falls more within the province of the social anthropologist than that of the psychologist or psycho-analyst, although the latter can assist the anthropologist by examining the nature and inter-connexions of the data clustered at the sensory pole of ritual symbolism. He can also, I believe, illuminate certain aspects of the stereotyped behaviour associated with symbols in field contexts, which the actors themselves are unable to explain. For, as we have seen, much of this behaviour is suggestive of attitudes which differ radically from those deemed appropriate in terms of traditional exegesis. And indeed certain conflicts would appear to be so basic that they totally block exegesis.

THE INTERPRETATION OF OBSERVED EMOTIONS

But can we really say that behaviour portraying conflict between persons and groups, who are represented by the symbols themselves as being in harmony, is in the full Freudian sense *unconscious* behaviour? For the Ndembu themselves in many situations outside Nkang'a, both secular and ritual, are perfectly aware of and ready to speak about hostility in the relationships between particular mothers and daughters, be-tween particular sub-lineages, and between particular young girls and the adult women in their villages. It is rather as though there existed in certain precisely defined public situa-tions, usually of a ritual or ceremonial type, a norm obstructing the verbal statement of conflicts in any way connected with the principle and rules celebrated or dramatised in those situations. Evidences of human passion and frailty are just not spoken about when the occasion is given up to the public commemorations, and reanimation, of norms and values in their abstract purity.

Yet, as we have seen, recurrent kinds of conflict may be *acted* out in the ritual or ceremonial form. For on great ritual occasions common practice, as well as highest principle, receives its symbolic or stereotyped expression. But practice, which is dominantly under the sway of what all societies consider man's "lower nature," is rife with expressions of conflict. Selfish and factional interests, oath-breaking, disloyalty, sins of omission as well as sins of commission, pollute and disfigure those ideal prototypes of behaviour which in precept, prayer, formula, and symbol are held up before the ritual assembly for its exclusive attention. In the orthodox interpretation of ritual it is pretended that common practice has no efficacy and that men and women really are as they ideally should be. Yet, as I have argued above, the "energy" required to reanimate the values and norms enshrined in dominant symbols and expressed in various kinds of verbal behaviour is "borrowed," to speak metaphorically in lieu at the moment of a more rigorous language, from the miming of well-known and normally mentionable conflicts. The raw energies of conflict are domesticated into the service of social order.

I should say here that I believe it possible, and indeed necessary, to analyse symbols in a context of observed emotions. If the investigator is well acquainted with the common idiom in which a society expresses such emotions as friendship, love, hate, joy, sorrow, contentment, and fear, he cannot fail to observe that these are experienced in ritual situations. Thus in Nkang'a, when the women laugh and jeer at the men, tease the novice and her mother, fight one another for the "porridge of *chipwampwilu*," and so on, the observer can hardly doubt that emotions are really aroused in the actors as well as formally represented by ritual custom. ("What's Hecuba to him or he to Hecuba, that he should weep for her?")

These emotions are portrayed and evoked in close relation with the dominant symbols of tribal cohesion and continuity, often by the performance of instrumentally symbolic behaviour. But since they are often associated with the mimesis of interpersonal and inter-group conflict such emotions and acts of behaviour obtain no place among the official, verbal meanings attributed to such dominant symbols.

THE SITUATIONAL SUPPRESSION OF CONFLICT
FROM INTERPRETATION

Emotion and praxis, indeed, give life and colouring to the values and norms: but the connexion between the behavioural expression of conflict and the normative components of each kind of ritual, and of its dominant symbols, is seldom explicitly formulated by believing actors. Only if one were to personify a society, regarding it as some kind of supra-individual entity, could one speak of "unconsciousness" here. Each individual participant in the Nkang'a ritual is well aware that kin quarrel most bitterly over rights and obligations conferred by the principle of matriliny. But that awareness is situationally held back from verbal expression: the participants must behave *as if* conflicts generated by matriliny were irrelevant.

This does not mean, as Nadel considers, that what is not verbalised is *in fact* irrelevant either to the participants or to the anthropologist. On the contrary, in so far as the anthropologist considers problems of social action to fall within his purview, the suppression from speech of what might be termed "the behavioural meaning" of certain dominant symbols is highly relevant. The fact is that any kind of coherent, organised social life would be impossible without the assumption that certain values and norms, imperatives and prohibitions, are axiomatic in character, ultimately binding on everyone. But for many reasons, the axiomatic quality of these norms is difficult to maintain in practice, since in the endless variety of real situations norms considered equally valid in abstraction are frequently found to be inconsistent with one another, and even mutually to conflict.

Furthermore, social norms, by their very nature, impose unnatural constraints on those whose biopsychical dispositions impel them to supranormal or abnormal behaviour, either fitfully or regularly. Social life in all organised groups appears to exhibit a cyclicality or oscillation between periods when one set of axiomatic norms are observed and periods when they give way to the dominance of another set. Thus since different norms govern different aspects or sectors of social behaviour, and, more importantly, since the sectors overlap and inter-penetrate in reality, causing norm-conflict, the validity of several major norms has to be reaffirmed in isolation from others, and outside the contexts in which struggles and conflicts arise in connexion with them. This is why one so often finds in ritual that dogmatic and symbolic emphasis is laid on a single norm or on a cluster of closely, and on the whole harmoniously, interrelated norms in a single kind of ritual.

And yet, since at major gatherings of this sort people assemble not as aggregates of individuals but as social personalities arrayed and organised by many principles and norms of grouping, it is by no means a simple matter to assert the clear situational paramountcy of the norms to be commemorated and extolled. Thus, in the Ndembu boys' circumcision ritual, relationships between social categories, such as men and women, old men and young men, circumcised and uncircumcised, and the norms governing such relationships, are given formal representation. But the members of the ritual assembly come as members of corporate groups, such as villages and lineages, which in secular life are in rivalry with one another. That this rivalry is not mysteriously and wonderfully dispelled by the circumcision ritual becomes abundantly clear from the number of quarrels and fights that can be observed during public dances and beer drinks in the intervals between phases of the ritual proper. Here people quarrel as members of groupings which are not recognised in the formal structure of the ritual.

It may be said that any major ritual which stresses the importance of a single principle of social organisation only does so by blocking the expression of other important principles. Sometimes the submerged principles, and the norms and customs through which they become effective, are given veiled and disguised representation in the symbolic pattern of the ritual: sometimes, as in the boys' circumcision ritual, they break through to expression in the spatial and temporal interstices of the procedure. In this essay we are concerned principally with the effects of the suppression on the meaning-structure of dominant symbols.

For example, in the frequently performed Nkula ritual, the dominant symbols are a cluster of red objects, notably red clay (*mukundu*) and the *mukula* tree mentioned previously. In the context of Nkula, both of these are said to represent menstrual blood, and the "blood of birth," which is the blood that accompanies the birth of a child. The ostensible goal of the ritual is to coagulate the patient's menstrual blood, which has been flowing away in menorrhagia, around the foetus in order to nourish it. A series of symbolic acts are performed to attain this end. For example, a young *mukula* tree is cut down by male doctors and part of it is carved into the shape of a baby, which is then inserted into a round calabash medicated with the blood of a sacrificed cock, with red clay and with a number of other "red" ingredients. The red medicines here, say the Ndembu, represent wished-for coagulation of the patient's menstrual blood, and the calabash is a symbolic womb. At the ideological pole of meaning, the *mukula* tree, and the medicated calabash, both represent (as the milk-tree does), the patient's matrilineage, and, at a higher level of abstraction, the principle of matriliny itself. This is also consistent with the fact that "*ivumu*," the term for "womb," also means "matrilineage." In this symbolism the procreative, rather than the nutritive, aspect of motherhood is stressed. But Ndembu red symbolism, unlike the white symbolism of which the milk-tree symbolism is a species, nearly always has explicit reference to violence, to killing, and, at its most general level of meaning, to breach, both in the social and natural orders. Although informants, when discussing this Nkula ritual specifically, tend to stress the positive, feminine aspects of parturition and reproduction, other meanings of the red symbols, stated explicitly in other ritual contexts, can be shown to make their influence felt in Nkula. For example, both red clay and the *mukula* tree are dominant symbols in the hunter's cult, where they mean the blood of animals, the red meat of game, the inheritance through either parent of hunting prowess, and the unity of all initiated hunters. It also stands for the hunter's power to kill. The same red symbols, in the context of the Wubanji ritual performed to purify a man who has killed a kinsman, or a lion or leopard (animals which are believed to be reincarnated hunter kin of the living), represent the blood of homicide. Again, in the boys' circumcision ritual, these symbols stand for the blood of circumcised boys. More seriously still, in divination and in anti-witchcraft rituals, they stand for the blood of witches' victims, that is exposed in necrophagous feasts.

Most of these meanings are implicit in Nkula. For example, the female patient, dressed in skins like a male hunter, and carrying a bow and arrow, at one phase of the ritual performs a special hunter's dance. Moreover, while she does this, she wears in her hair, just above the brow, the red feather of a lourie bird. Only shedders of blood, such as hunters, manslayers, and circumcisers, are customarily entitled to wear this feather. Again, after the patient has been given the baby figurine in its symbolic womb, she dances with it in a style of dancing peculiar to circumcisers when they brandish aloft the great *nfunda* medicine of the circumcision lodge. Why then is the woman patient identified with male bloodspillers? The field context of these symbolic objects and items of behaviour suggests that the Ndembu feel that the woman, in wasting her menstrual blood and in failing to bear children, is actively renouncing her expected role as a mature married female. She is behaving like a male killer, not like a female nourisher. The situation is analogous, though modified by matriliny, to the following pronouncement in the ancient Jewish Code of Qaro: "Every man is bound to marry a wife in order to beget children, and he who fails of this duty is as one who sheds blood."

One does not need to be a psycho-analyst, one only needs sound sociological training, acquaintance with the total Ndembu symbolic system, plus ordinary common sense, to see that one of the aims of the ritual is to make the woman accept her lot in life as a child-bearer and rearer of children for her lineage. The symbolism suggests that the patient is unconsciously rejecting her female role, that indeed she is guilty; indeed, "*mbayi*," one term for menstrual blood, is etymologically connected with "*ku-baya* (to be guilty)." I have not time here to present further evidence of symbols and interpretations, both in Nkula and in cognate rituals, which reinforce this explanation. In the situation of Nkula, the dominant principles celebrated and reanimated are those of matriliny, the mother-child bond, and tribal continuity through matriliny. The norms in which these are expressed are those governing the behaviour of mature women, which ascribe to them the role appropriate to their sex. The suppressed or submerged principles and norms, in this situation, concern and control the personal and corporate behaviour deemed appropriate for men.

The analysis of Nkula symbolism throws into relief another major function of ritual. Ritual adapts and periodically re-adapts the biopsychical individual to the basic conditions and axiomatic values of human social life. In redressive rituals, the category to which Nkula belongs, the eternally rebellious individual is converted for a while into a loyal citizen, In the case of Nkula, a female individual whose behaviour is felt to demonstrate her rebellion against, or at least her reluctance to comply with, the biological and social life-patterns of her sex, is both induced and coerced by means of precept and symbol to accept her culturally prescribed destiny.

MODES OF INFERENCE IN INTERPRETATION

Each kind of Ndembu ritual, like Nkula, has several meanings and goals which are not made explicit by informants, but must be inferred by the investigator from the symbolic pattern and from behaviour. He is able to make these inferences only if he has previously examined the symbolic configurations, and the meanings attributed to their component symbols by skilled informants, of many other kinds of ritual in the same total system. In other words, he must examine symbols not only in the context of each specific kind of ritual, but in the *context of the total system.* He may even find it profitable, where the same symbol is found throughout a wide culture area, to study its changes of meaning in different societies in that area.

There are two main types of contexts, irrespective of size. There is the action-field context, which we have discussed at some length. There is also the cultural context in which symbols are regarded as clusters of abstract meanings. By comparing the different kinds and sizes of contexts in which a dominant symbol occurs, we can often see that the meanings "officially" attributed to it in a particular kind of ritual may be mutually consistent. But there may be much discrepancy and even contradiction between many of the meanings given by informants, when this dominant symbol is regarded as a unit of the total symbolic system. I do not believe that this discrepancy is the result of mere carelessness and ignorance, or variously distributed pieces of insight. I believe that discrepancy between *significata* is a quintessential property of the great symbolic dominants in all religions. Such symbols come in the process of time to absorb into their meaning-content most of the major aspects of human social life, so that, in a sense, they come to represent "human society" itself. In each ritual they assert the situational primacy of a single aspect or of a few aspects only, but by their mere presence they suffuse those aspects with the awe that can only be inspired by the human total. All the contradictions of human social life, between norms and drives, between different drives and between different norms, between society and the individual, and between groups, are condensed and unified in a single representation, the dominant symbols. It is the task of analysis to break down this amalgam into its primary constituents.

THE RELATIVITY OF "DEPTH"

Perhaps this can best be done within different analytical frameworks. I was formerly in favour of talking about "different levels of analysis," but the term "level" contains an implication of depth which I now find misleading, unless we can agree to take "level" to mean any class of abstraction whatsoever. The question of the relative depth of different ways of interpreting symbols is still very much under dispute. For example, psycho-analysts assert that their interpretations of ritual symbols are "deeper" than those of social anthropologists. On the other hand, anthropologists like Monica Wilson hold that at their "deepest level" rituals reveal values, which are socio-cultural facts.

I have suggested in this essay that different aspects of ritual symbolism can be analysed within the framework of structur-alist theory and of cultural anthropology respectively. As I have said, this would be to treat ritual symbols as timeless entities. Many useful conclusions can be arrived at by these methods. But the essential nature, both of dominant symbols and of constellations of instrumental symbols, is that they are dynamic factors. Static analysis would here presuppose a corpse, and, as Jung says, "a symbol is alive." It is alive only in so far as it is "pregnant with meaning" for men and women, who interact by observing, transgressing, and manipulating for private ends the norms and values which the symbol expresses. If the ritual symbol is conceptualised as a force in a field of social action, its critical properties of condensation, polarisation, and unifica-tion of disparities become intelligible and explicable. On the other hand conceptualising the symbol as if it were an object, and neglecting its role in action, often lead to a stress on only those aspects of symbolism which can be logically and consistently related to one another to form an abstract unitary system. In a field situation, the unity of a symbol or a symbolic configuration appears as the resultant of many tendencies converging towards one another from different areas of bio-psychical and social existence. The symbol is an independent force which is itself a product of many opposed forces.

CONCLUSION: THE ANALYSIS OF SYMBOLS IN SOCIAL PROCESSES

Let me briefly outline the way in which I think ritual symbols may fruitfully be analysed. Performances of ritual are phases in broad social processes, the span and complexity of which are roughly proportional to the size and degree of differentiation of the groups in which they occur. One class of ritual is situated near the apex of a whole hierarchy of re-dressive and regulative institutions which correct deflections and deviations from customarily prescribed behaviour. Another class anticipates deviations and conflicts. This class includes periodic rituals and life-crisis rituals. Each kind of ritual is a patterned process in time, the units of which are symbolic objects and serialised items of symbolic behaviour.

The symbolic constituents may themselves be classed into structural elements, or "dominant symbols," which tend to be ends in themselves, and variable elements, or "instrumental symbols," which serve as means to the explicit or implicit goals of the given ritual. In order to give an adequate explanation of the meaning of a particular symbol it is necessary first to examine the widest action-field context, that, namely, in which the ritual itself is simply a phase. Here one must consider what kinds of circumstances give rise to a performance of ritual, whether these are concerned with natural phenomena, econ-omic and technological processes, human life-crises, or with the breach of crucial social relationships. The circumstances will probably determine what sort of ritual is performed. The goals of the ritual will have overt and implicit reference to the antecedent circumstances and will in turn help to determine the meaning of the symbols. Symbols must now be examined within the context of the specific ritual. It is here that we enlist the aid of indigenous informants. It is here also that we may be able to speak legitimately of "levels" of interpretation,

for laymen will give the investigator simple and exoteric meanings, while specialists will give him esoteric explanations and
more elaborate texts. Next, behaviour directed towards each
symbol should be noted, for such behaviour is an important
component of its total meaning.

We are now in a position to exhibit the ritual as a system
of meanings. But this system acquires additional richness and
depth if it is regarded as itself constituting a sector of the
Ndembu ritual system, as interpreted by informants and as
observed in action. It is in comparison with other sectors of
the total system, and by reference to the dominant articulating
principles of the total system, that we often become aware that
the overt and ostensible aims and purposes of a given ritual
conceal unavowed, and even "unconscious," wishes and goals.
We also become aware that a complex relationship exists
between the overt and the submerged, and the manifest and
latent patterns of meaning. As social anthropologists we are
potentially capable of analysing the social aspect of this relationship. We can examine, for example, the relations of
dependence and independence between the total society and
its parts, and the relations between different kinds of parts, and
between different parts of the same kind. We can see how the
same dominant symbol, which in one kind of ritual stands for
one kind of social group, or for one principle of organisation,
in another kind of ritual stands for another kind of group or
principle, and in its aggregate of meanings stands for unity
and continuity of the widest Ndembu society, embracing its
contradictions.

THE LIMITS OF CONTEMPORARY ANTHROPOLOGICAL COMPETENCE

But our analysis must needs be incomplete when we consider the relationship between the normative elements in social
life and the individual. For this relationship, too, finds its way
into the meaning of ritual symbols. Here we come to the
confines of our present anthropological competence, for we are
now dealing with the structure and properties of psyches, a
scientific field traditionally studied by other disciplines than
ours. At one end of the symbol's spectrum of meanings we
encounter the individual psychologist and the social psycho-

logist, and even beyond them (if one may make a friendly tilt at an envied friend), brandishing his Medusa's head, the psycho-analyst, ready to turn to stone the foolhardy interloper into his caverns of terminology.

We shudder back thankfully into the light of social day. Here the significant elements of a symbol's meaning are related to what it does, and what is done to it by and for whom. And these aspects can only be understood if one takes into account from the beginning, and represents by appropriate theoretical constructs, the total field situation in which the symbol occurs. This situation would include the structure of the group which performs the ritual we observe, its basic organising principles and perdurable relationships, and, in addition, its extant division into transient alliances and factions on the basis of immediate interest and ambitions. For both abiding structure and recurrent forms of conflict and selfish interest are stereotyped in ritual symbolism. Once we have collected informants' interpretations of a given symbol, our work of analysis has indeed just begun. We must gradually approximate to the action-meaning of our symbol by way of what Lewin calls "a stepwise increasing specificity"[11] from widest to narrowest significant action-context. Informants' "meanings" only become meaningful as objects of scientific study in the course of this analytical process.

[11] Lewin, *Field Theory in Social Science*, p. 149.

3

F. G. Bailey

TWO VILLAGES IN ORISSA (INDIA)
[written in 1958]

In this essay I attempt to mark the place of social anthropology between history and the study of culture on the one
side, and, on the other side, economics and political science.
Since these essays are intended, in part, to describe problems
encountered in analysing field material, I shall hinge the discussion on two disputes, which I recorded between 1952 and
1955 in the Kondmals, a sub-division in highland Orissa. This
essay is a record of what I did, rather than a universal formula
of what ought to be done. I have sometimes phrased the
conclusions in general terms, but it is fair to remind the reader
that where I draw bounds around "social anthropology," I am
in fact drawing them for one particular piece of research and
its analysis; different problems might require further, or on the
other hand less extensive, ventures into other disciplines.

Nevertheless, although the boundaries shift according to the
questions asked and although I shall be arguing from limited
evidence, I shall try to indicate broadly what kind of problems
belong to social anthropology, and what kind belong elsewhere.
Social anthropology has its own subject-matter and its own
techniques. I shall argue that the subject-matter need not be
solely primitive societies, and that the techniques are still useful
when the social anthropologist enters into the study of complex
societies. By doing so, he does not become an amateur historian,
or a naïve political scientist, or a watered-down economist.
On the contrary, he brings to the study of complex societies

forms of understanding which are complementary to, but quite distinct from, those of the disciplines named.

BISIPARA

On the outskirts of the Oriya village of Bisipara there is a temple. This temple is built on Bisipara land, and the Brahmin and other officials who care for it are Bisipara men, but the temple belongs to all Hindus in the Kondmals, and an annual excursion is made by the priest and his assistants to collect contributions for its upkeep.

The Bisipara Pans, a caste of untouchables, hearing of the Temple Entry Act,[1] organised a procession to the temple and announced that they would go inside, since they now had a legal right to do so. When the Pans came to the temple they found it guarded by the clean castes of Bisipara, headed by the Warriors.[2] The police were then called by the Pans, who demanded that their right to enter the temple should be enforced. The Warriors asserted that they, as men of Bisipara, were merely the custodians of the temple and not its owners; they would stand aside and permit the Pans to enter, providing that all other clean-caste Hindus in the Kondmals were first consulted. After a few days tempers cooled; the police went away; the Pans made no further efforts to enter the temple.

Some time afterwards the village council, on which clean castes alone sit, announced that the Pan privilege of music-making and licensed begging on ritual occasions had now been withdrawn and would be allotted to a different untouchable caste. The Pans did not, to my knowledge, make any formal protest against this decision. Instead they did two things which seem to me implicitly to accept, and even to welcome, the withdrawal of their traditional privileges. They met in council and announced a series of measures which in effect denied their untouchable status. They would no longer act as scavengers for the village and they would not cart away and flay dead cattle. They would no longer drink alcohol. They would be

---

[1] This Act makes it an offence to exclude people from places of worship on the grounds of untouchability.

[2] For a fuller description of this case, see F. G. Bailey, *Caste and the Economic Frontier* [1957]. The caste there called Boad Outcastes is here called Pan.

vegetarian. From that time onwards they were no longer Pans, but Harijans—"children of God"—the name by which Gandhi dignified untouchables. Finally, as another gesture of independence and equality, they built their own temple in their own street.

In 1953 an elderly Pan was returning in the evening from market. His path lay through the centre of the village and along a narrow track on a bank above the water-logged rice-fields. On this track he met a youth of the high Warrior caste, returning from fishing in the fields. They came face to face on the pathway; there was a scuffle; the youth fell into the muddy field. The youth ran home, roused the village, and a council meeting was called. This meeting summoned the Pan. A message came back that he would attend in the morning. During the night the Pans sent an appeal to the police, eight miles away, saying that their houses had been attacked by the clean castes. The police came in the early morning and took statements from both sides. That same day a Minister from the Orissa Government happened to be touring in the area, and the Bisipara Pans intercepted his party and asked for his protection. This resulted in a second police enquiry by a higher official. The police decided that there was no case to answer. The Pans then appealed to the Magistrate. The case was heard in 1954 and the Magistrate ordered both sides to keep the peace.

In the closing months of 1953 (I left the village at the end of that year) the tension between the two sides seemed to me curiously compartmented. Everyday economic relationships—casual labour hired by clean castes from among Pans to work on the farm or about the house—went on as usual, and there was nothing that I could distinguish in the behaviour of master and servant to indicate communal tension. But the village council behaved as if in a state of siege. Pans were no longer allowed to lounge outside the meeting-house and hear what was going on. There were frequent warnings against careless talk, and threats to fine any clean-caste person who revealed to a Pan— even inadvertently—what the council had decided to do. Money was levied to pay the expenses of witnesses at court, and there was even talk of hiring a lawyer. I was told many times that the Pans no longer knew their place; allegations that they were unfit to be received in decent human society were bolstered by stories of their nauseating personal habits; in short, the incidents of 1953 brought into the open great bitterness and the emotions which we associate with racial conflict.

BADERI

In 1955, in the Kond village of Baderi, which is half an hour's walk from Bisipara, some Baderi Pans sat down at a wedding feast beside the visiting Pan musicians who came with the bride's escort.[3] A Baderi Kond, named Liringa, abused the Baderi Pans and drove them away. That night the Baderi Pans slashed the skins of the visitors' drums. The visitors complained, and the Konds of Baderi, who hold in that village a position analogous to that of the clean castes in Bisipara, met in council and summoned their Pans. The Baderi Pans attended, and at once complained that when they were driven away from the wedding feast, their caste had been publicly insulted. In a very short time Liringa and the Pan elders were shouting at one another. Then one of the Pans struck Liringa and another Kond who stood at his side. Both men were struck across the face, openly, and in full view of the council. The Pans then fled and the council broke up in disorder.

The Kond council met again at the instigation of Liringa and decided to impose an economic "lock-out." Pans would no longer be employed as labourers or retained as clients. Land or any other form of property given to them must be resumed. The village would no longer employ them as musicians. All this was written into a document together with the reasons for the lock-out: the Pans no longer obeyed or respected their Kond masters "since the Government started calling them Harijans." and they therefore would no longer be granted the privileges of servants. The names of all present were written on the document together with an agreement to pay a fine of Rs. 25 if they broke its provisions.

In fact the document came to nothing. No one dismissed a Pan; no one resumed his property; a few months later, when the agricultural season began, the Baderi Pans were working as

---

[3] For a more detailed description of this dispute, see F. G. Bailey, *Tribe, Caste, and Nation* [1960], Ch. VI.

labourers in Kond fields, as they had always done. Even before that, at a ceremony held in one of the hamlets which constitute Baderi village, they had appeared with their drums and provided music and had been paid for it.

The attitudes of the Konds towards untouchables differs from the attitude of the clean castes in Bisipara. It is true that they put forward many of the same reasons to explain the behaviour of their Pans; especially they insisted that this kind of conflict was caused by the Government using the term "Harijan." But some of them said that in Baderi there was no real Harijan problem. The fault was Liringa's; with a little more tact he might have smoothed the whole thing over. Whatever was happening elsewhere, this argument ran, there was no real problem in Baderi; the Pans could be kept in their places.

After they assaulted Liringa the Pans made no further move to protect themselves or to assert their rights. They did not call in the Administration, as the Bisipara Pans did. They made no proclamations about reforming themselves. They continued to behave in the manner of the traditional Pans.

Within a few days the excitement died down, and the incident appeared to have been forgotten.

THE PROBLEM

In some ways the events in these two villages resemble one another. Both cases arose from an encounter between individuals, and both immediately mobilised groups on each side of the barrier of untouchability. Both in Baderi and in Bisipara an untouchable assaulted a person of clean caste, and in both villages this breach of the rules of ritual avoidance was the occasion, but not the sole cause, of the conflict. In both cases the village council met, first as a judicial body summoning the Pans to stand before it as before a court. These summones were ignored or frustrated, and when the councils met again later, they met as councils of war, determining how to deal with an opponent whose equality they thus implicitly acknowledged.

There are also differences, not so much in the actions of the clean castes, but in the way in which the two sets of untouchables conducted their case. The Baderi Pans, after their two acts of violence (damaging the drums and assaulting Liringa), did nothing to embarrass the Konds and quickly resumed their normal posture of subservience. The Bisipara Pans, on the other hand, were defiant: they made several appeals to the Administration and one to a Minister, and by doing so they kept the Bisipara clean castes on the defensive for a year. They made vociferous claims that their rights, as citizens of India, should be respected. They made a general issue out of the assault case, and used it to demonstrate that they were no longer subservient to the clean castes, and in particular to the Warriors. The consequences of this was that the dispute in Bisipara was much more bitter and more protracted than the dispute in Baderi.

These cases pose two questions. Firstly, why did these disputes occur at all? This is not the historical question: Why did these particular unique events occur at that time? Rather it is the question: Can these events be understood as aspects of regular behaviour, as social regularities, as part of a system? Secondly, how can a sociologist explain the differing course of the two disputes, the greater initiative shown by the Bisipara Pans, and the relative lack of political enterprise apparent among the Baderi Pans?

EXPLANATIONS FROM CULTURE

In the first place there are certain cultural items, the significance of which must be known if one is to understand why the actors behaved as they did. One must, in other words, have some knowledge of Hinduism and of the symbolic values which Hindus attach to certain places and certain forms of behaviour.

One has to know that an untouchable is so called because if he comes into contact with persons of clean caste he pollutes them, and some form of ritual cleansing becomes necessary before the polluted person is fit again to carry out his normal tasks.

Knowing this, one better understands why the assaults, neither of which did apparent bodily harm, nevertheless caused such an uproar—and that among a people who readily use violence to gain their ends. In each case the blow was struck by an untouchable on a person of clean caste, and the effect upon clean-caste public opinion was much the same as when we read of attacks on women and children. The incidents were seen by the clean castes not so much as assaults on individuals, but rather as attacks on a fundamental principle of morality.

The attempt of the untouchables to gain entry to the Bisipara temple has the same significance. The temple is an object of ritual purity; the untouchables are polluting. Knowing this, one better understands what the trouble was about. The same point comes up again in the fact that Pans are not members of the village council in Bisipara, although they are permitted in normal times to stand outside the meeting-house and listen to what is going on. But the meeting-house itself is also a shrine, which would be polluted by the presence of Pans.

Another point which would be obscure without a knowledge of Hindu culture is the significance of the methods employed by the Bisipara Pans to make themselves respectable. Vegetarianism and the avoidance of alcohol are habits which bring spiritual merit; they are also the habits of the much respected priestly caste, the Brahmin. Conversely, any form of violence to the cow, including the handling of dead cattle and hides, is a sin. Such forms of behaviour are indices not only of spiritual merit, but also of social prestige.

These are cultural values which Hindus hold, and if we know them, we understand better the significance of various ways of behaving in the two disputes. But there arise further questions:

(*a*) Does a knowledge of these cultural items answer the two questions posed above? By understanding Hindu culture, do we understand sociologically why these disputes occurred? And can we account, in this way, for different behaviour in the two villages?

(*b*) Do we need to explain these cultural items, and if so, how is the explanation to be made?

It seems to me that a knowledge of the culture is only the beginning of the effort to understand sociologically why these disputes occurred. In each case the cultural description poses, at a higher level of abstraction, a sociological problem. A knowledge of Hindu values gives us to understand that when the Bisipara Pans imposed on themselves a ban on eating meat and drinking alcohol and handling dead cattle, they were making an attempt at social climbing. But cultural symbolism will not explain *why* they were trying to better themselves. By knowing the meaning of "untouchability" and the symbols associated with it, we also know that in trying to enter the temple, and in striking a person of clean caste, the Pans were making an attack on the established social order. But we do not know yet what is that social order, nor why the Pans were attacking it. A knowledge of Hindu culture will not help us to understand why these disputes took place; that knowledge only helps us to realise that there is a problem.

Does it, then, help us to understand why the dispute in Baderi was so much shorter and less complicated than in Bisipara? One might be able to show that Kond values differ from Oriya values, and that, in contrast to Bisipara, the dispute in Baderi involved values which were less strongly held and less readily aroused strong emotions. There could be such an explanation: but the facts did not warrant it. It is true that no Kond temple was involved, and that the Kond council does not meet in a shrine. But the attitudes towards untouchables do not differ among the Konds from the attitudes of the clean castes in Bisipara. Certainly an assault by an untouchable on a man of high caste has the same emotional and moral significance in both villages. One cannot therefore account for the difference in the course of the two disputes by saying that the Konds are less "caste-minded" than the Oriyas. In so far as the problem is a sociological one, it cannot be explained only in terms of culture.

In discussing the disputes I have taken as given the Hindu concepts of untouchability and Hindu values about the cow and about vegetarianism. These items concern two different kinds of expertise: psychology, and—to lump a lot of disciplines together—Indology. Are we, then, being naïve in the way we use the concept of untouchability and ideas about cattle in India? Would we *better understand our own problems* (as distinct from being more knowledgeable) if we attempted to train ourselves as psychologists or Indologists?

Turner's essay deals with psychology and I can add nothing to this. To analyse the rituals of untouchability would be a different problem from the one with which I am concerned; and I have made the judgment that I can begin my analysis from my informants' conscious and explicit ideas about untouchability and the sacredness of the cow and the spiritual merit of being a teetotaller and a vegetarian.

The concept of untouchability, and the ritual value of the cow, are traits which the people of Bisipara and Baderi share with the greater part of the population of India. These concepts are also part of a theological corpus contained in sacred books, commented upon and analysed with great skill and infinite subtlety by Hindu theologians. Would it help us to understand the disputes in the two villages if we were equipped with the Indologists' expertise? More generally, can we expect to work successfully as sociologists in civilised countries if we are not versed in the sacred literature and the classical literature of those civilisations? Professor Evans-Pritchard has written that the anthropologist in India ought to have a knowledge of Sanskrit literature. "If one has any regard for scholarship one cannot be a student . . . of Indian peasant communities without having some knowledge both of the literature of their language and of Sanskrit, the classical language of their ritual and religious tradition."[4]

This view has also been expressed, in more detail, by Dr Marriott in *Village India*. Marriott argued that a village in India cannot be "satisfactorily comprehended and conceived as a whole in itself";[5] and, developing the late Professor Redfield's ideas, that the village on the one hand, and the greater culture and greater society on the other, are mutual determinants of one another. There are many sides to this argument: here I am concerned with the point that village culture (or, as Redfield calls it, "little tradition") and the greater culture (or "great tradition") are mutual determinants of one another. Obviously they are; and although the demonstration of the social links involved in this interconnexion (uncovering what Redfield calls "the social organisation of tradition")[6] is extremely difficult, no one would deny that there is some connexion between, for instance, the Siva who appears in sacred

    4 E. E. Evans-Pritchard, *Social Anthropology* [1951], p. 15.
    5 McKim Marriott, *Village India* [1955], pp. 171-222.
    6 Robert Redfield, *Peasant Society and Culture* [1956], Ch. III.

texts and the Siva who is worshipped in Bisipara. Does it then follow that I must know what this connexion is, and trace its every link, before I can appreciate the significance of the Bisipara temple in the dispute between the clean castes and the Bisipara Pans? Must I know what is written in the Sanskrit texts about untouchability before I can understand why the clean castes of the two villages took such a serious view of the assaults?

The nuances of social relationships only become apparent to one familiar with the culture in which those relationships are expressed. The better one is able to absorb Hindu values and Hindu culture, the more penetrating is likely to be one's insight into social relationships. Yet the Hindu culture which helps us to sharpen the dissecting knives of sociology is not, on the whole, the distillation and systematisation which appears in the sacred books in the Sanskrit language. There is a link, as Marriott and others argue, between the "great tradition" and the "little tradition" of the village: but they are nevertheless separable when we regard a knowledge of culture as a tool which helps us to frame particular sociological problems. Our knowledge of the "little tradition" we acquire partly from reading about the manners and customs of the people of India, and partly (and more satisfactorily) by seeing how people behave and listening to the explanations they give of that behaviour. If one ventures very much further into the literature, it is because one is interested, not because familiarity with the more academic side of Hinduism is required for the under-standing of peasant social relations.

To many this will seem the attitude of a Philistine. But it is not; it is merely specialisation. To explain culture traits in a village by relating them, either genetically or through morpho-logical similarity, to traits described in the sacred literature or found in the courts of kings or in the great religious centres, is another problem, different from the one with which I am concerned. It is a cultural problem which is left behind, un-answered and not needing to be answered, in the process of abstracting a system of social behaviour. In the language of this book, it is a problem about which one can afford to be naïve, just as Marriott, in his discussion of festivals and deities, could afford to abstract away, or ignore, or be naïve about, the social relations involved in those festivals and in the worship of those deities.

Neither dispute would be in the least comprehensible unless one traced out the alignments of the protagonists, and realised that only in the beginning were these disputes between individuals; in one case about who was to have priority on a narrow pathway, and in the other case about who was to share in a feast. In both disputes groups immediately mobilised behind the protagonists. These groups were not simply gathered to prosecute the quarrel, but possessed a relative degree of permanence, existing apart from this situation. They were, in other words, part of the structure of social relationships.

An elementary knowledge of Hindu culture and Hindu values was indispensable, as I showed in a previous section, to understand what was going on, although it did not help us to understand why the disputes took place, nor why they followed different courses in the two villages. Does an analysis of the rôles of the people concerned, and a comparison of social relationships in the two villages, explain why the disputes took place, and why they developed differently in the two villages?

Baderi consists of nine nucleated hamlets dispersed in, and at the mouth of, a valley. The greatest distance between any two hamlets is about two miles, but three-quarters of the population live within a mile of one another. Bisipara has a single "suburb" about half a mile from the main village; the rest of the village live in a compact settlement, which is divided into streets, roughly on the basis of caste. Bisipara contains 700 people; Baderi 500. In Bisipara, Pans are 21 per cent of the population; in Baderi, Pans are 17 per cent. Of the clean-caste group in Baderi, Konds are 84 per cent: but in Bisipara the clean-caste group is divided into eighteen different castes, two of which contain half the clean-caste population.

In none of this information is there any fact which would explain why the disputes arose, nor why they followed different courses in the two villages. The proportion of Pans in the population of each village is roughly the same, and the villages themselves do not differ greatly in size. We might seem to have a clue to the different behaviour of the clean-caste groups in the fact that the Baderi group is virtually one caste and one lineage, and might therefore need less institutionalised efforts to display unity in the face of the Pan threat. The division of the Bisipara group into different castes might require greater organisation to achieve unity. On the other hand, the Baderi clean castes are dispersed over different settlements, while those of Bisipara live compactly. These clues might help later, but it would be premature to attribute the difference in the two disputes to structural differences of this kind. In any case, in these structural differences there is no hint why the disputes broke out in the first place.

If the explanation does not lie in the gross structural differences between the two villages, it might lie in the roles which the different protagonists play in sub-systems within the village. The different course of the disputes might be accounted for if, for instance, an unimportant man had been assaulted in Baderi, and a person of standing and influence attacked in Bisipara. Exactly the reverse is true. The victim in Bisipara was a youth, and the alleged assault was committed by an elder. Youth owes respect to age, and had the two persons belonged to the same caste, the older man would have had every right to cuff the youngster out of his way. In Baderi the victim was one of the leading men of the village. In Bisipara the assault took place in the dusk out in the fields, with no witnesses, and could easily have been dressed up as an accident. In Baderi the blow was struck, deliberately and openly, in full view of the village council, and in no circumstances could anyone have pretended that it was an accident. In this situation one would have expected the Baderi dispute to be the more bitter and to be fought out more strenuously. In fact, the opposite happened.

One could explore various other roles and attributes of the protagonists—their economic activities, their education, the offices which they held, and so forth—in an effort to explain the different courses of the two disputes, but there is no space to do so here, and in any case it would be to explore blind alleys. In the end, one would be brought to the conclusion that the significant role in both cases is caste membership, and the structural relationship which might throw light on what happened is the relationship of the two groups across the barrier of pollution: the relationship between the clean castes and the untouchables.

The nature of this relationship is well known and I have described it, with reference to these disputes, in the books noted earlier; here I can be brief. The traditional relationship —and from the point of view of the high castes, the proper relationship—lies in the political, economic, and ritual subordination of the untouchables. The Pan families should be attached to families in the clean castes, in particular to the Warriors in Bisipara and to the Konds in Baderi. The Pans work for their clean-caste masters about the house and on the farm, and they themselves own only such property as their masters choose to give them. They achieve political representation only as the servants of their masters, for they themselves may not sit on the village council; and if they wish to bring a matter before the council, their masters must act for them. Their humble position is symbolised by ritual behaviour, in particular by the usages of untouchability, by their habit of eating and drinking substances which are degrading in the view of Hindus, and by their exclusion from places of ritual importance in the village.

In this outline of groups and institutions are contained some of the clues which explain the behaviour of the disputants. Hindu ideas about pollution explain why the blows which were struck were not simple assaults, but were also attacks on a fundamental moral principle, governing the relationship between clean caste and untouchable. This ritual relationship is now seen as one part of a complex in which political and economic interests are also involved. The blows now appear not only as an offence against village morality, but also as an attack on the established political order of the village. Given that the rituals of untouchability symbolise also political inferiority, these assaults were tantamount to a revolution. So also was the attempt by the Bisipara Pans to enter the Kondmals temple.

A structural analysis, carried out to this depth, and confining itself to the two villages concerned, tells us, putting it briefly, only what is the normal expected behaviour between clean caste and untouchable, and what issues are involved in that behaviour; it tells us who are the actors, how they are expected to act, and what political, ritual and economic interests lie between them. It also shows what village institutions come into action when there is a breach of these rights and obligations: in both the disputes the village council was concerned to restore equilibrium and to sanction correct behaviour.

But such an analysis of village groups and village institutions cannot explain why these institutions failed to restore the balance. In Bisipara, institutions which do not appear in a structural analysis of village relations, in the end prevented the dispute from becoming more violent; in Baderi, the action taken by the village council failed, and normal relations were restored in spite of, rather than because of, its intervention.

In both disputes the action taken by the Pans was tantamount to a revolution. It is obvious, from the course of the two disputes, that the Bisipara Pans wanted a revolution and the Baderi Pans did not. In order to explain this, one has to take into account the relationships which the villagers have with persons and groups outside the village, and which are not part of the village structure; and one has also to take into account institutions which do not belong within the village system.

EXTERNAL RELATIONSHIPS

In neither village does this structural description fit the reality of political and economic relationships. The Pans of Bisipara number among them several schoolmasters, and this profession, by the standards of wealth in the Kondmals, is well paid, and, money apart, carries a high social prestige. There are also several men who make a good living through trade, and the land owned per head of the Bisipara Pans is not so very much less than that owned by the Bisipara Warriors. Even the poor Pans are not, as a rule, tied as clients in a serf-like bond to individual Warrior families, but usually sell their labour on an open market. In short, they are not, in any sense, the complete economic dependants of the Warriors and the clean castes.

The Pans of Baderi are by no means so advanced, and can boast of no men in the professional classes. But they depend for much of their living on outside sources. Some make a

E

precarious living by weaving for the market. In the summer many find work as casual labourers on the roads. And they too, like the Pans of Bisipara, are seldom tied as clients, but in almost every case sell their labour on a day-to-day basis.

In the traditional structure of the village, the Pan had no political role except as the client of his master. This master had to speak for him in the village council, and had to be prepared to defend him against other people. But the reality now is different. Both the Pan and his master stand equal as citizens of India. The Pan can (in practice, with many difficulties) enforce his rights in the Government courts, and he can enforce them even against the Warriors of his own village. Or at least he can try to do so, and the Warriors can no longer legally use force against their Pans. In other words, many of the political functions of the village council have been taken over by the Government courts, and the locus of ultimate power has certainly shifted from the council to those courts and to the Administration.

In Bisipara at least, the Pans have political and economic privileges superior to their former masters. They owe this to the policy of the Government which has been trying for many years to improve the lot of untouchables. Untouchables have preference over clean-caste men for appointment to certain jobs in the Administration; there are special scholarships for them; they are the favoured wards of Government. There is not this difference in Baderi, since the Konds too, having the status of Adibasis (members of primitive tribes) are qualified to receive similar privileges.

By taking into account the political and economic relationships which the people of the villages have with the world outside, and the effect of these relationships on village structures, we can explain why the untouchables of both villages made their protest. We can understand why a quarrel between individuals quickly became generalised into a conflict between castes. Since the Pans are no longer politically entirely subordinate and no longer economically entirely dependent on their clean-caste masters, they were unwilling—in Bisipara at least—to follow out the usages of ritual subservience. Earlier I said that the Bisipara Pans wanted a revolution; it would, perhaps, be more correct to say that they want recognition of a revolution that has already taken place. They want to be acknowledged, or, more accurately, their leaders want to be acknowledged, as the political and economic equals of the clean castes. That is one reason why they tried to enter the Kondmals temple; that is the reason why they threw off customs—drinking alcohol, meat-eating, scavenging—which are associated with an inferior status; that is the reason why they were so ready to call in the police, and it is also the reason why the clean-caste council tried to keep the matter within the village and have it settled by the village council. Both sides knew that in the village council an assault by an untouchable on a person of clean caste is a heinous offence, but that in the courts the caste status of the persons involved would be considered irrelevant. That is why the Pans refused to come before the village council, and planned to get the case heard outside the village.

By taking into account relationships going outside the village, we can explain also why the dispute in Bisipara was so much more bitter than in Baderi. The Baderi Pans were less wealthy, relatively to their own clean castes, than were the Bisipara Pans; they had no men of influence; they had no educated men and no one in touch with outside political movements, while among the Bisipara Pans there was a Congress agent and two men who were candidates for the Orissa Legislative Assembly. In short, there had been no revolution in Baderi: the Pans were still very much dependent for their living on the Baderi Konds, and they were too ignorant of their constitutional rights to exploit these rights efficiently.

We have now reached a third level of understanding. The values of Hinduism—vegetarianism, untouchability, and so forth—explain the emotional significance of various actions. An analysis of groups and their interrelationships within the village sorts out the actors, provides a picture of normality, and enables us to see what is at stake—that is, what interests (political, economic, and ritual) are involved in these relationships. Finally, by looking at relationships outside the village, we see how these enabled certain groups within the village to challenge, and, to some extent, to overthrow, the established order.

I have used a phrase "levels of understanding": but I do not mean by this that the three explanations are arranged in

order of profundity, nor that any one gives us "deeper" understanding than any other. I could have presented them in a
different order—beginning, for instance, with events outside
the village, examining their effects on the structure of the
village, and coming finally to the "given" of Hindu values.
These three explanations are complementary to one another:
one is not discarded and rejected when another is taken up.

Yet, to the investigator trained in social anthropology (in
Britain anyway), these three explanations are not of the same
interest. The one which I have taken second—the structure of
groups and the institutions which regulated their interrelationships—has a special interest for us. We want to concentrate
on this and to cut down our excursions into the first and the
third field. I have already (above, pp. 57-62) discussed cultural
explanations. I now turn to what is, to me, a more difficult
problem: How, and in what circumstances, and at what point,
we can cut off our investigations of social relationships going
outside the social system which we have chosen to investigate?
I do this with reference to three problems: firstly (below,
pp. 68-70), with reference to events which are conventionally
studied by political and economic historians; secondly (pp.
71-74) with reference to systems which are conventionally
studied by economists and political scientists; thirdly (pp. 74-79)
with reference to the social ties which the Bisipara Pans have
with the Harijan movement.

HISTORY

Some events which intrude into and affect the social system
which we are studying, we have no difficulty in treating simply
as accidents, although we know that there are causes for these
events and that, in many cases, the events can be studied as
systematic regularities. If half the population is wiped out by
a plague, we do not feel bound to study the medical etiology
of the disease. We are naturally curious, and if there is a
medical explanation available in terms we can understand,
then, by knowing this explanation, we feel we have pushed
back the frontiers of our ignorance one degree. But if the
explanation happens to involve concepts peculiar to medical
science, the significance of which we could not grasp without a

training in medicine, then we are satisfied to say simply that half the population died of a plague, and begin our analysis of the effects of this disaster on the social system. We do not feel naïve in limiting our investigations in medical etiology at this point. The same can be said of a crop-failure due to blight, or a drought, or excessive rainfall or a landslide, or any one of the countless other "acts of God" which change the course of social development.

Why do we feel justified in accepting without regret our own ignorance in these matters? Firstly, it is because these events are understandable in terms of sciences which do not belong to the *social* sciences. Secondly, it may be because they seem to be "one-way" chains of causation and do not seem to have that element of *inter*connexion which might qualify them for inclusion in our social system. Nothing done by the people whose life we are studying has, in our science at least, brought on the drought or the floods. I do not deny that, in certain circumstances, these may be connected: certain kinds of flooding may be connected with soil erosion caused by slash-and-burn agriculture; the spread of a particular disease may be understandable only in terms of the social relations of the people who contract the disease. But these are not our problems, unless we choose to make them so; and the existence of these problems does not invalidate the assertion that certain natural events can be treated as accidents, the effects of which we study while ignoring their genesis. Thirdly, events like a plague or a crop-failure have a "given" quality; they are a starting-point, both for our explanations of their effects on society and for the biological explorations into their cause. If the medical research worker or the agricultural scientist lights on an explanation which subsequently proves to be wrong, then his mistakes do not affect our studies of consequences, any more than a wrong diagnosis of the cause of death alters the fact of death.

This quality of being "given" belongs also to certain events which are conventionally within disciplines concerned directly with man, particularly within history (when history is considered as a chronicle of what happened). For instance, an historian considering the privileges granted to Harijans and Adibasis in Bisipara and Baderi might trace these privileges back and connect them with the Partially-Excluded Areas provisions of the 1935 Act, and, more generally with the activities of the late Dr Ambedkar and the ambitions of the Congress Party and of the ruling power. Were the material available, an economic historian could trace back the steps by which the export of turmeric and oilseeds from the Kondmals grew—the building of roads, the opening of railways, the demands of the Calcutta industries for dye; this trade has much to do with the superior wealth of the Bisipara Pans, and is therefore an *historical* cause contributing to the disputes in Bisipara described above. Yet I consider that we can treat the policies decided upon in the 1935 Act, or the opening of roads into the Kondmals, as *given* events affecting the social system which we are studying. We need to look at their effects, but we need not be concerned with their historical genesis.

Again, one asks why this is possible. It cannot be because these events, like those discussed above, belong to the physical sciences; they belong to history. Nor is it so easy to see them as "one-way" causes. The Administration's decision to favour Pans and Adibasis was at least in some degree affected, if not by Bisipara and Baderi, at least by the totality of villages in India. These were not "acts of God," but were events and policies shaped and framed, to some extent, by what went on in the villages. But the third parallel with the physical sciences holds. We can take it as a fact that the Bisipara Pans have been able to better themselves; whether in surveying outside causes, we attribute this (wrongly) to the activities of the missionaries or (correctly) to economic growth and the policy of the Government, is neither here nor there. A wrong diagnosis of anterior causes will not—in the case of these "given" events—invalidate our analysis of their effects in the social system of the villages.

This is not a plea for ignorance: it is, as I said with reference to Indology, a claim that we must specialise. Nor, to redress the balance a little, can we claim that the superior political and economic opportunities of the Bisipara Pans have quite the same stark "given" quality as a plague or crop-failure. It is rather a very complex series of events over a relatively long time, which we must describe as fully as we can, and about which we must know at least as much as our informants think they know, but behind which we need not go in order to find historical causes.

POLITICAL SCIENCE AND ECONOMICS

Besides being treated as the end of a chain of historical causes, some events which intrude into and affect the social system chosen for study can also be studied as elements in a political or economic system. The examples are obvious. The dispute in Bisipara finally went before the Magistrate. His actions, both in this case and in others, are to be explained not only by what is brought before him, but also by the fact that he stands at a certain point in the administrative hierarchy and has relationships with those above and those below him in the hierarchy. His relationship with his superiors is one of the determinants of how he will act in the case of the Bisipara Pans, and, conversely, his decision in that case could affect his relationship with those superiors. One can be very easily led into the examination of a quite different system of relationships—the administrative hierarchy—and find oneself enquiring into their methods of recruitment, their charter or constitution, and so forth. In just the same way, the Education Department stands behind the Pan schoolmasters as one of the determinants of their actions in the case; and the same can be said for the police.

All the time the material throws up questions, the answers to which seem to lie in systems of relationships outside the one we have chosen for study. For instance, the Bisipara Pans allege that untouchables find it more difficult to approach the Administration than do men of high caste; to understand why this is true (if it is), in spite of the legal equivalence of persons irrespective of their caste membership, one would have to look not only in the village, but also at the Administration, its method and sources of recruitment, the degree of latitude allowed in the interpretation of orders, and so forth. Yet, more often then not, we need not ask these questions. If we do not choose to follow up these lines of investigation, it is not only because we have not the time and the training, but also because the answer to our own problems does not depend on the result of these investigations.

I have stated this in "black-and-white" terms, as if it were possible to draw a line and put questions on one side or the other, as being relevant or irrelevant. Obviously, this is not so, and my argument does not mean that one can remain literally within the village, being content to know, for instance, that Harijans and Adibasis receive preferential opportunities for employment in Government service. One then asks why all Harijans in the village do not have such jobs; or why more of them in Bisipara are employed in salaried occupations than there are in Baderi. The answers to these questions lie outside the villages. In the second case, the answer is that Oriya-speaking Pans (such as those in Bisipara) are better qualified for jobs in an Oriya-speaking administration than the bilingual, but mainly Kui-speaking, Pans of Baderi. In other words, one has to know the fairly simple *fact* that Oriya is the language of administration. But the answer to the first question—why all Bisipara Harijans do not have salaried jobs— could lie not only in their lack of qualifications, but also (as they sometimes allege) in the fact that the administrators are biased against them. To find out whether that is true or false, one might have to study the Administration, and one might well be led into asking what proportion of the administrators in the Kondmals come from high castes, or from very caste-conscious areas of India. But it may be impossible, for various reasons, to make this kind of verification. At that point there is no way out of the *impasse*, except the commonsense one of phrasing one's explanation cautiously, and saying that it has not been verified. The same would have to be said of an explanation which connected events in the village with the degree of bureaucratic inefficiency among (or alternatively the lack of adequate checks upon) members of the Civil Service. One tries to handle only intrusive *events*; but one may be forced back to allow *hypotheses* to intrude from another science. I think this can only be accepted as a necessity, provided one has exhausted all the possible explanations within the system one is studying (*i.e.*, providing one is not evading sociology), and provided that we recognise the intrusion for what it is: something which we cannot verify, but which is, in theory at least, capable of verification. In my explanation of the two disputes I have, on the whole, used as explanations external political and economic events (*i.e.*, historical facts) rather than hypotheses from economics and political science.

The difference between anthropology, and political science

or economics, lies in the type of relations studied. Both the latter disciplines work at a higher degree of abstraction than social anthropology. They concern themselves with specialised, or single-interest, relations; in the one case relationships involving power, and in the other case relations involving the exchange of goods and services. We do not abstract to this level; indeed our whole attention is focused on the way different relationships—economic, political, and ritual—are linked to one another. In other words, we are interested in social systems in so far as actual relations between persons tend to carry more than one interest—in so far as they are multiplex. As a rule of thumb, I found myself following single-interest relationships to one link only. One would go as far as, for instance, a decision by the Magistrate; or the salary that policemen received; or the rule by which schoolteachers had to work in villages not their own. From that point onwards one would become involved in the single-interest relationships of the Administration, or the police, or the educational system, and at that point it was possible to draw a line. I am aware, of course, that the example of the Magistrate may be a peculiarity of the Kondmals and other Agency areas, and would not apply everywhere. In some areas the community and caste affiliations of the Magistrate himself are of importance in understanding his relations with the villagers. In the Kondmals they were not, although they might have been had the Magistrate been, for instance, an untouchable.

Probably no regular relationship is truly single-interest, since the individuals involved get to know one another and to treat one another as individuals, rather than simply as incumbents of particular roles. Nevertheless there is a discernible difference in, for instance, the relationship of two village headmen in the Kondmals and the relationship of either of them with the Magistrate. Between a headman and the Magistrate the relationship is near to the single interest of *imperium*: between two headmen ties of caste and kinship are likely to be involved, as well as their relationship in the political system. In short, our investigations stop at the point where relationships tend to become single-interest and specialised, and therefore of interest to, and adapted to the techniques of, political scientists and economists.

In considering the relations of social anthropology to economics and political science, I also argue that where, within these systems of single-interest relationships, it seems necessary to regard some relationships as multiplex, then social anthropology can come back. These are the areas which lie at the margins of the purer style of economics or political science. A factory, a parliamentary assembly, a trade-union movement— in all these the purely economic or the purely political system is achieved only by quite drastic abstraction from actual behaviour. Yet in reality the alignments in an assembly are to be understood not only in terms of a constitution and of party manifestoes, but also in terms of caste, linguistic, and regional interests, and even through the kinship and other obligations of the members of the assembly.

THE WIDER SOCIETY

One reason why, in studying behaviour within a village, it seems legitimate to take as given the system of administration and the wider economic system, or such historical events as the developments of these systems, is that these systems and events "belong" to other disciplines. We are willing to make a minimal excursion, partly because we fear that through inadequate training our handling of their concepts may be trivial or naïve, and partly because we tell ourselves that it is at least possible that the required research may be done by an expert in those disciplines. In many cases this is unlikely, as Lupton and Cunnison have pointed out: nevertheless I think it justifies our making minimal use of these disciplines, but it would not, of course, justify totally ignoring them.

In the various sections of this essay I have examined different disciplines which seem to attract me in the course of trying to explain social behaviour in my chosen unit of observation, and I described in general why I have concluded that I could in most cases take the findings of these disciplines as "given." I also showed that both these other disciplines and social anthropology start from the same given events or facts and, in attempting to explain these, they work away from one another in different directions.

From our vantage point inside the village we see these other disciplines as analysing many relationships which connect the people of our village with outsiders: the relations, for instance, of the village people with the administrators, or with the merchants and traders; or, more nebulously, the relations through which Hindu culture has come and continues to come to the village ("the social organisation of tradition"). But besides these relationships there are various others, which we cannot so easily treat as "given" and which seem to demand to be treated, not by political science or economics or Indology, but by our own social anthropological skills.

Firstly, there is the social hinterland of the village, the way in which the people of our own village interact with people of other villages. In the northern part of India *de jure* or *de facto* village exogamy is frequently practised, and it is clearly part of our business to analyse and explain uterine and affinal links which run between villages, and in doing so we will be practising nothing but social anthropology. Secondly, in many parts of traditional India, the framework of politics and descent used for the analysis of African societies can be applied, for instance among the Rajputs of northern India, or among the Konds themselves. If this has been done less frequently than the analysis of caste relations within a village, that is no reason for assuming that it cannot be done. Thirdly, there are the relationships within one caste between people dispersed over many villages: the study of caste councils, the limits of their jurisdiction, and so forth. This is, I suppose, another aspect of kinship, and several ventures have been made, or are being made, into this field. Fourthly, there is the political organisation of small traditional kingdoms. It would probably be difficult to make a contemporary study of this field, but there is much to be gleaned from the literature.

These four examples (which could be multiplied) of relationships which go beyond the village and yet are susceptible to analysis by social anthropologists have this in common: they do not, except, possibly, for the fourth example—the study of traditional kingdoms—lead us into any field which belongs by convention to another social science. They are qualitatively distinct from the relationships which connect villagers with the Administration or with an expanding capitalist economy.

The second category of social relationships which go beyond

the village I find more difficult to handle, because it does not so clearly belong to social anthropology, at least to the type of social anthropology which we have so far practised. If we venture into this field we may have to develop new techniques, or take over—with the risk of being incompetent—techniques developed by other social sciences. I find it hard to define these relationships, and I will therefore indicate what I mean by an example.

In former days, before the Bisipara Pans began to become independent of their masters in Bisipara, their ties with the Pans of other villages were almost exclusively those of kinship. They had no economic relationships with one another, and the Pans of several villages were not organised as a corporate group with common interests and a common policy. Indeed, as I have noted, even within one village the Pans were not a group with political interests, but depended for their political rights on their individual Warrior masters. I conjecture that when the Baderi Pans damaged the drums of the visiting Pans (above, p. 55), they may have been angered because the visitors refused to act with the Baderi Pans against the Baderi Konds (as they could have done by refusing to take further part in the wedding) and said that what went on between Baderi Konds and Baderi Pans was no affair of outsiders.

At present there is an ever-increasing consciousness among the Pans of the Kondmals, particularly in Oriya villages, that they are a group not only in their own village but perhaps to the limits of the State or even to all-India limits. This consciousness of caste-unity over a wide area is now a common phenomenon, among other castes as well as the Pans, but its especial development among them and other untouchables has been fostered partly because they are separately classified and preferentially treated by the Administration, and partly because of the activities of the Harijan movement and the leadership of the late Dr Ambedkar. It will be remembered that I used the Bisipara Pans' knowledge of, and allegiance to, that movement as one link in a chain of explanations for their aggressiveness and self-confidence.

What is to be done about the allegiance of the Bisipara Pans to this all-India group? It might be said that the Harijan movement falls within the view of political science, for the activities of its members are very much within the arena of state and national politics, and the function of the group is partly the orthodox political one of gaining more power for itself. It can easily be viewed as a pressure-group.

If these connexions with state and national politics did not exist, then we might easily classify these relationships with other caste relationships, considering them (to use Professor Srinivas's word) "horizontally," as part of the complex of inter-village links. But they are clearly more than this. They are a link between the "village level" and the national or State level.

Can we then, with a clear conscience, push these links, which go outside the village, into the same methodological category as the Administration or the national economy? If we choose to be strict we can do so. We can begin our analysis by taking the presence in Bisipara of an untouchable Congress agent and two would-be Members of the Legislative Assembly of Orissa as "given," and see what the effect of their activities is upon the traditional structure of the village. This is, in fact, what I have done in the descriptions of the Kondmals I have so far written.

Yet, in another way, the links of the Bisipara Pans with the larger Harijan organisations are not the same as the links of the villagers with the Administration or with the agents of the capitalist economy. These links in the Harijan movement represent the genesis of a new *group*, a new corporate group with political interests but recruited not solely on the basis of political interest. The social anthropologist, as distinct from the political scientist or the economist, is peculiarly fitted to study the basis of this recruitment, because such a study involves a knowledge of village structure and of Hindu values. The same would not apply to the relationship of the villagers to merchants or the Deputy Commissioner, who do not form a group. Secondly, the Bisipara Pan allegiance to the all-India Harijan group represents a diminution of the unit we have chosen to study. In other words, the fact that these wider relationships exist, diminishes the area of intra-village relationships which are explicable without holding other things equal. We now have to take as "given" the Congress agent and the other links with the outside, in order to understand Pan-

Warrior relationships; whereas formerly Pan-Warrior relationships were entirely explicable within the structure of the village. Our field is diminished by the villager-Magistrate link or the villager-merchant link. But the difference is that we are qualified to examine and analyse the Harijan movement (at least in its more local manifestations) because it is a group, and because this group is held together by multiplex links, in that it has political aims, is recruited on a criterion of ritual (untouchability), and is potentially at least a group which will be held together in part by kinship links. To a greater degree than most political parties in India (Communist, Socialist, or Congress, for example) the Harijan pressure group contains multiplex ties. A similar example would be the Jharkand party, which is recruited from and represents the interests of Adibasis in Bihar and northern Orissa.

I am not arguing that one *must* analyse relationships within the Harijan movement—say in Orissa or even in the Kondmals —before one can understand what goes on in Bisipara between the Pans and the Warriors. Clearly the time for research is limited, and it seems legitimate to take his wider organisation as one of the "given" factors. But I am arguing that an investigation of this Harijan movement—and similar groups arising within the modern complex State political system—is both feasible for us and the logical next step in our research. An investigation of the Administration or the economic system, using the methods and concepts of political science or economics, is not the next step; it is a field better explored by someone else.

Research into these larger groups is logically the next step, because the more such supra-village-level relationships come into being, the more difficult will it be for us to isolate a significant system of social relationships located roughly in a village. The more such relationships exist, the more is the village integrated in a larger whole, and the more it comes to resemble, for instance, a London middle-class suburb where the sole link comes near to being that of living close together, while all other activities are conducted elsewhere. The nearer to this condition the villages come, the more the social anthropologist needs to be prepared to interest himself in relationships outside the village. If the explanatory value of analysing the social structure of the village becomes very low, and a relatively large number of factors have to be taken as "given," then the social anthropologist must be prepared to select, using the criteria discussed above (pp. 72-74), those "given" elements which seem susceptible to social analysis by his own techniques, or by techniques and concepts which he may devise to analyse them; otherwise he runs the risk of losing touch with the contemporary reality. Those "given" elements which belong clearly to economics or political science, he can safely leave alone.

CONCLUSIONS

In order to understand what happened in the disputes in Bisipara and Baderi, I did not try to find out what was the "world view" of the people of these villages, nor to see their culture as the product of an interchange between folk and urban traditions. Rather I have tried to understand behaviour in so far as it could be related as one part to other parts in a system.

No one who uses the concept of social structure is so naïve (or no one ought to be so naïve) as to imagine that by identifying regular relationships he has understood the totality of behaviour. Again and again he comes up against facts which he has to write off as "given" or as, from his point of view, accidents. The process of abstracting regularities from actual behaviour is like chipping away the unwanted parts and rubbing down what is left until it is logically sound, or, to follow the metaphor, aesthetically pleasing. When we have carved out the regularities we are left with a great detritus of "unexplained." Other people sometimes look with horror at the mound of unexplained facts, and complain that social anthropology is arid or merely academic, or they ask if we know that we are dealing with human beings. Yet our limitations are obvious: if we venture to forecast, we do not imply that we have understood the totality of behaviour by saying "x will happen," but rather "If x happens, then y also will happen, because x and y have been shown to be linked (other things being equal) in one system."

In this essay I have been preoccupied with the "detritus"

of unexplained facts. It is natural that anyone who studies Indian society would be brought harder against this problem than are those whose studies deal with the "primitive isolate," as Redfield called it. The "isolate" is not always so easily isolable in practice, and there is always an element of the arbitrary in the lines we draw round even the most primitive societies. It is so much the harder to draw lines around a village of peasants which is part of one of the world's great nations.

In so far as a village in India or Latin America or in our own country is not primitive, we are concerned not so much to delineate a unit for study, as to define the bounds of different disciplines. To an economist or a political scientist, what pass for economic or political data in a primitive society seem so jejune and so far removed from his experience that he does not feel professionally involved in what social anthropologists say about primitive economics or primitive political systems. But this is not the case in India. The events which we consider in the villages are also part of a literate tradition, and of a known sequence of historical events, and are appropriated and studied by economists and political scientists.

In other words, what I have classified as detritus is in fact the subject-matter of other disciplines, or of anthropologists who bring to this discipline an outlook different from the one taken in this essay. I have picked four categories out of the "given": the disciplines of Indology and history, economics and political science. These fall conveniently into two categories, and I will summarise my argument by considering each of them separately.

In dealing with the two former disciplines we have to steer a way between Scylla and Charybdis. The Scylla is that, through ignorance of, for instance, the value of Hinduism, we might fail to appreciate the significance of particular actions and relationships. To take an extreme instance, I might have treated the two disputes as arising from simple assaults, and not realised the significance of untouchability. In the case of history, I might, in ignorance of the Government's policy of favouring untouchables, have tried to explain the dispute between clean castes and untouchables solely within a system of regular behaviour.

The Charybdis, on the other hand, consists in too quick a

resort to the "given" and the evasion of a sociological explanation by an appeal to values or historical accidents. The disputes, for instance, would not have been explained sufficiently by stating the moral issues involved between clean castes and untouchables, and ignoring the fact that this relationship also has political and economic aspects.

It is clear that, even if in our analyses of social regularities the cultural facts and the historical background are left tacitly unconsidered, it would be foolish not to know as many of these facts as we can. But it does not follow that we have to become Indologists or historians. There is no universal formula for knowing where to draw the line; each case has to be considered on its own. A sociological study of a Buddhist monastery is likely to require considerable familiarity with sacred literature, while fieldwork among a tribe such as the Chenchus would require practically none.

But there is a line to be drawn between the knowledge of culture (or history) required to understand social relations, and the study of that culture (or historical sequence) as an end in itself. To trace historically the growth of Dr Ambedkar's movement, or to plot the distribution of particular traits of Hinduism on a criterion of morphological similarity, or to discover the link between the "great tradition" and the "little tradition" manifestation of those traits, are questions to which we may be led by interest, but not by the requirements of sociological analysis.

The difference between social anthropology on the one hand and economics or political science on the other, is that we have grown used to analysing multiplex relationships, while economics and political science deal usually with single-interest relationships. We abstract to a lower degree and we are nearer to reality. It is from this fact, as I argued above, that we can expect to find areas where we can work in a field that by convention belongs to political science or to economics.

Finally we have to recognise that not only have we moved, in studying India or our own country, into a more complex field, but also that many fields which once were primitive isolates are tending more and more to become complex and permeated by specialist single-interest relationships. I am not arguing that there are no longer any primitive isolates; still

F

less am I arguing that we have completed the study of primitive isolates and can turn to other fields. But I am arguing that our techniques, even as they exist now, do not rule us out of the more complex field.

When we study problems in a factory, or a mining township, or a parliamentary assembly, our techniques might be modified and developed, but they will still be different from the techniques of the orthodox economists and political scientists; because our interests are different. By venturing into this field we do not make ourselves half-trained economists or incompetent political scientists: to think so would be to confuse data with analysis.

4

A. L. Epstein

URBAN COMMUNITIES IN AFRICA

[written in 1957]

INTRODUCTION: THE "COMMUNITY STUDY"

Whatever the position may have been in the past, the groups and institutions which social anthropologists elect to study today are rarely isolated and self-sufficient units; more generally they form part of, or at least have close links with, some wider and more extensive politico-economic system. The general problem raised in this volume is particularly relevant in the study of the new urban communities now so rapidly developing throughout Africa: in this essay I have attempted to examine briefly the way in which it emerged in the course of my own field-work in a mining community on the Copperbelt of Northern Rhodesia.

But before turning to the Copperbelt itself, it may be useful to state the problem as it has arisen in the field of urban studies in general. The urban community represents a distinctive form of social life going on within an environment which has not only been artificially created, but is continually changing: it has therefore a highly complex form of social organisation, the study of which presents a number of immediate difficulties. As the Lynds found when they came to undertake their pioneer study of Middletown, the town presents itself to the observer as some kind of phantasmagoria, a succession of dim figures caught up in a myriad of diverse activities, with little to give meaning or pattern to it all. Faced with this problem, the Lynds held that "some kind of orderly procedure in such a maze" was to be found in the approach of the cultural anthropologist. Taking the community as the unit of study, they decided to approach Middletown as the anthropologist would a primitive tribe.[1] At the time the assumptions underlying this approach appear to have been accepted uncritically. It was only with the gradual development of the "community study," and in particular the anthropological analyses of social class in American society, that students began to raise the serious objections that can be levelled at this kind of approach. For the town cannot be handled in the same way as the tribe for these purposes: they belong to different orders of social organisation. The tribal community is, in general terms, an isolable unit, culturally self-sufficient: it exists in its own right. By contrast, the modern urban community has no independent existence. As Goldschmidt observes, the urban community cannot be treated as a "microcosm of culture" or world-in-little, because it exists only within and as part of a wider system.[2] Major decisions which affect most intimately the life of the community are taken in remote power centres; the institutions which flourish in the town, and most deeply influence behaviour, frequently have a national or regional, not a local, referent.

This situation poses a serious dilemma for the anthropologist. Much of modern anthropology has tended to concern itself with systems of social relations and with the processes of social interaction studied within the narrow context of local communities. In anthropological thinking the local community has come to provide, not only the working laboratory, but also the point of reference for analysis. But when we turn to the study of town life we find so many phenomena important in guiding the behaviour of urban dwellers which are not themselves explicable in terms of, nor directly referable to, the structure of the local community.

The general point I am making here is particularly well illustrated in the case of the towns of the Northern Rhodesian Copperbelt. Discussing urban growth in the United States, Hallenbeck[3] has associated the development of cities with

[1] Robert S. and Helen Lynd, *Middletown* [1929], p. 3.

[2] W. Goldschmidt, "Social Class in America—a Critical Review," in *American Anthropologist* [1950], pp. 483-98 ff.

[3] W. Hallenbeck, *American Urban Communities* [1951], p. 15.

national development. He observes: "In the social and economic evolution of a nation there comes a time when certain functions require cities." But in Central Africa towns have grown up in response, not to any indigenous or national need, but rather to those of colonial expansion. Towns such as Kitwe, Luanshya, or Chingola owe their present existence entirely to the development of the copper-mining industry— an industry which is organised and controlled by corporations based and operating far beyond the boundaries of Northern Rhodesia. Linked thus to a world economic system, the life of these towns is very much at the mercy of movements in the price of copper and other developments on the world market. Linked similarly to a wider political system, social relations within the town reflect the pronouncements of Colonial Office policy, or the activities and manœuvrings of other foreign governments. More immediately, however, the "colonial" origins of the towns are to be seen in their social composition and character. The set of pre-existing conditions which Hallenbeck[4] has specified as essential for the indigenous development of cities was absent in Central Africa. Power, labour supply, capital, etc., and the various technical, administrative, and managerial skills to direct and control them, have all had to be imported. Consequently the new urban populations are multi-racial, culturally heterogeneous, and marked by sharp divisions of wealth, power, and privilege: behaviour in many situations is closely affected by the ideologies and attitudes which individuals have brought with them from their original homes. Within the "colonial" structure there develops, too, a "national" structure which also has its part in shaping events within the urban community. Thus many of the matters of closest concern to urban Africans, such as housing or labour conditions, fall within the province of relations between the African employees and the mine managements; but they are also affected by the policies of the Central Government on urban stabilisation, agricultural development, and so on, as well as by the relations between the mining companies and other European employers of labour.

There is very little novel in affirming that the modern towns of Africa form part of a national and colonial structure.

[4] *Op. cit.*, pp. 15-16.

If I have laboured the point, it is only because certain writers now seem to hold that the external factors are of such over-riding importance, and that regional and national scales and standards have become so much a part of the local scene, that the studies made by anthropologists of urban communities are of little sociological interest. Thus in a recent critique Mills writes:

> Most local community studies [of prestige], so often the unit of sociological study, are of merely local interest. One cannot even say that they are of interest beyond that because of methodological innovations they make possible, for in truth most of these methodological advancements are suitable only for what they have been worked out for—local community studies.[5]

Mills's strictures carry a good deal of weight, particularly where they are directed against the tendency to generalise from small town to society at large.[6] If he appears unduly harsh, certainly the case he presents is so strong that it behoves the anthropologist to define more carefully the limits within which he is working, and to indicate more specifically what he can hope to achieve within those limits. The present essay is designed as a tentative contribution to this discussion.

THE POLITICAL PROCESS AND THE SOCIAL STRUCTURE OF THE LOCAL COMMUNITY

Each of the mining towns of the Copperbelt is made up of two adjoining but otherwise quite distinct administrative and residential units, the one known as the "Mine Township," the other as the "Government Township." Each township in turn is divided into two spatially segregated areas for Europeans and Africans. These African areas are referred to here respectively as the "Mine Compound" and the "Municipal Location." The Mine Township includes the working area of the mine itself: but within it are the houses provided by the mining company for all European and African employees, the hospital, recrea-

---

[5] C. Wright Mills, *The Power Elite* [1957], p. 368.

[6] It may be worth noting in this connexion that although the Lynds disclaim any typicality for Middletown, their book carries the sub-title: *A Study of American Culture*.

tion centres, and so on. The Government Township has developed as a kind of service centre for the mine: here are to be found the town's business premises, and public offices, as well as the residential areas for those who are not employed on the mine. There are of course close relations between the two townships, which are dependent upon one another for a number of services. But otherwise each is a quite distinct and independent unit, possessing its own governing body. The Central Government, and ultimately the Colonial Office, is directly represented in the town through the office of the District Commissioner, who has important functions, particularly in regard to the African residents of the town. Thus the town as a whole possesses a complex economic and administrative structure, the main features of which stem from the social and political dominance of the Europeans. The Europeans, whether as "settlers" or expatriate colonial officials, control the centres of power within the community, and thus provide and maintain the structure within which African social life in the towns is largely organised.

In my own field-research, I was primarily concerned with problems of social organisation amongst the African section of the urban population, in particular the emergence of African political institutions in the towns. Already in an earlier study of the African urban courts I had come to see African political life in the towns as dominated by a struggle for power within the existing administrative framework. Now, therefore, I was interested to investigate further the nature of the cleavages operating within the urban communities, the processes of group formation, the relations between these groups, and the type of leadership associated with them. When I began work at Luanshya I was at once struck by certain differences between the Mine Compound and the Municipal Location. For example, it was soon apparent that in the Mine Compound there was general consensus on who were the leaders in the African community: in the Municipal Location I found no such consensus and questioning generally drew forth a stereotyped response to the effect that every tribe or group considered its own leaders to be most important. As the study progressed, it also became clear that there were marked differences as between Compound and Location in the way political groups had developed there, and the degree of internal cohesion and influence they had been able to achieve. By virtue of their training and interests, anthropologists who enter the field of urban studies in Africa tend to be predisposed in the direction of the African section of the urban community, especially to the problems of social change involved in the Africans' adjustment to urban conditions. This is a quite legitimate interest, and one which I have myself followed. But springing directly from it, I suggest, is a tendency at times to see the urban community as a kind of ragbag, drawing its population from different regions and cultures, but having no social system of its own; with this approach there is associated a further tendency to interpret African behaviour in the towns against the background of the tribal system. When it came to interpreting my own observations of urban political life, I found this conceptual approach not merely unhelpful, but even misleading, and I was led to try to account for the various differences I had encountered between Compound and Location in terms of the different modes of economic organisation in the Mine and Government Townships, and the different forms of administration associated with each.

The mining of copper today is a highly technical process which demands, for maximum efficiency, a complex organisation. On the Copperbelt, everyone working on the mine is an employee of a common employer, and every employee must live on mine premises; work and wages are controlled and directed by the common authority. But in the conditions under which mining developed in Northern Rhodesia, the organisation which has been built up by the mining companies extends far beyond what would be required by the immediate tasks of copper-production: housing, health, and, in earlier days, feeding, all fell within the responsibilities assumed by the mining company. The African who joins the mine passes through an induction school, and is then allocated to a labour gang which has its African boss-boy or charge-hand and European supervisor, and he carries out regular tasks according to planned schedules. Off duty, he drinks his beer at the beer-hall on the mine; he attends the cinema at the mine welfare centre, and when he and his wife and children are ill they are treated in the hospital provided and staffed by the mining company. In short, social life is linked at nearly every point with the organisation built up and administered by the mining company. In sharp contrast, a location in the Government Township is merely a a large housing area which lacks any central organising principle; here there is no common authority which integrates the various activities of the African population in work and leisure. The location residents, for example, are in employment with a wide variety of employers. By law, employers are responsible for the payment of rent on the houses of their employees. In effect, houses are tied to jobs: when a man loses his job he also loses his house. Thus each individual is dependent upon and has to turn to his own employer for support in this matter. Moreover, for large categories of workers there is no standardisation of wages or working conditions such as obtains on the mines which might tend to create a sense of community of interests amongst location residents.

These differences in organisation obtaining in Mine Compound and Municipal Location are best brought out perhaps in comparing the positions of the two key personalities in their respective administrative structures—the African Personnel Manager on the mine, and the Location Superintendent. The former is responsible for the maintenance of discipline amongst the African labour force; he is responsible for all matters connected with the running of the Mine Compound, and so on. (It may be added that so insistent is mine-management on the importance of the Personnel Manager's position and authority that the General Manager himself rarely visits the compound: more than this his position is also jealously guarded against any encroachment of the Central Government in the person of the District Commissioner.) But, above all, it is the master/servant element which is important in his relationship with the Compound residents. The African Personnel Manager "hires and fires" labour; he deals with workers' grievances; and nowadays he negotiates with the African Mine Workers Trade Union on behalf of the mine management in matters affecting wages or working conditions. By contrast, the Location Superintendent is largely concerned with providing accommodation, collecting rents, and maintaining the general cleanliness of the Location. There is no element here of the master/servant relationship: the Location Superintendent has no concern whatsoever with questions of wages or working conditions affecting those African who live in the location.

Given these differences in the social organisation of the two townships, we are in a better position to understand other differences between them, as in forms of social grouping, in patterns of behaviour, and in values and attitudes on a wide variety of matters. Thus, in the course of a study of mass communications on the Copperbelt, Professor Powdermaker found considerable differences in reading and other habits as between the two townships.[7] In the political sphere, likewise, we can trace out some of the consequences that follow from these differences of social structure. On the mine where, as I have argued, so much is channelled through the mine-organisation itself, certain Africans who occupied key positions in the structure as intermediaries between the African public and the European Compound officials tended to be thrown up as leaders. For instance, at an election for the local Urban Advisory Council which took place during my stay in Luanshya, of the eleven Mine Compound respresentatives elected, five were employed as clerks in an office immediately adjoining that of the African Personnel Manager: here, of course, they were constantly on hand to act as interpreters in the cases continuously being brought before the Manager. These men were younger and better-educated in the main than the Tribal Elders who at one time had provided such African leadership as there was in the Mine Compound, and with whom they soon came successfully to compete for positions on various official representative councils. The respect accorded to Tribal Elders rested, at least initially, on a whole complex of values and attitudes deriving from tribal society; the prestige and authority of the younger men had its sources within the urban community itself, so that when trade-unionism was introduced to Africans in Northern Rhodesia, and the African Mine Workers Trade Union established, it was these younger men who provided the leadership. The African Mine Workers Union flourished, and it rapidly grew in strength. Gradually it began to acquire functions which would nowadays in this country be generally regarded as falling outside the scope of trade-unionism. Trade-unionism amongst

[7] H. Powdermaker: unpublished report presented to the Rhodes-Livingstone Institute by the author. For a fuller discussion see her *Copper Town* [1962].

Africans is not, of course, confined to mine-workers. There are a number of other unions today which cater for shop-assistants, drivers, general workers, and so on. Since these cater for a membership living in the municipal locations and peri-urban settlements, they may here be collectively termed "location unions." Some of them can claim a territory-wide membership, but in fact none has been able to achieve anything like the strength of the Mine Workers Union. The story of the location unions provides indeed a striking contrast with that of the Mine Workers Union: it is one of dissension between leaders, vacillation in policy and action, and a record showing few positive achievements. In many cases branches of location unions only have a nominal existence.

It is important to try to explain these differences, and I think we can go some way towards this in terms of the hypothesis suggested earlier. As already indicated, the African Personnel Manager was responsible for matters touching nearly every aspect of African life in the Compound, on which he always had to be approached and consulted. In the same way, the local African union leaders came to be seen by members as possessing, though from a different point of view, a similar range of responsibilities, extending far beyond the matter of wages and working conditions of union members. In this particular context it seems appropriate to describe the African Personnel Manager and the local Branch Secretary as occupying positions structurally equivalent but opposed. The Mine Workers Union indeed worked within a framework of organisation created by the mining company for its own purposes: an examination of the internal organisation of the local branch would show that it tends at almost every point to be geared into the organisation of the mine itself. The location unions, on the other hand, face serious problems of organisation very different from those which obtain on the mines. Serving different and competitive industries, the location unions are themselves divided. In the mining industry, wage-rates and working conditions are generally standardised, so that on any specific issue union members are likely to have a certain amount of common ground between them. In smaller and less tightly organised industries, there is more room for variation in these respects, and therefore less likelihood of union members, by whatever firm they are employed, taking a stand upon a common issue. Again, in terms of union organisation, the wide scatter of members, in respect of residence and employment, makes it virtually impossible to hold the vast branch public meetings such as are called regularly in the Mine Compound, and which serve to strengthen awareness of the union as a vital entity. Among location unions, such meetings of the branches as take place are of small working and residential groups, and tend to make for division rather than unity.

The difficulties of organisation confronting the location unions are presumably not insuperable—but they demand of officials qualities which the present leaders do not possess. The location unions have acquired as permanent officials very young men who not only lack organising skill but have little knowledge of the industries with which their unions are associated, and no experience of negotiation. This is not altogether accidental, and accords, I suggest, with the form of social organisation characteristic of the Location. I have argued that on the mine, mine-organisation itself served to focus attention on certain key personalities who thus came to be widely known and recognised by Africans as their spokesmen. Moreover, there had been on the mine, from the very beginning, some form of consultation by management with African committees of various kinds. Meetings of the African Personnel Manager (or Compound Manager, as he was called in the early days) with Tribal Representatives, with the Boss-Boys, and later with the Works Committees, brought the African spokesmen into regular contact with the common authority, and enabled them to acquire some experience of negotiation. A further factor of possible significance is that, in earlier days, when the total population of the Government Township was very small, and opportunities for employment were few, the ablest Africans were drawn to the mines. At all events, when the African Mine Workers Trade Union finally emerged there were already available relatively older and more experienced men to take office.

The Locations, on the other hand, lacking the same strong centralising tendency working within the social structure, have not thrown up in the same way individuals who have come to be widely acknowledged as spokesmen for the whole community. Within the Location there exists a multiplicity of different groupings, each catering for a different set of interests; there is a multiplicity of leaders, each with his own small following: amongst these the union leaders do not stand out as being very different in kind or influence. In the same way, and for the same reasons, there has never been in the Location the same close relationship between African representatives and the Location Superintendent such as exists on the mine. It is true that there have been from the beginning Tribal Elders in the Location whose function it was to assist the Location Superintendent in various ways in the administration of Location affairs. In the main, their duties have been confined to the settling of domestic disputes, and to providing hospitality for strangers newly arrived in the town until they have been able to find their own kinsmen. In short, their work has conformed largely to the traditional concept of eldership as it operated in the villages; it has never extended to the discussion of labour questions as did the work of Tribal Representatives on the mines. In this connexion, it is perhaps worth noting, as a final illustration of the differences obtaining between the two Townships, and as further support for the hypothesis advanced, that while tribal representation was abolished a few years ago at the instance of the Mine Workers Union, similar attempts by location union leaders to oust the Location Elders have so far been unsuccessful. On the contrary, Tribal Elders appear to continue to hold the respect of large numbers of location residents.[8]

Thus far in my analysis I have been discussing certain regularities in political behaviour which I observed in the field, and have sought to account for them by relating them to local community structure. There were, however, other events which fell within the scope of my enquiry which could not so easily be handled within this framework. In working out the differences between Mine and Government Townships, I have found it convenient to distinguish between the "unitary" structure of the one and the "atomistic" structure of the other. I describe mine society as "unitary" in the sense that so much of what goes on in the mine is channelled or controlled through

[8] It is interesting to note that a number of committee members in location unions are also Tribal Elders.

the mine bureaucracy: the term "atomistic" is used simply to suggest the very sharp contrast presented by the situation obtaining in the location. I argue beyond this that because it develops within a unitary structure, the African Mine Workers Union itself tends to take on certain unitary characteristics and to assume widespread responsibilities to its members. The ascription of unitary character does not, of course, imply the absence of internal cleavage and division. Africans on the mine are divided amongst themselves in all sorts of ways; therefore where the Union comes to express the unity of African employees at a political level, it must also contain within its own structure the cleavages which operate in the wider mine society.

The problem of cleavages within groups, and of fission leading to the emergence of new groups, had attracted my attention early in my field-work; it was thrust into sharper focus by an election for the office of Branch Chairman which took place while I was in Luanshya, and, shortly afterwards, by a number of important developments touching the question of African advancement in the mining industry. To take the election first: there were four candidates for the position, three of whom were mine clerks. One of these was the retiring Chairman, who was standing for re-election, while another had been Branch Chairman in the past. The fourth, who won finally by a handsome margin, was a boss-boy who had spent the best part of his working career—some twenty-odd years— underground. In marked contrast to the other candidates, he was uneducated, spoke little English—and that haltingly—and was widely known throughout the Compound for his physical toughness and fearlessness, particularly where Europeans were concerned. The election of the boss-boy represented a radical departure from the kind of leadership which had hitherto prevailed in the Union: at the same time the whole conduct of the election threw into relief some of the divisions which were operating within the African mine community. Thus the spontaneous comments of the voters which I was able to record as they moved to and from the ballot boxes suggested at first hostility between underground and surface workers. The latter include the various labour categories employed at the concentrator, the smelter, the engineering, and other departments, as well as those in the personnel and administration departments. Yet it was only against the last that underground workers launched their diatribes. It was the relatively small category of clerks, from which hitherto the leadership had been drawn, that alone was singled out for vilification and abuse. The charges laid against the clerks were couched in terms of their education, and the aloofness and arrogance to which it was alleged to give rise. But behind this there lay, too, a view of the clerks as having a different kind of interest in the industry. "People who speak English are cowards," was an expression heard frequently throughout the election. Africans on the Copperbelt who are proficient in English are still relatively few, and they are generally to be found as clerks, hospital orderlies, welfare assistants, and the like. Indeed, for those with a Standard Six education, who count as highly educated in comparison with the mass of their fellows, there are still few jobs beyond these to which they can aspire. Since these jobs, which carry relatively high wages, are still fairly rare outside the mines, there is keen competition for them. Mine clerks tend, therefore, to be amongst the most stable element in the labour force. By contrast, manual labourers are easily replaceable, and find less difficulty in switching from job to job. Consequently, they tend to see mine clerks and others in high labour categories as being too circumspect in their behaviour. They accuse the clerks of being dominated by a fear of losing their jobs. Given their position, the argument runs, how could they be expected to prosecute with full vigour the cause of the mass of their fellow-Africans who were unskilled labourers? The new Chairman, on the other hand, was a man who had worked underground, and knew how Europeans treated Africans there. He was not afraid of anyone, and would himself assault any European who used insulting language to an African worker. He possessed the quality which above all the voters seemed to demand of a leader—the quality of militancy, which the other candidates lacked.

If these events were to be viewed solely within a local context, they might be taken as evidence of the existence of a clearly-demarcated class structure within the African Mine Compound: in these terms, the election of the new Chairman might then be interpreted as evidence for asserting the emergence of a militant "working-class" leadership. The divisions

within the Mine Compound which were highlighted throughout the whole conduct of the election are undoubtedly real; but
the only effect of a "class" or "local" interpretation of the
election would be to obscure a crucial element in the situation,
namely the internal political struggles going on within the
African Mine Workers Union as a whole. If the new Chairman
had the kind of personality and approach that enabled him to
carry a mass meeting with him, he was at the same time more
amenable to the influence of his politically more agile and
perceptive Branch Secretary, who was a permanent paid
official of the Union, and a member of the Union executive.
And, indeed, it was clear that the election of the new Chairman
was due in large measure to the skilful manipulations of the
Branch Secretary. Previously, the union branch committee was
composed of representatives drawn from the different departments of the mine, and the Chairman was elected by the
committee. On this occasion, however, the Secretary had been
successful in persuading the branch to hold a popular election
by secret ballot as being a more democratic procedure. The
Branch Secretary was bitterly opposed on personal and political
grounds to the leadership of the General President who ran the
Union headquarters at Kitwe. Thus the election of the new
Chairman, who on a number of occasions had shown he was
not the kind of man to be browbeaten by the General President,
clearly strengthened the position of the Luanshya branch in its
opposition to headquarters.

Shortly after this election the importance of intra-union
politics began to emerge more strikingly, for the internal
struggle was now being further exacerbated by the discussions
taking place around the central problem of African advancement in industry. Space does not permit the discussion of this
complex issue in any detail. Very briefly, then, the present
talks were addressed to finding a formula whereby Africans
could advance to positions of greater skill and responsibility in
the mining industry without affecting too seriously the position
of European workers. The interested parties to these talks were
the mine managements, the European Mine Workers Union,
the European Salaried Staff Association, and the African Mine
Workers Union. There had been innumerable discussions and
conferences in the past on the issue of African advancement,

but they had always broken down, mainly because of the European Union's insistence on the acceptance of the principle of equal pay for equal work throughout the industry as a condition of African advancement to posts of higher responsibility. The European Union's case rested, of course, on the assumption that advancement on any other terms would open the way to a cheap labour policy, and thus constitute a serious threat to White living standards, and indeed the whole position of the Europeans in the community.

The African Union was itself divided on the question of the equal-pay formula. Some of the leaders appear to have been prepared to accept it: but there was also an important opposing faction which took the line that advancement on these terms would benefit only a tiny handful, who would be promoted to jobs of relative importance and responsibility, while the vast majority of the unskilled and semi-skilled would find their position unchanged. In these circumstances, members of the opposing faction argued, the former would probably join a counterpart of the European Salaried Staff Association, while the latter would come to see themselves as having been betrayed by their leaders and the power of the Union would thus be broken. During the months that the talks on advancement proceeded, there was much discussion of the matter amongst the Africans themselves and it seems clear from the comments I was able to gather that the question was viewed differently in different sections of the community. Thus while some in high-labour groups saw advancement as providing an opportunity to take over posts at present filled by Europeans at European rates of pay, labourers and others spoke merely in terms of an overall improvement in wages and working conditions.

At length the discussions ended in deadlock. Immediately, there was a rapid decline in membership of the African Union, while at the same time branches of an African Salaried Staff Association began to appear all over the Copperbelt. The upshot of these developments was a sudden intensification of strife within and between the various African organisations. This found its expression in a protracted period of industrial unrest which, after a series of rolling strikes, culminated in 1956 in a declaration of a State of Emergency in the Western Province, and the swift removal to detention camps of many of the leaders—notably of the opposition faction—of the African Mine Workers Trade Union.

The mere recital of these events is sufficient to show the extent to which the life of a modern urban community is bound up in the developments taking place in the wider social field of which it forms part. At the same time it raises in acute form the problem of handling the relationship between behaviour observed in the local community and events and relationships which go on outside. Thus I have referred to the opposition faction within the union leadership which was opposed to the acceptance of the equal pay for equal work formula. The leaders of this faction were also frequently outspoken nationalists, and at least one held high office in the African National Congress. They opposed the policies espoused by the General President of the Union and his followers on the grounds that it would promote a rift in the African ranks: Africans would no longer present a united front *vis-à-vis* the Europeans. Acceptance of such policies, they argued, would sharpen awareness of African "class" divisions, and result in the emergence of an African counterpart of the European Mine Salaried Staff Association, a possibility which they violently denounced. In the end the "Congress" faction lost the struggle, though I have no means of knowing what particular form the struggle took, or what particular pressures led to its being decided one way or the other. What does stand out is that many of the events taking place within Luanshya can only be satisfactorily understood if they are seen as forming part of a complex system of relationships whose boundaries stretch far beyond the town. We may, if we like, see the emergence of an African Salaried Staff Association at Luanshya as an obvious reflexion of the cleavages I described as operating within the African mine-community there; but the cleavages do not explain how or why such an association should have come into being at that time. Here a fuller understanding would have to take into account the policies and aims of the mining companies, and the ways in which these were affected, for example, by the question of foreign investment, as well as relations within and between various European and African organisations. But here we move into an area where the data required, as well as the technical means of handling them, are not normally available to the anthropologist. To take a simple example, it would appear to be a reasonable assumption that the mining companies considered it to their advantage to have a "buffer" between themselves and the African Mine Workers Trade Union. It is possible, therefore, that the African Salaried Staff Association's existence owed more than a little to the support given it by certain mine Personnel Managers. But these can be assumptions only: I, at least, have not adequate evidence to support them, nor the material to make the necessary analysis.

LIMITS AND LIMITATIONS

I have been attempting here to look at the theme of this book in the light of two problems which emerged out of field-work in a mining community on the Copperbelt. The range of my enquiry was limited to the development of political groups and institutions amongst urban Africans. The analysis given here should serve to make at least one point clear: that the urban community cannot be regarded as being made up of a number of independent ethnic communities. The process of urbanisation has sometimes been regarded as a movement from the ordered ways of tribal life to the anarchy of the urban jungle. Here the use of terms such as "disorganisation" or "malaise" applied to the urban situation suggest a profound methodological error, for they imply the assessment of urban conditions against a model of the traditional tribal system: such concepts help little in understanding the kind of phenomena described in this essay. In fact, of course, the town is not a jungle; it has its own specific and highly complex form of organisation into which the African who comes to town has to fit himself. In a word, we have to view the town as a single field of social relations in which the different, and sometimes opposed, sections of the urban population are also closely linked by ties of interdependence.

Approaching the town in this way, I have sought to show how we can make a useful beginning by explaining certain differences in the behaviour of urban Africans in the domain of politics by relating these to the different forms of organisation obtaining in a mine compound and a municipal location. On the other hand, the town is not an isolated or self-sufficient unit: it is closely integrated into a wider politico-economic system which is continuously influencing events within the local community. Therefore we can also expect that other problems within that same domain of politics should compel us to raise our sights beyond the immediate level of the local community being studied. It is at this point, I think, that we become most acutely aware that we are approaching the limits of our anthropological competence, and exposing ourselves to the charge of naïvety.

An analysis can be naïve in at least two ways: in the lack of sophistication with which it handles concepts and data or in the lack of awareness of the relevance of other factors which would strike specialists in other disciplines as at once obvious. On the first score, it seems scarcely necessary to observe that my picture of the urban social system is considerably over-simplified; there are also many factors present in the situation which find no mention in my analysis, but which might well have a direct bearing on the growth and development of African political institutions in the town. In particular, I have offered no detailed analysis either of economic organisation or administrative structure. In drawing a comparison between the Mine and Government Townships I was presented with a crude polarity of forms, economic and administrative, which I could use without making the detailed analysis that would in any case have been beyond my competence. Such naïvety, I would argue, is necessary at certain stages in the development of analysis, and justifiable in the present circumstances on the grounds that I was working within the limits of relevance. Detailed examination of these and other factors was not necessary in terms of the problem posed, and would have contributed little further to our solution of it.

The risk of exposure to the charge of naïvety in the second sense is likely to be stronger when we are compelled to move beyond the confines of the local community being studied, as in the discussion of fission and group formation amongst Africans on the mine. Here, as we have seen, we are confronted more sharply with the limits of knowledge, of available data. Many of the decisions, and much of the political by-play, even when they are taken and take place in the community being studied, represent material which is inaccessible to the observer.

But a more serious handicap is that as we move further from our own theoretical base we are likely to be more unaware of other factors and variables of direct relevance to our problem. Here again I would argue that, in a field of enquiry still relatively uncultivated, a measure of naïvety in the handling of the wider system may be justified; but I would be less ready to affirm in the present case that a closer acquaintance with political science or the history of trade unionism elsewhere might not have led me to a different view of the problem.

The issue I have just been discussing raises what I may call the problem of the limits of the discipline. For certain purposes it may be convenient to regard a town as having its own internal structure; but in other contexts it is essential to bear in mind that a town represents the point of intersection of a number of different activity systems. In these circumstances, therefore, the anthropologist has to become increasingly aware of the possible importance of external factors, and accordingly of the concepts and methods of other academic disciplines impinging on his field. This problem arises in its most acute form when, as in the case of Lupton and Cunnison's workshop studies, a number of different urban studies have been conducted with the same general problem in mind, and one has to seek an explanation for the differences that emerge. Thus if the hypothesis suggested earlier in this essay were to be tested out in other urban communities in Africa—say Elisabethville or Bulawayo—or if one were to try to explain why tribal associations and tribal unions have developed to such a high degree in West Africa whereas they are relatively unimportant in Northern Rhodesia, the procedures adopted in Luanshya might not be sufficient. One might well have to take into account and analyse many of the factors and variables which in Luanshya I was able to accept as given or to exclude as irrelevant—such as the attitudes and policies of colonial powers, the views of local governments on urban stabilisation and agricultural development, the cultural background and personalities of those making up the population of the new towns, and so on. It is at this point where the anthropologist, compelled like Lupton and Cunnison to handle a cluster of external variables, may have to become a naïve historian, a naïve economist and political scientist—and possibly a naïve anthropologist.

We are compelled, then, to recognise that the study of urban communities sets certain limits to what can be achieved by orthodox anthropological techniques and concepts. But such studies are not thereby necessarily deprived of sociological interest. The anthropologist who studies the system of social relations within a single town may not be able to generalise about society at large. On the other hand, this essay will have served its purpose if it does no more than remind sociologists and others who demand a large canvas, that while the social life of local communities is being continuously moulded and affected by external forces, the social structure of these communities is also important in determining how these external forces will be received.

5

Tom Lupton & Sheila Cunnison

WORKSHOP BEHAVIOUR

[written in 1957]

In this paper we discuss the problem of handling the relation-ship between behaviour observed in industrial workshops and events which happen outside. The problem arose in the analysis of material from studies of three workshops in the Manchester area.[1]

In these studies, which we began in 1955, we set out to investigate the social factors influencing the level of output of industrial workers. Knowledge of previous work in the field led us to expect to find customary social norms of output, at variance with the formal expectations of management, and enforced by an informal pattern of sanctions. We chose par-ticipant observation as our main technique of research, since, if we were to describe in detail the way in which norms are established and maintained, we would have to work in the workshop itself. Our material on workshop social relationships is very detailed. We also have records of the output and earnings of the workers. We can, therefore, give a detailed description of events in the workshops, and an analysis of their inter-relations. But we cannot be satisfied with this. We have to explain the behaviour we observed, and it is in the attempt to do this that we have encountered our problems.

We noted that the behaviour of workers in a garment-making workshop we investigated differed radically from the behaviour of workers in an engineering workshop. We have attempted to explain these differences by reference to differ-

---

[1] Fuller accounts of these workshops are published in T. Lupton, *On the Shop Floor* [1963], and S. Cunnison, *Wages and Work Allocation* [1965].

ences in the degrees of competition in the two industries, the proportion of labour cost to total cost, and the strength of trade unions in the workshops. It seemed to us that these external factors could be adduced to explain different patterns of behaviour. But our research techniques had given us scanty data about these factors, and our training as sociologists, does not equip us adequately to handle such concepts as the degree of competition. We shall presently be discussing some of our field data and referring to these external factors, but first we place our particular problems in a wider perspective.

In our work we have tended to extend the limits of plausibility. We have drawn a picture of the relationships between events in the workshops and what one might call the economic and social environment of these workshops, a picture which is based, so far as the context is concerned, upon scanty data. Our material from the workshops describes actual social relationships. Our material on the economic context consists of abstracted economic relationships, rather than detailed field research on the behaviour of managers in different market situations. There are, to our knowledge, no data of this kind in the literature of economics. Many, though not all, economists operate with a naïve psychology, and the propostions about the behaviour of entrepreneurs and managers which one finds in the textbooks are logically derived from doubtful psychological premisses.

We could, of course, have ignored external factors. We could have said: "We can make so much sense out of the behaviour we have observed by reference to internal factors, our job is done, and we can hand over to the economists and psychologists, or even historians—we have used some naïve history too—and they can throw light in the dark places we have left." This would have been unsatisfactory. In the first place, we doubt whether these persons would be greatly interested in our problem. Secondly, in some cases we have not been able to make much sense out of our material without reference to external factors. Take, for example, the case of Dee Garment Company. Here we found relatively little social cohesion amongst the workers, associated with relatively high output. The behaviour of management, faced with high labour turnover and an ageing labour force, was inexplicable unless one took into account factors operating in the market for the product and unless one examined the history and traditions of the industry. Then it began to make sense.

If we have extended the limits of plausibility, we are in distinguished company. George Homans and Lloyd Warner have dealt with problems of relationships between internal and external factors, Homans in his analysis of the Bank Wiring Observation Room data in *The Human Group*,[2] and Warner and Low in *The Social System of the Modern Factory*.[3] Homans's attention is focused on the small group, and Warner's on the local community. Each has detailed material only on his chosen area. Outside these areas they rely, as we have done, on partial data, and on shaky generalisations.

Homans admits that he lacks sufficient data to study adequately the relationship between internal and external factors. Yet this does not deter him from setting up an elaborate conceptual scheme to handle the relationship between the two. Homans uses three concepts: environment, external system, and internal system. The two latter, in mutual dependence, make up the social system of the group, and react back on the environment. Environment, in Homans's usage, includes everything outside the group being studied. He enumerates production planning, supervisory organisations, other workers in the company, Chicago in the early years of the depression, membership of other groups like family, church, social class, and American culture—without much attempt at classification. Having stated, as a self-evident proposition, that there is a relationship between the environment and observed behaviour in the group, Homans then attempts. so far as we can see, to handle this relationship by abstracting certain parts of the environment for inclusion in his concept of external system. He defines the external system as "The state of these elements and of their interrelations so far as it constitutes a solution . . . not necessarily the only possible solution to the problem . . . How shall the group survive in its environment?" The elements referred to are sentiment, activity, and interaction. In the external system of the Bank Wiring Room, sentiments are motives for working, activities are the jobs performed, and interactions those required by the productive process. Having abstracted these factors, *e.g.*, motives, from the environment, Homans can then trace their effects upon behaviour in the workshop. This is an ingenious method of internalising external factors for convenience in analysis, but it tells us very little about the relationship between the group and its environment: we learn only that the group is in some sort of equilibrium with it, and nothing about the process by which the equilibrium is established.

But the external system is not the whole social system. There is also the internal system which is again defined as the interrelation of the three elements of behaviour. It is a growth out of the external system arising because men elaborate their relationships beyond the requirements of the task in hand, so increasing interest and satisfaction. Homans calls this process the Mode of Elaboration. Further, norms and values tend to become similar among men who associate with one another —the Mode of Standardisation. Thus clique formation and restriction of output are explained in terms of the internal system.

This formulation of the relationship between external and internal factors leaves several loose ends. What, for example, is the relation between the norm of output of the group and the notion, from the environment, of a "fair day's work for a fair day's pay," the latter specifically mentioned by Homans? What is the influence of social-class expectations on the relationship between management and worker? Again, this scheme makes the analysis of social conflict difficult. Indeed, Homans takes over the conclusion of the Bank Wiring Room observers, that hostility between workers and management is to be explained as an unconscious desire of groups to protect themselves, and that it is not an independent determining factor in behaviour.

Warner's approach is less elaborate and requires less discussion. His analysis of occupational and social class structure, and in particular his concept of the break in the skill hierarchy, are useful since they help explain why managers and workers make different evaluations of the same facts, *i.e.*, the existence of social conflict in industry. But there is little analysis of workshop and factory relationships to show how production is carried on despite cleavages created by the break in the skill hierarchy. Warner's analysis of workshop relationships is made partly by projecting into the factories the social class, ethnic, and occupational cleavages within Yankee City. About actual relationships inside the factories his data are much less detailed. However, he produces some interesting correlations between ethnicity and solidarity, between solidarity and high earnings, high status and high earnings, and supply and demand for labour and the level of earnings. These are enough to whet our appetite for more detailed material on the process by which such correlations arise.

It will become obvious as we discuss our own field data that Warner's approach has been of much more help than Homans's has. But some of the external factors which have seemed crucial to us are absent from Warner's analysis. In criticising Homans we must remember that his interests were essentially different from ours. While we are interested in explaining behaviour observed in three workshops, he is attempting to find a method to analyse behaviour in very diverse groups ranging from the Norton Street gang of Chicago to the Tikopean family. For this purpose his concepts may be considered adequate.

We now look at our own material, and attempt to analyse the relationship between observed behaviour and social context. We have not space to present a detailed analysis of behaviour in the three workshops. We therefore attempt, first, to show the way in which external factors affect observed behaviour in one workshop. We look first at the informal group structure of assemblers in Dee Garment Company. Next we look at the problems which arise when we compare observed behaviour in the three workshops, with particular reference to the presence or absence of collective controls over output.

THE WORKSHOP AT DEE GARMENT COMPANY

In the workshop at Dee Garment Company about 60 people were engaged, some full-time, some part-time, on the assembly of garments of many different styles and cloths. The garments were of a special type whose production is localised in three main areas of Britain. Men and women worked alongside one another on two operations, machining and assembly. An

assembler co-operated with a machiner, working on bundles of
several garments. Garments passed back and forth between
assembler and machiner several times during making up.
Workers were paid by the piece, and piecework prices for each
garment were calculated from a negotiated Price List which
comprised practically all the operations which might go into
the making of a garment. Anomalies in the Price List resulted
in some work being easy, and some work difficult to make
money on, in "good" and "bad" work as it was known in the
workshop. This distinction was important in the social life of the
workshop. Also important was the variation in the supply of
garments to be made up, a result of the seasonal nature of the
garment trade. Work was scarce during the study and for
several weeks there was not enough to keep all the workers busy
the whole of the time. The shop was personally supervised by
the manager who allocated the work; in this he was assisted
by the chargehand.

Unlike the Bank Wiring Room, there was no collective
norm of output. The only norm seemed to be that of hard work.
Earnings varied greatly from worker to worker. Two reasons
for this were differences in skill and effort. But there were other
reasons: in particular, earnings were much affected by the
allocation of work within the workshop. Earnings for each
worker also varied from week to week. Sometimes these
fluctuations can be related to shortage of garments; sometimes
they are due to anomalies in the Price List referred to above.

There was a fairly well defined informal group structure,
particularly among assemblers. This was so in spite of high
labour turnover. But informal groups did not arise in the way
that Homans suggests in his analysis of the external and internal
systems. Interactions between assembler and machiner in the
productive unit did not lead *via* sentiments of liking and dis-
liking to the formation of informal groups. Indeed, the productive system generated much hostility between assembler and
machiner so that they rarely belonged to the same groups.
There were many reasons for this hostility. Changes in style of
garment, for example, often affected assemblers and machiners
differently. Absence of a machiner often caused overloading of
other machiners with work, and breakdowns in the productive
units. This affected the earnings of the assemblers with whom

the machiners co-operated. The productive system did not set rigid limits to the informal group structure. Groups were more closely related to spatial arrangement. But since workers were able to move their places of work and occasionally did so, spatial arrangement must be considered as an effect as well as a determinant of group membership. Thus the productive system did affect group structure, but neither in the way nor by the process suggested by Homans. Among the factors affecting relationships between assemblers and machiners we mentioned absence and changes in style of garment; these factors occur haphazardly from the viewpoint of a single workshop; neither comes into Homans's scheme.

We also criticise Homans's failure to examine in detail the interrelation between the pattern of informal groups within the workshop and the roles of workers and managers in social systems outside it. We demonstrate the importance of this interrelation at Dee by the following analysis of informal groups there.

Among the thirty to forty assemblers there were four main groups, the Old Workers, the Fliers, the Back Table, and Levine's Lot. There were also a number of workers who belonged to no particular group; space does not allow us to include them in the discussion, but their inclusion would not have altered the main points of the argument.

The Old Workers were nearly all men and nearly all Jewish. Their ages ranged from forty to over seventy. They were highly skilled and had all worked at Dee for nearly twenty years, one or two of them for nearly forty years. The Fliers were all women and all Christian. Their ages ranged from the late twenties to the early forties. They were not very skilled and had been at Dee for six or seven years. The Back Table were Christian women in their forties and fifties. They had worked at Dee for only two or three years though they had all been in the trade for much longer and were skilled workers. Skilled also were Levine's Lot, who had come to Dee about six months before the study began when Levine's factory had closed down one of its workshops. They were all Christian, aged between forty and fifty-five.

The grouping of workers was thus associated with their positions in different social systems external to the workshop.

It was associated with differences in sex and religious affiliation; these two were connected in that most of the men in the
trade were Jewish while most of the women were Christian.
It was associated with differences in age in a trade in which
the labour force as a whole was ageing. Age was also connected
with sex; the men in the labour force were on the whole older
than the women. It was associated with differences in skill.
Formally there was no differentiation between workers as
regards skill: all who had finished their training were on the
same piece-rates. But skill varied widely within the force,
depending in large measure on the period at which workers
learned their trade. Thus it too was connected with age and
sex. Those who had entered the trade in the nineteen-twenties
or early nineteen-thirties tended to be more skilled than those
who entered afterwards. Occupational experience in later years
was also important; some firms tended to make a distinctly
higher grade of work than others. Length of service, a characteristic linking internal and external social systems, also
distinguished between one group and another. The practice in
the trade of "last in first out" which operated during a recession
meant that short service tended to snowball, and the short-
service workers at Dee had a very different occupational
history from the very-long-service workers.

As we have already remarked, workers at Dee could and
did move their places within the workshop. The groups which
we have just described may therefore be explained partly as
the association of persons with like interests derived from
similar positions in a number of specified systems external to
the factory. The tendency to group so was probably strengthened by the way in which certain characteristics were linked—
for instance, age, sex, and religious affiliation. This mode of
grouping was one way in which positions in external systems
affected the structure of groups within Dee. Another was
through the allocation of work. This we shall now discuss.

Groups could be distinguished from one another according
to the type of work that their members were allocated:
whether it was made from heavy- or light-weight cloth, and
whether it was of high, medium or cheap quality.[4] By and large,

---

[4] Work made from heavy-weight and light-weight cloth is henceforth referred
to as heavy and light work.

heavy work was "better" than light, and medium quality "better" than high quality. Cheap quality, almost invariably light work, was the best of the lot, so long as it was made up quickly without too much attention to neatness and precise fit; if made with the care necessary for high and medium quality it did not pay so well. The second point about allocation is that, in the slack period, members of different groups spent different lengths of time waiting for work.

Members of the Old Workers were allocated heavy work. Much of this was high-quality work of intricate design. Members of the Fliers were allocated predominantly light, cheap-quality work. During the work scarcity, however, there was no cheap-quality work and they were then given heavy work. They spent more time waiting for work than any other group. When they had cheap-quality work they made it fast and carelessly and as a result one or two then earned a higher hourly rate than the Old Workers who certainly worked more consistently. But in the slack times when the Fliers made heavy work, their hourly earnings were lower than those of nearly all the Old Workers. Then their percentage drop in weekly wages was bigger than that for any of the other three groups. Members of the Back Table and Levine's Lot were allocated light work of a medium quality. This work too was in short supply during the period of slack trade, though not so scarce as the cheap-quality work, and so during the shortage these two groups too were allocated a share of the heavy work. Levine's Lot worked harder than the Back Table and their average hourly earnings tended to be higher. Both were below those of the Fliers and the Old Workers.

The allocation of different types and quantities of work to different workers tended to create interest groups among them. For instance, those workers who were persistently given heavy work came to feel that they had an interest in the productive system which was distinct from the interest of those who were given light work: the technical problems of making the work up differed; the prices were arrived at independently; and most important, the money which could be earned on it differed.

So far then we have shown that there were four groups which could be distinguished in two ways, firstly by the positions of their members in specified systems external to the factory, and secondly by the type and quantity of work allocated to them. This much was observed within the workshop. And from this we have deduced that groups were formed partly by free association of people with like interests outside the workshop, partly by the creation, through the allocation of work, of like interests in the productive system.

What was the connexion between these two processes by which groups were formed? The answer to this requires a further analysis of the way work was allocated. At this point we can no longer rely entirely on direct systematic observation, but have to gather our ideas additionally from occasional interviews with the manager of Dee and with other managers; from reports made to us by the workers at Dee of their conversations with the manager; from opinions expressed by the workers; and from our own reasoning. Our evidence is thus thinner and much less sure. With this warning to ourselves and to our readers we proceed in pursuit of our argument.

First we consider the factors influencing the manager's decisions about the allocation of work. Allocation is not to be explained as part of a management policy of "divide and rule." Workers were not given different types of work solely because they belonged to one group or another, though, as we point out later, this was of some importance. The factors affecting allocation can be most easily understood in context of the problems faced by the manager in producing for this unstable and highly competitive section of the garment trade. We examine the kinds of considerations the manager had to make in allocating the high-quality and the cheap-quality work, in allocating the heavy and light work, and in sharing out scarce work during the shortage.

(1) *High Quality and Cheap Quality*

The market was differentiated: high-quality work was required in some sections while in others cheap quality was wanted and speed of delivery was more important. It was not always easy to get high-quality work made because only some of the more skilled workers were capable of turning out top-class garments. These top-class garments were usually intricately designed; they involved a lot of fitting, trimming, and handling. Workers were not paid for this but only for actually joining together pieces of cloth. Garments of the highest quality were usually made in heavy cloth. As a result of this and their intricate design they were almost invariably "bad" work. They were given to the Old Workers because there was no one else who could make them. Another factor may have been that the Old Workers were unlikely to leave even if they were given "bad" work, because their length of service meant a certain security of employment in the slack times. The medium-quality light work tended to be of a similar design. When made in a light cloth it was given to the Back Table and to Levine's Lot, but rarely to the Fliers because of their lesser skill and slap-dash ways of working.

(2) *Heavy and Light Work*

In sharing the heavy and light work the main considera-tion involved was that of keeping labour at Dee. The trade is seasonal; wholesalers do not carry big stocks and the burden of fluctuations falls on the producers. The skill of assemblers and machiners, but particularly of assemblers, is specific to this section of the garment trade. As a result all firms suffer from a labour problem: in the busy periods there is never enough labour; in the slack periods firms hesitate as long as possible before getting rid of workers, because speed of delivery might be crucial in obtaining an order and because workers will be at a premium when the upswing occurs. Within the trade labour is traditionally very mobile, going from one shop to another as work is most plentiful first at one and then at another, and following any increase in prices above the union rate. This exaggerated the labour problem for a firm like Dee which was important in the employers' federation and willing to pay only very little above the union rate.

Now, in the trade in general and in Dee in particular, women were marginal labour in that most of them were secondary wage earners and were thus freer to take the risks involved in moving from one firm to another. This may be argued in spite of the fact that women form the majority of the labour force. In the busy periods women were in a powerful bargaining position and they then refused to make

H

heavy work, but in the slack periods they eagerly accepted a share of it. This issue is somewhat complicated by the fact that the men were more highly skilled than the majority of the women and much of the heavy work was high quality. But there were one or two of the women, belonging to the Back Table, who could have done high-quality work in the busy times, but who were not given it. (Levine's Lot had not worked at Dee during a busy time.) The sharing of the work in this way was no doubt influenced by the custom in our society that men do heavier labour than women.

(3) *Sharing Scarce Work*

This again related to the labour problem. Trade was slack during the study and assemblers sometimes had no work. A few left because, they said, wages were too low. Yet over the six months there was a net gain in labour because new assemblers, all of them highly skilled, were taken on after the worst of the shortage was over. During the worst part the policy of the manager seemed to be to prevent anyone's wage falling so low that he or she would leave. One of his ways of doing this was to take account of differences in family responsibilities, those of the men as opposed to those of the women, and of the differing responsibilities of the women.

The Old Workers who were, as men, the main breadwinners, did not have to wait. They were, too, the backbone of Dee's labour force. It was understood that the manager would "look after" them in slack times, in so far as he was able. It would have been a blow to him if any of them had left. The Fliers, in contrast, had to wait more than any other group. On the whole the Fliers were doing well at Dee; they had found how to handle the cheap-quality work in such a way that it paid them better money than they would earn elsewhere; it was not likely that they would leave. It was more likely that some of the Back Table or Levine's Lot would do so. These latter two groups of women were kept busy while the Fliers sat and waited. When the Fliers complained to the manager he replied, they said, that these women already earned less than any of the Fliers and he could not let their wages fall any further. Moreover, he pointed out that they had children to support while the Fliers as it happened had not.

These three examples show how, in allocating work, the manager took account of certain characteristics of his workers, characteristics which affected their performance or potential performance as producers of garments for Dee. The discussion reveals the second way in which the positions of workers in social systems outside the workshop were connected with informal group structure. Moreover, the connexion between the two processes giving rise to groups is now clear. The social characteristics which the manager took into account when allocating work—namely, skill, sex, financial responsibilities, and length of service at Dee— were the same as, or were linked with, the characteristics influencing association along lines of interest outside work. The two processes thus reinforced one another. Together they resulted in the four groups; and these groups held together even though, as groups, they exercised no control over the major concern of their members in coming to work —*i.e.*, over earnings—either directly or indirectly through norms regulating output.

One thing that was remarkable about the resultant groups was the degree of hostility they expressed towards one another. Hostility was couched mainly, though not exclusively, in terms of work allocation. Each group had some reason to feel resentful and envious of another. The Old Workers resented the Fliers who made light cheap-quality work and were able to make higher earnings than they themselves could on the heavy work. The skilled Back Table and Levine's Lot resented the Fliers who were allowed to "get away" with careless work, and they too were envious of their higher earnings. The Fliers themselves grumbled constantly when they had to wait for work while other groups did not.

Though not in intent a policy of "divide and rule," work allocation was in effect precisely this. Clearly the structuring of hostility along intergroup lines made the manager's task of allocating work easier. Workers who saw the kind of work they wanted being made by others, immediately said that this was not fair, and that those workers had been currying favour with the manager. While workers thus blamed one another, the manager could give them the type of work that it suited him to. Yet the structuring of hostility did put some limits on the way the manager shared out the work. Intergroup hostility was matched by warmth and friendliness within the several groups. When the manager treated members of the same group very differently, for example, giving one heavy work and another light, this disturbed the pleasant and easy relationships. Sometimes he did this: the variety in style and weight of garment, and the sudden demands for orders made it inevitable. Up to a point there were mechanisms within the group which enabled members to disregard different treatment, but beyond that point it threatened to disrupt relations and cause workers to leave.

Now, workers often stated that allocation was unfair, and while they blamed the manager for this, they directed their hostility more frequently towards the groups they thought were favoured. Why, if they considered it to be unfair, did workers aquiesce in the current pattern of allocation? Joint action on the part of the majority would have been necessary if the pattern were to be changed. But joint action was never taken. Seeking reasons for this we note firstly that the workers at Dee did not feel that the manager was *entirely* responsible for the way work was shared. And in a way he was not. It was open to any worker to try and persuade the manager to give him the kind and quantity of work he wanted; there were many opportunities when he could be seen alone in his office and workers took advantage of these. But he could not satisfy everyone; the quantity of work was limited; some was "good" and some "bad"; and so he had to choose whom to satisfy and whom to disappoint. The pressures that workers could apply came into these choices, precisely because these pressures were relevant to his problems as the co-ordinator of production. But it may be argued that if the Back Table and Levine's Lot had never suggested to him that they might have to leave on account of their low wages, he might have made them wait more than he actually did. Yet the Fliers complained in vain; they would not leave and the manager knew it; so they waited. In the final instance it was the pressure of keeping the firm going in these highly competitive labour and wholesale and retail markets which determined the manager's decisions.

Workers were not unaware of the manager's crucial rôle in allocating work. There were other reasons why they did not come together to try and construct and enforce their own order of priorities. They were structurally divided, one group against another; each group felt that another was favoured; not only this, each group felt that it had an advantage over the other, in terms of job security, low waiting time, and so on. To act together would have been to forgo these advantages. Thus the structural arrangement of hostile and competing groups and the pattern of allocation were mutually dependent. This structural arrangement itself explains why workers would not act together, and why allocation continued along lines which divided them. We mention also the high labour turnover: Levine's Lot in particular felt unsettled at Dee and talked of leaving: they did not have enough interest in what went on at Dee to warrant the effort which would have been necessary to control allocation.

Again, however, we feel it is necessary to follow certain threads of argument which lead us outside Dee. We draw attention again to the highly competitive, unstable cost-conscious nature of the garment trade. The current experience of the workers was of seasonal slackness and uncertainty in employment; their past experience in the nineteen-thirties, when the big slump hit the trade hard, was of bitter unemployment. The very nearness of Dee workers to their trade environment meant that they saw themselves at its mercy; it was something to which they could adapt, and from which they could protect themselves, but which they could not control. Hence they were predisposed to compete with one another for scarce work and for jobs. There was a tradition of each for himself; and it mirrored the fiercely individualistic competition among the small firms comprising the trade.

Finally we comment on the way piece-rate prices were fixed and maintained. Seasonal sufficiency and scarcity of work was a major cause of allocation problems. Anomalies in the Price List and resulting "good" and "bad" work were another. Now, it is clear that the manager could rarely afford to pay any more than the union price on the "bad" work: the keen competition between firms made this very difficult, of course much more so in the slack periods. "Good" and "bad" work or prices are common in workshops where there is variety in the goods produced and where payment is by the piece. But at Dee the difference between the "good" and the "bad" appeared to be rather large, and it became more noticeable in the absence of any mechanisms for sharing work or controlling output. We are not suggesting that, under piecework and rapid style changes, "good" and "bad" work could be eradicated, only that the workers might have tried to narrow the difference between the two. Taking as given the existing method of pricing by means of an itemised list, there were two ways of tackling the problem: first, at workshop level by bargaining with the manager over any particular "bad" garment; and second at top level by re-negotiating the relative prices of outstanding anomalous items.[5]

Bargaining at workshop level would require joint action on the part of the workers. All the arguments we have used to explain why workers did not combine to control allocation are relevant in explaining why they did not combine over prices. And there are more. Combination for such a purpose not only lacked the blessing of the union, it was expressly against the rules. The union was a small local organisation catering only for workers in this localised section of the garment trade. It boasted a single full-time official, the General Secretary, and a lay executive committee elected at an Annual General Meeting. Workshop committees had existed for a short period in the past, but they had been abolished ten to fifteen years ago. There were, however, shop stewards in many workshops. Their official union tasks were collecting dues, handing out notices, and reporting any infringements of union agreements first to the manager, and then, if not satisfied, to head office. The shop steward at Dee was also the "chargehand" (she was not formally accorded this status) who assisted the manager in allocation and in calculating weekly wages. She refused to argue with the manager about prices; it was, of course, outside her union duties; and it was left to individual workers to state their own case when they felt that a garment was very "bad" work. In sum, by its rules and procedure the union firmly discouraged all joint action *at the level of the workshop*.

[5] This would probably not resolve the trouble, since a "bad" garment might be the result of a large number of slightly "bad" items.

Trying to remove anomalies by means of central negotiation between the employers' federation and the union was
impossible since, with the last revision of the Price List, it was
officially agreed that all anomalies should be considered to have
been removed. In any case, since there were upwards of a
thousand items, some priced as low as ⅛d., the job of relating
them fairly to one another was in the state of current knowledge of measuring work and effort probably impossible.[6] To
attempt the task would have meant entering into lengthy
negotiations. Yet workers at Dee claimed that there were still
anomalies; they wanted these removed, but said they could not
make themselves heard by the executive committee when they
tried to voice the issue. Citing this and other evidence, they
stated that the union was run on authoritarian lines. While this
is clearly a biased judgment in the sense that it is made by a
few members of the rank and file upon their executive and
secretary, it is also clear that the union was indeed highly
centralised, and that it discouraged activity among the rank
and file except through the channel of the Annual General
Meeting, and even here workers said that they were often not
allowed to raise the issues they wanted to. An explanation of
this policy of centralisation regarding prices may be that the
union was desperately trying to bring some uniformity and
order into the trade. It saw the Price List as a way of imposing
some minimum standards. Yet it is inescapable that in attempting to enforce the Price List, the union did in effect support
the existence of anomalies, and hence played a part in per-
petuating within Dee a pattern of allocating work which
divided workers into the mutually hostile groups we have
described.

To explain the structure of the informal groups of assemblers
at Dee, we have had to go right outside the workshop and look
at the roles of both workers and manager in other social systems.
Emphasis has been placed on the role of the manager in the
relationships of the market and its effect on workshop behaviour. Here we have made what may be regarded as shaky

---

[6] It is possible to criticise the whole system of pricing as unsuitable to the type
of product and method of production at Dee. Some workers suggested that each
new garment be timed, and a price fixed, in co-operation with the union, on the
shop floor.

generalisations on the basis of unsystematic data. We have also looked at the role of workers in the garment trade as a whole, their specialised skill, their age, and their mobility between firms. We have mentioned the role of women in family financial responsibilities, and contrasted it with that of men. And we have mentioned the effect of the union on some aspects of workers' behaviour. Such data provide a partial explanation of the structure of informal groups though, at the same time, we emphasise that the particular way in which these external factors affect internal structure depends on other factors internal to the workshop, in this case on the nature of the productive system.

THE THREE WORKSHOPS COMPARED

In the light of this exposition of the structure of one workshop, we now consider the range of problems which emerges when comparative analysis of the three workshops is attempted, for we lack space to analyse the other two workshops at similar length.

All our studies focused upon the social factors affecting output. From this viewpoint, the most striking difference between the workshops studied was in the existence of a norm of output in the engineering workshop and the absence of such a norm in the garment workshops.[7]

In the engineering shop, a wide variety of electrical transformers were assembled, almost entirely by hand, and from components supplied by other departments. The incentive offered to the workers was a weekly cash bonus, calculated from records of the time saved by the workers on the time allowed for each job. The allowed times were arrived at after time-study, but were also the subject of hard bargaining between the firm's ratefixer and the worker and his shop steward. Trade-unionism was strong in the workshop, and the shop steward was important in workshop life.

The norm of output was defined by the workers as a "ceiling" to the amount which ought to be declared as having been saved on any job. By observing the norm, a worker did

[7] We use the term "norm" to refer to a behavioural convention. By definition, a "norm" will carry with it a pattern of sanctions to discourage deviation.

not necessarily lose some of his weekly bonus. As a result both of errors made in computing allowed times, and of the bargaining process, some times were "loose" and some were "tight"— *i.e.*, some paid the workers well, while others paid them badly.

By observing the ceiling when recording time taken on "loose" jobs, time saved over and above the ceiling could be "banked" by a worker to offset bonus losses made, or expected, on tight jobs. When work was held up, as it very often was, for shortage of components, "banked" time could also be used to offset the effects of waiting time, which was paid at the lower time-rate.

Workers described this mode of behaviour as "the fiddle." They claimed that it worked to their advantage in the following ways:

1. It safeguarded them against rate-cutting.

2. It was a useful device for ironing out fluctuations in earnings.

3. It gave them a measure of control sufficient to enable them to balance work and leisure during working time against cash profit and loss.

There was no "cross-booking" technique such as this in the garment workshops, nor was there any other attempt by the workers collectively to control the level of output and earnings. We have already suggested some of the reasons for this in our discussion of the Dee workshop. At Wye, the other garment shop, the method of production was to a much greater extent responsible for fluctuations in earnings. In Wye, market conditions were much more stable, since much Government contract work was done. In contrast to Dee, the work of garment assembly was subdivided and carried out by semi-skilled workers, each of whom was responsible for a small number of operations. Co-ordination of the work of operatives within the units of sixteen workers was incorporated into the arrangements for flow of work as planned by the management. The industry price list did not operate at Wye, prices being based on time-study data. The marked fluctuations in the earnings of most workers were traceable to breakdowns in the flow of work, which involved transfer of workers to unfamiliar tasks. But absenteeism was often caused by circumstances outside the workshop. Changes in the design of garment often presented new problems of assembly and affected earnings. And then, as always, there were "tight" and "loose" prices. But in Wye the workers made no collective attempt to offset the effects of these factors on the level and stability of earnings.

Thus, in terms of our problem, the main difference between the engineering and the garment workshops related to the presence or absence of informal collective controls over output and earnings. In all three shops there were external factors operating to affect output and earnings, factors formally beyond the control of the workers. Yet in one case the workers combined to devise and operate a system of control on their own. In the other cases no such attempt was made. It will already be clear that it is not possible to explain these differences fully by using Homans's scheme of analysis. Nor is Warner's scheme of much help since it allows only of general statements about the relationship between managers and workers.

There were certain broad similarities of social structure between the three shops. In each case, jealousies and hostilities were generated between individuals and groups. These were sometimes generated by the system of allocating work and by the mode of production. Sometimes they could be seen to be related to age and sex differences, and to differences in length of service. Sometimes the two sets of factors operated simultaneously, one reinforcing the other.

But in the engineering shop the "fiddle" acted as an integrating institution across all groups. There were different institutions in the garment workshops (for example, the tea-break groupings at Wye), which cut across the competing productive groupings. But these were less effective and did not act as controls over output and earnings.

Although some of the differences we observed will yield to analysis using Homans's concepts, we must turn to the consideration of external factors if we are to attempt a fuller explanation. When the structure of the garment industry is compared with that of the engineering industry some significant differences can be discerned. The engineering industry is highly capitalised. It is dominated by a few large-scale units of production, and the large firms and combines in the industry exercise a high degree of control over the level of prices. By contrast, the garment industry is made up of a large number of small firms in fierce competition for orders. No one firm or combination of firms controls the level of prices, for the market is dominated by the wholesalers and retailers. This situation combined with a technology demanding only a small amount of capital, makes it possible in times of brisk demand for an operative to set up a small workshop and enter into competition with his former employers.

It is not here necessary for us to attempt a detailed explanation of these differences. But it seems to us that the garment industry has developed and maintained a flexible structure by way of response to the demands of the market for its product. The demand for heavy electrical equipment, though fluctuating from boom to slump, has been stable and predictable over sufficiently long periods to favour large-scale enterprise, formation of cartels, and the like. The level of technology and the scale of enterprise have mutually affected one another in the two industries. In each case, the workers have had to adjust their behaviour in the light of their own interests and goals. In the garment industry, where uncertainty is chronic in the labour and product markets, workers have tended to look after their interests as individuals, acting individually. This attitude has perhaps been reinforced by the persistence of traditional values from the time when both employers and employees were predominantly Jewish, and where a predominant motive was the achievement of independence by setting up on one's own.[8] Historical factors such as this cannot be ignored in analysis, especially in this case, where the trade-union organisation in the industry has obviously been affected. In engineering one finds a set of traditions which differ remarkably, a trade-union movement with great power in the workshops, and great solidarity.

Another point of contrast between the two industries relates to the proportion of costs of labour to the total cost of the product. In engineering the pressure to keep costs of labour low

[8] See H. Neustetter, "Demographic and other Statistical Aspects of Anglo-Jewry," in *A Minority in Britain: Social Studies of the Anglo-Jewish Community*, ed. M. Freedman [1955], p. 109.

is less urgent. Economies can be made elsewhere, or the increased cost passed on to the consumer. This is not possible in the garment industry, where labour cost is high.

The element of uncertainty in the garment industry due to rapid changes in demand, made for greater fear of unemployment and reduced the workers' power in negotiation. In engineering, the workers were able to put pressure on management, for besides having greater security, more alternative employments were available to them.

It seems to us that the competitive nature of the garment industry, together with the concomitant pressure to keep wages down, was an important factor affecting workers' behaviour. It is easier to trace the connexion in Dee than in the other shops, for here the workers were at but one remove from the market, and market changes were direct in their effect. In the other firms, which were larger, and which had specialised management functions, it was more difficult to trace the effect of changes in the market on sales and pricing policy, hence on the behaviour of managers and workers.

We do not attempt to trace in detail the interrelations between the external factors we have enumerated—the structure of the industry, the level of technology, the degree of capitalisation, the strength of trade-unionism in workshops and so on. We think they *are* systematically related, and we have attempted to show how, directly or indirectly, they influence workshop behaviour. Although it is not possible, with present knowledge, to assess the relative significance of the various external factors, we nevertheless feel justified in advancing the hypothesis that in industries characterised by clusters of factors such as a high degree of competition, easy entry of new units of production, high labour cost, and weak unionism, collective control over output by workers is less likely to be found than in industries where the reverse is true. We would also say that these clusters of characteristics are more commonly found in some industries than in others. For example, we can think of few industries with a constantly fluctuating market, where one finds strong trade unions, large units, and high capitalisation. We are, of course, aware of instances of collective control over output in the absence of trade unions. But we have stated our hypothesis in terms of clusters of variables. There are few other studies with sufficient data on both workshop behaviour and external factors, which we could use when formulating our hypothesis.

In our discussion of Dee Garments and in the comparison of the three workshops, we have been treating the workshop as a system of social relationships, included within wider systems —the factory, the market for the product, and so on. We think it is possible to make such general statements about the relationships of the part to the whole without going beyond the limits of plausibility. But any attempt to analyse the relationship in detail raises the problem of dealing with systems which are organised on principles different from those which have been properly regarded as the province of sociology and social anthropology, and with facts about large-scale administration, production engineering, and the movement of economic variables.

It is easy to be critical of Homans and Warner, and to state the difficulties that have attended our own efforts to handle the relationship between external and internal events. In conclusion, we summarise our own ideas as to how the problems we have raised may be handled.

If the attention of the observer is focused on workshop life, he will find it easy to mark off his area of study. Workshops are bounded by four walls, and these set limits to what can be observed. The difficulty seems to be to define the social context, or environment, or whatever one chooses to call it. It seems to us that when we are dealing with workshop life we have to handle in analysis a number of overlapping systems. According to this notion of overlap there are segments of different social systems which are latent in a single workshop. For instance, a man's role as a father, or as a member of a social class, may affect his behaviour in the workshop.

In our analysis we have also talked of the workshop as being included within larger systems, as when we spoke of the influence of the market on the economic structure of the industry. We therefore refer to the relationship between the workshop and its context in terms of both overlap and inclusion. For example, the problem of the deviant from workshop norms, which we have not mentioned here, can be treated in terms of overlap. This has been done in an article by Collins,

Dalton, and Roy.[9] The behaviour of the manager in Dee would involve analysis in terms of inclusion and overlap.

The role-set or role-cluster of any individual is the point of interaction of the workshop system, and its overlapping and inclusive systems. So in addition to studying the social systems of the workshop, and, say, of the family, we also need to study the social mechanisms by which conflicting sets of rights and obligations are reconciled in a specific social situation such as a dispute about rates on the shop floor.

Our notions of overlap, inclusion and role-set give us a crude frame of reference for our workshop studies, which enables us to handle observations about social relationships in small groups, and facts about the structure of the industry, and social class systems. Our approach is empirical. We do not wish to build elaborate conceptual models, but to map out a guide for field research and analysis which will ensure that relevant facts are neither ignored in the field, nor their importance undervalued in analysis.

The notions of overlap and inclusion involve some confusion, for they are not mutually exclusive. For instance, an industrial trade union would fall into both categories, because it can be looked at from both points of view. But this approach brings out some interesting problems, for example, the relationship of the overlap system of social class to the inclusive system of occupational structure within the industry.

Though we have attempted to look at our field of study with this frame of reference in mind, we cannot pretend to any systematic collection of data or analysis of social systems other than the workshop. We were not so clearly aware of the extent of influence of social context on behaviour when we embarked on the study. Our treatment of external factors has been *ex post facto* as well as *ad hoc*. We have looked at the three workshops in turn and seen where the external system seemed to influence observed behaviour. And we have looked at the three workshops with the same questions in mind. That our explanation is couched so much in terms of the different industrial complexes of the garment and the engineering industries, is a function of the polar differences between the industries, and

[9] O. Collins, M. Dalton, and D. Roy, "The Industrial Ratebuster, a Characterization," in *Applied Anthropology VII* [1948], pp. 5-18.

of our problem. Had we been studying another problem, it is possible that we would have been led to emphasise other external factors.

We turn briefly to the problem of research methods. How do we get data on the overlapping and inclusive systems, and yet retain our focus on the workshop? Inclusive systems, at least at the level of the factory and industry, seem the easier to deal with. At this level, we have abstracted economic relationships from social relationships. Participant observation studies of management in the factory where workshop observation is going on would seem the logical solution at factory level. At industry level, formal interviews with managers, employers and trade union officials, and study of trade-union and employers' association documents where these have been preserved, would be required.

Studying overlapping systems of family, church, local class structure and so on tends to be more difficult. Where workers come from a fairly small community, it would be possible to study the social institutions of that community. But where workers come from many different places, it would be difficult to get such information from each one, and still more difficult to relate it to the workshop. Intensive interviews with the families of workers may enable us to map out kinship networks, to discover financial obligations to kin, and the present occupation, educational and occupational histories, and leisure-time activities of the worker and his family.

It is inevitable that, in studying modern industrial societies, sociologists and social anthropologists will be dealing with the same areas of social life as economists, political scientists, social historians, and psychologists. Therefore at least an elementary knowledge of the work of these other students of society, and of their methods of analysis, is called for. A possible alternative would be interdisciplinary team research.

The choice will, to some extent, depend on the problem selected. And the chief difficulty here is the difficulty of getting members of an interdisciplinary team to agree upon a problem. We would therefore favour research by social anthropologists and sociologists, either working singly, or in groups so organised that each person specialises in a different aspect of a common problem.

Note

Since we wrote this paper we have come to question whether the concepts of internal and external factors, as we have used them in our analysis, are adequate. We used them, and defined them as we did, because of the way we stated our problem, and because of the limitations on our data which our research technique imposed. Our problem led us to lay stress on the individual's role as a producer; our research technique limited our observations, with respect both to space and time. So we were led to treat of other roles of the individual, in the situations we observed, as somehow external. And similar considerations influenced our treatment of the market position of the firm, and its history and traditions, as external factors.

To treat of our present problem and our data in this way has been fruitful, but we now think that it might be more useful and enlightening if we were to regard workshop social situations, and indeed all social situations, as points of articulation of several rôle systems. We would then look at the individuals whose behaviour and relationships define our situations, as bearers of values and expectations typical of such systems. To see things this way would be to avoid the stress on productive roles, and make it possible to analyse the process fully by which certain types of social situation stress certain kinds of role behaviour. Thus the problem to be studied would be couched in terms of the situational relationship of elements within the social context, rather than with performance in an abstracted role system. This would involve the collection of data about other role systems and thus the scope of the investigation would be widened. Yet it would have the advantage that, by avoiding the arbitrary abstraction of role systems in terms of the internal-external dichotomy, it would make possible a more sophisticated analysis of the behaviour of individuals in workshops.

We have not attempted to recast our present analysis in these terms, largely because of the limitations set by our problem, and by the related inadequacies of our data.

6

W. Watson

SOCIAL MOBILITY AND SOCIAL CLASS IN INDUSTRIAL COMMUNITIES

[written in 1957]

The problems discussed in this essay arose out of field-work carried out some years ago in a Scottish coal-mining community. The object of the research was to investigate the connexion between the educational achievements of children and the occupational and social standing of their families. Children who were considered to be the most successful achieved a literary secondary course (the equivalent of a grammar-school education in England), with its implications of a professional career on leaving school. As the majority of the population of the Burgh was working-class, this success presaged the possibility of a discontinuity in occupational and social status between these children and their parents. Most of the successful children would eventually leave the community altogether and take up careers and residence elsewhere, for within the community there were not many posts for professional people. Hence certain classes in the senior secondary school trained selected children for positions and a mode of life which could not be observed within the local community. The educational institutions within the Burgh, which were the main channel for occupational and social mobility, were part of a national system. Although the Burgh had its own local system for evaluating the social prestige of individuals, the people were in fact involved in a process of occupational and social mobility, which extended beyond the social and geographical boundaries of their community into regional and national spheres.

As a result, any analysis of the Burgh's internal social system, based only on such data as could be collected while working in the community soon turned out to be quite inadequate. The external system had to be taken into account, and the connexions between it and the Burgh examined. But a review of the sociological literature on social class and on occupational and social mobility failed to provide a satisfactory conceptual framework within which to trace these wider connexions. The concepts of social class current in sociological theory appeared to be too blunt an instrument for a satisfactory comprehension of the different prestige systems involved, and the connexion between them, particularly as there is a good deal of occupational and social mobility in the Burgh. In these circumstances the external system could not be accepted as given: it was necessary to attempt to construct a more serviceable picture of the wider and inclusive society and to formulate a theory about the national system as a whole.

This picture, of course, is based only on my own studies in sociology and my own field-work experience. What follows, therefore, is a tentative outline, and its implications and refinements, together with its further application to local community studies, remains to be worked out in further study and field-research.

INDUSTRIAL ORGANISATION AND THE LOCAL COMMUNITY

In studies of Western society, social anthropologists have so far confined themselves to communities with well-defined social, economic or political boundaries.[1] Current social anthropological theories are based on the study of small-scale societies with simple technologies, and to test out these theories in Western society the social anthropologist has tended to search out relatively isolated villages or the smaller towns, particularly those with distinct geographical boundaries. But nowadays in Britain even the most remote fishing or farming village is rarely in a state of even relative isolation. The people use elaborate technical apparatus, manufactured elsewhere and often serviced from without, and enjoy the same Government

---

[1] For example, see R. Frankenberg, *Village on the Border* [1957]; and N. Dennis, C. Slaughter, and F. Henriques, *Coal is our Life* [1956]. These followed such pre-war studies as C. Arensberg, *The Irish Countryman* [1937].

social services as the rest of the country. They are often members of industrial, trade, leisure, and other organisations with a national basis. In fact they are linked by innumerable economic, political, and social bonds to people in other communities, and the whole makes up our complex social system. Hence the investigation of a local community tends to draw the social anthropologist further and further outside its boundaries, however determined.

This state of affairs has accompanied a growing trend in the British economy as a whole, namely the emergence of large-scale national organisations of production, exchange, consumption, services, etc. In the public sector of the economy, such large-scale organisation is characteristic, but the same trend is also present in the private sector.

Such large organisations often take over small local firms and absorb them, so that there is a continuous movement away from local independence towards centralised control and direction. Some organisations may indeed operate on an international scale.[2] The extent to which this has occurred appears when we examine the number of persons now employed by large organisations. The publicly owned corporations alone now employ over 2,000,000 persons; while, in the private sector of industry organisations with 10,000 or more workers now employ approximately 20 per cent of all employees. In addition, the State has now extended its services to include even the smallest and most isolated community; the Civil Service has doubled in size since 1938.

These developments have affected both the physical and social environment in a multitude of ways, *e.g.*, the concentration of the English population into six great conurbations,[3] or the growth in size of trade-union membership. As a result, most communities selected for study, however small, are now penetrated by one or more large-scale national organisations which may have workshops or branches or offices in many other communities. This has affected social behaviour. In the larger towns and conurbations people often live in one district,

[2] See T. E. Chester and G. Forsyth, "Sociological Aspects of Management Development," a paper presented to the International Congress of Sociology [1959].

[3] As defined by the Registrar-General, *Report on Greater London and five other Conurbations, Census* 1951.

work in another, and spend their leisure in yet another. This mobility of the population for different interests creates certain difficulties in defining and examining social relations within any given "local community," particularly where it is part of, or adjacent to, a larger unit. But before turning to the local community, I would like to outline one further social phenomenon that appears to be a consequence of large-scale organisation and centralised control.

INCREASE IN PROFESSIONAL OCCUPATIONS

Industrial and other organisations have not only grown in size and scale of operations, they have also developed a new complexity of technique, through the application of scientific discoveries and methods. This has resulted in a concomitant elaboration of professional and technical skills as well as the emergence of new professions and technologies, with a great increase in the number of persons who have acquired these skills. The Census tables show that between 1921 and 1951 the professional and technical sections increased by 84 per cent, while during the same period the occupied population as a whole increased by only 19 per cent.[4] In addition, the increased size and complexity of operations in industry and commerce have not only increased the actual number of managers, supervisors, and administrators, but have also altered the kind of skills such people need to operate effectively. Some productive processes are such as must be supervised by technologists and specialists of various kinds, and these skills are already recognised as professional occupations, as for instance in the Institute of Production Engineers. Other aspects of industry, too, such as administration and labour-management, are organised by highly-trained specialists, such as the members of the Institute of Costs and Works Accountants. This development is illustrated in the growth of the number of such specialists as business-efficiency consultants, labour-managers, time-study engineers, and dieticians, which rose from 6,000 in 1931 to 17,000 in 1951.[5]

The extension of State services, too, has provided another

---

[4] *Census* 1951 *(England and Wales). Occupation Tables.*
[5] *Op. cit.*

field of employment for technical and professional people, as shown by the increase in the number of such persons classified by the Registrar General as workers in Social Welfare, who grew in numbers from 7,200 in 1931 to 32,200 in 1951. The apparatus of central and local government has also expanded in recent years, and consequently there are now many more officials of higher grades who have a professional status, such as the executive, professional, and technical grades of the Civil Service, nationalised industries, and local government.

To meet the increasing demand for persons qualified in the old and new professions and technologies, universities, colleges, and training institutions have expanded, and it is now national policy to speed up this expansion.

These developments have considerably altered the distribution of professional occupations among the population. Thirty years ago, the engineering, building, and scientific professions amounted to less than half of those of medicine, law, and religion; today they outnumber them by two to one.

In such a rapidly-developing situation, the exact definition of those occupations which are "true" professions may be a matter of controversy. There can, however, be little doubt that "one of the distinctive features of change in occupational distribution in the twentieth century is the apparently never-ending birth of professions."[6] This change in the occupational structure has obvious social implications, particularly in any analysis of the social class structure of society as a whole. But its consequences can be seen most readily if we consider the concept of social class as it operates among the residents of a local community.

LOCAL COMMUNITIES AND THE CONCEPT OF SOCIAL CLASS

Industrial society may be regarded as composed of a large number of local residential communities, which differ in the number and character of the occupational groups to be found within each one. Each has a particular local culture and consequent variations in the standards by which occupational status and social prestige are judged. These local communities are linked together by a variety of productive, administrative,

6 D. C. Marsh, *The Changing Social Structure of England and Wales* [1958], p. 149.

servicing, and other hierarchies, both private and public, as well as by a number of associations and institutions with a national basis. Although each local community has its own internal system of social prestige, whose determinants vary from one to another, all are linked together into the larger system, with certain values common to all. But because of local variation, we can only determine a national class system in the broadest sense, for social standing is largely an outcome of the prestige systems of limited social groups. This pluralistic concept of social structure and social class is opposed to current theories that society can be divided into a unitary hierarchy of social classes based on the relative status of occupations and of relations to property, theories that subsume the classical conception of capitalists, middle class, and working class. This Neapolitan-ice theory, which divided society into horizontal layers, even though the borders between the layers might be considered to be indefinite, is not a useful concept for dealing with modern complexities, however valid it may have been in the past. The "middle class" alone contains many disparate social elements: professional people, small shopkeepers, farmers, etc. To arrange these on a unitary social scale does not effectively help the sociologist to estimate either the relative position of one occupational group in relation to another, nor to assess the class positions of individuals in any given community.[7]

Here the field material from two community studies made in Britain since the War in terms of this pluralistic concept may briefly be outlined. The first is a study of the Derbyshire manufacturing town of Glossop made by members of the staff of Manchester University,[8] and the other the study of a coal-mining burgh in the East of Scotland that has already been mentioned.

Until 1914 Glossop apparently had a pyramidal social structure in which different occupational and social groups could be easily stratified in terms of upper and lower social classes. At the peak of the social hierarchy was an aristocratic landowning family. Beneath them came the industrialists who owned the mills and works in the town, some of them very wealthy. At the bottom of the pyramid were the great mass of

---

[7] For a criticism of unilinear scales, see T. Caplow, *The Sociology of Work* [1954].
[8] A. H. Birch, *Small-Town Politics* [1959].

factory hands, and in an intermediate position were a relatively small number of professional people, shopkeepers, and clerical workers. Two industrialist families dominated, both economically and socially. These two families represented opposed religious and political standards, the Tory Anglicans and the Liberal Dissenters. They competed for leadership and dominance within the town, a rivalry of some local benefit, for one family endowed the hospital, built the baths, and laid out the park, while the other contributed a library and a public hall. In the course of their competition both families acquired a number of honours and titles. The town could be regarded as stratified horizontally by economic and occupational differences, and divided vertically by religious and political differences, for the majority of the population followed the leadership of the two competing industrial families.

After the Great War, and particularly in the nineteen-thirties, this clear-cut economic and social structure was considerably modified. The manorial estates were sold in 1925, and the aristocratic family left the area. The dominant industrialists did not survive as independent owners. One of the families went bankrupt, the other sold its interests, and the mills and factories were taken over by impersonal public companies and combines. Eleven new firms came into the town, of which four were foreign. Only five of these were concerned with textiles—and not mainly with cotton, the former staple industry in Glossop—and six were industries quite new to the community. The old paternalistic rulers were replaced by salaried managers, most of whom were incomers. The social relationship of these new managers with the rest of the population was quite different from that of the former owners. In addition, national and local government services expanded. At the beginning of the century the only civil servants in Glossop were the staff of the Post Office. Now there are five Government departments, together with the regional boards of two nationalised industries. This meant a great increase in the number of officials living and working in the town, and few of these were local people. Even among the eight senior borough officials, only one was a native of Glossop. About four-fifths of the persons now in the most influential positions—the chief industrialists, the senior public officials, the clergymen, the headmasters—are immigrants to the town. Hence, although Glossop now maintains a large number of professional people, scientists and engineers, industrial welfare officers, public officials, and office workers, few of them are natives. Those Glossop children who achieve a grammar-school course and further education tend to leave the town and seek positions elsewhere. The brightest young people are in fact siphoned off by the educational system and channelled into careers in other places. Political allegiances too, have changed: the Labour Party has replaced the Liberal Party, and political loyalties are no longer directly related to religious differences. Finally, the physical boundaries of the town have been blurred by new building.

What now distinguishes Glossop from other similar small towns in the area is a distinctive local culture. The kind of work the people do, the way in which they use their leisure, the public and private services and amentities they enjoy, and the clothes they wear, are common to adjacent communities. Glossop people are linked to other members of the conurbation and the rest of Britain through their industrial organisations, through their professional and trade-union and political associations, and through certain regional and national recreational pursuits. They are distinguished from other industrial communities by distinctive variations in history, housing, dialect, and nuances of social behaviour.

The present social structure of this manufacturing town shows a broad correspondence with that of the Scottish coalmining burgh.[9] From quite different historical and economic beginnings, the two communities have converged.

The Burgh has a long history as a fishing and mining community. The coalmines in the area were the property of a private company, largely owned by a distinguished aristocratic family which had been in the coal trade for centuries. They had dominated the community socially as well as economically. Unlike Glossop, the Burgh had no great industrial development in the nineteenth century, apart from the collieries, but many Burgh families had owned shares in the small fishing-boats; and, after the aristocratic family, these people formed the most important social and political group. Fishing declined in the latter half of the nineteenth century, and had virtually dis-

[9] Unpublished MS. by W. Watson.

appeared by 1918. During the early years of this century, therefore, the Burgh was almost entirely dependent on the collieries.

After the depression of the early nineteen-thirties, some
manufacturing and other industrial enterprises took root in the
Burgh and its neighbourhood; and after 1938, stimulated by
rearmament and by the War, the number of workers in industries other than coal began to rise, and the percentage of the
population engaged in coal-mining began to fall. This process
continued after the War, and the Burgh became merged in a
larger industrial and mining area. This economic development
and the growth of both the Burgh and its contiguous communities produced a much more variegated occupational
pattern and less physical isolation. The population now includes
factory-owners and managers, professional people, local and
national civil servants, shopkeepers, hotel-owners, clerks and
officials, as well as skilled and unskilled workers in many
different trades. Finally the nationalisation of the coal industry
after the War replaced the former private owners, and their
functions were taken over by salaried managers and officials.
The social dominance of the former coal-owners disappeared.

In 1947 the total number of men and boys at work was
5,900, of whom 3,000 worked in the collieries. About 13 per
cent of the rest of the male working population was engaged in
clerical or supervisory work or in shopkeeping, and about
33 per cent in skilled manual work. These were employed in a
number of trades and industries, most of which operated on a
small scale; apart from the collieries, the largest single work-
place in the whole area of employment of which the Burgh
formed an integral part was an iron and steel foundry a few
miles outside the Burgh boundary, which employed about
1,400 men.

Only thirty people of professional occupations actually lived
in the Burgh, and a considerable proportion of these were
doctors and ministers of religion, whose occupations obliged
them to live within the Burgh boundaries. Most other professional people whose work lay within the Burgh boundaries
lived outside, in villages along the coast.

In certain broad respects, the Burgh, therefore, had come
to resemble Glossop. In both communities, the aristocratic
families had ceased to be an important economic, political, or

social factor. The dominant occupational groups are the professional people, the managers of the nationalised and other industries, the civil servants, and the small shopkeepers and local businessmen. Beneath them comes the great mass of wage-earners. Most of the professional people are immigrants to the communities. Both communities have an educational system which siphons off the brighter children and sends them out to positions elsewhere. In both places the physical boundaries are less obvious than in the past, and the people are affiliated to others in the country through their trade union and other associations, and in their leisure pursuits. Each community may be said to be comprised of three main economic and social groups: the salaried professionals, the burgesses (small shopkeepers and industialists, etc.), and wage-earners.

OCCUPATION AND SOCIAL CLASS

Populations are usually stratified into superior and inferior groups in terms of occupations, and in turn this stratification is used as a basis for assessing the social class of individuals and groups, as in the social-class scale devised by the Registrar General. The evaluation of the relative superiority or inferiority of given occupations is based on criteria which are assumed to be values common to our whole society. Generally, those occupations which demand most skill and the longest training also provide the highest pay, the most security, and the easiest working conditions, and are thereby held to be superior. But other factors are considered. Work which demands hard physical exertion under dirty conditions tends to have low prestige. In addition, the income provided is not simply a matter of the actual amounts earned, but also the spread of those amounts through a working life. Professional and highly skilled workers almost invariably start their careers with relatively low earnings which increase regularly with age and experience, a pattern most marked in the salaried professions.[10] Although these factors appear to be the main determinants of status for most occupations in the country as a whole, other factors affect the status of occupations in particular com-

[10] See H. Lydall, "The Life Cycle in Income, Saving, and Asset Ownership," [1955], pp. 131-150.

munities, and these arise from the actual constellation of occupations to be found within them.

In the Burgh, for instance, the standards by which social prestige are measured arise partly from the historical dominance of coal-mining in the area. Because coal-mining is arduous, dirty, and dangerous, colliers suffer in comparison with other manual workers, whatever degree of skill the collier may have. Furthermore, colliers have an unusual pattern of earnings. After an initial period of relatively low earnings while training, a collier who succeeds in getting on to the coal-face will rapidly increase his earnings, which are then based on his ability to produce more than the basic stint or task. Face-working is a peak earning period in a collier's working life-cycle. Usually he earns his highest wages between the early twenties and forties. After that, his earnings decline as he leaves piece-work, which demands intense physical effort, and takes up less arduous work paid at the minimum day-rate. Despite the post-War improvements in the pay and conditions of colliers as a whole, their work still has lower prestige than that of other skilled men.

Nor, in the Burgh, is social prestige solely determined by occupation. Social prestige is estimated by quite other characteristics. The amount of property a man owns, his mode of life, his educational level, and his social behaviour generally, are all elements that affect his standing in the view of his neighbours and fellow-citizens. These factors are obviously interrelated and at either end of the social scale—between, say, company directors and dustmen—produce two distinct modes of life using different material objects and with different social habits and expectations. Because the range of occupations in local communities is usually limited, professional and managerial people tend to exemplify the persons and mode of life with the highest social prestige, and unskilled manual workers exemplify the persons and mode of life with the lowest. These provide two consistent reference-groups by which to assess the social prestige of people whose occupational, economic, and social differences are not nearly so distinct.[11] Naturally the constellations of people with varied occupations

[11] For a discussion on reference group behaviour, see R. K. Merton, *Social Theory and Social Structure* [1957].

are greater in the large towns and conurbations, and here the rating of social prestige is much more difficult and obscure. But in such large communities the range of contact between different groups is much more limited, so that a general consensus of class position can scarcely be achieved.[12]

OCCUPATIONAL AND SOCIAL PRESTIGE IN THE LOCAL COMMUNITY

In the coal-mining Burgh, the social "class" of individuals cannot be assumed to correspond with their occupational category and social class as determined by such national scales of social class as that issued by the Registrar General. When people in the Burgh assign others to a social "class" they tend to consider a large number of factors, apart from occupation. They use the terms "middle class" and "working" class to describe social differences, but they include in these categories people of quite disparate occupations. The concept of two reference-groups is always present, a top and a bottom, and judgments of persons in particular social situations are made in terms of this concept. The social prestige of individuals is rated by the degree to which they are assumed to conform to or to depart from the standards of these reference-groups. This applies particularly to the great number of skilled workers in various trades and industries who have comparable occupations. Among these people factors other than occupation become of primary importance in determining their social prestige and class. A skilled worker who owns his own home and motor car, who is a deacon of the Church, and whose son is a university student, regards himself, and is regarded by others, as "middle class." In everything but his occupation, such a man conforms to the mode of life of the professional classes which form the upper reference-group. Social "classes" as distinct permanent groups with a precise definable membership do not exist. The social-prestige structure of local communities is based on a number of social groups and of individuals who compete with one another for prestige in terms of the two reference-groups which set the standards of competition. The social-class concept is a measure for assessing relative success and failure in a

[12] See J. Hall and D. C. Jones, "Social Grading of Occupations," [1950], pp. 31-55.

competitive prestige system. As such, the standards vary from one community to another, and these standards may vary considerably. What is common to them all is the concept of social "class."

In the Burgh, for instance, an individual achieves social mobility in terms of a prestige system of this nature. The particular system of the Burgh is complicated by the major occupational division between colliers and all other workers. Colliers form a group quite distinct from all other workers, owing to the special conditions of their work. Colliers work underground, "hidden away from the world," as one put it, on a shift system that does not correspond to the usual working times of industry; they may be paid on a contract system; and they have special skills which cannot readily be transferred to other kinds of work. Even the introduction of machinery has not altered this essential distinction between miners and other manual workers. Despite the amelioration of conditions in recent years, all underground activity still remains to a great extent isolated and dangerous and differs in type from other industrial work. In addition, colliers themselves are stratified by degrees of skill, special responsibilities, and different rates of pay. Some of them are oversmen or supervisors of one kind or another, and a number of skilled tradesmen also work underground. In spite of this, the division between colliers and others remains, and is important socially.

An individual can attempt to achieve higher social prestige by changing his occupation, but that is difficult. Usually an adult can change his occupation only within a very restricted range, particularly among the wage-earning population. A man may move from unskilled to semi-skilled work, or from skilled work to a supervisory position. He may transfer from one industry to another. Changes from one grade of work to another are difficult, because of the apprenticeship system and the rules for trade-union membership, which demand long periods of training. Alternatively, a man may save or acquire enough capital to open a small business and thus change his occupation. All such changes are within the category of non-professional occupations. An adult may only enter a profession through prolonged study in his spare time, to obtain an external degree or some other higher educational or technical qualification.

Occupational changes are difficult; it is easier for a man to acquire social prestige within the local community by participating in certain social activities outside the factory or colliery. He can be active in the Church, in a political party, in some recreational organisation, or in some other group. Prominence in such activities confers prestige on a man within his own particular social circle, and perhaps in the community as a whole; it may also help him to transfer to another social circle whose prestige is higher. Moreover, a man can achieve social prestige through his children, for if they reach an occupational level higher than his own, and particularly if they enter the professions, their acquired status is reflected back on his own. Drives for prestige are often combined with residential changes from one district to another. A man's occupation alone is by no means a certain indication of his social "class" within the local community. For instance, how is the social "class" of the following individual to be assessed in terms of a unitary scale based on occupation? This man was chairman of the local branch of a national political party, he was a baillie (municipal magistrate), a director of the football club, an elder of the Church, owned his own home, and had three children who had achieved a university education. He was in fact an unskilled worker. In terms of a social-class scale based on occupation, he should be rated in the lowest social class: but in terms of the social-prestige system of the Burgh, he was quite definitely "middle class," regarded himself as such, and was so regarded by others.

The social significance of professional people as a reference-group whereby social prestige and social class in a local community is judged is obviously important. The effects of the rise in number and influence of professional people in society as a whole are less clear and remain to be studied. I propose to outline briefly the characteristics of professions and to indicate the lines on which future research into their social significance should be developed.

THE CHARACTERISTICS OF PROFESSIONS

Professions may be divided by their basic skills and functions into two main categories: the scientific professions and the non-scientific.[13] The scientific professions are allied to the major divisions of science and technology, and may be grouped into sub-crafts which have multiplied in number as scientific knowledge has advanced. Thus the principles of mechanics are the basis of the profession of civil engineering, and from this in turn developed over time a number of sub-crafts such as the mechanical engineers, aeronautical engineers, naval architects, and so on. These scientific professions have proliferated as industrial organisation developed in scope and complexity. The close connexion between scientific advance, industrial organisation, and the professional status of persons with certain skills is indicated in the relative ages of the professions. Civil engineers achieved professional status in 1818, when they founded the Institute of Civil Engineers, while physicists were not classified separately in the Census until 1921. Since then physics has been the basis for the growth of a number of specialised professions. In the same way, the application of the principles of chemistry had led to an extensive proliferation of skills which are regarded as professional occupations.

Non-scientific professions may be grouped within broad categories of status associations, as opposed to sub-crafts, for instance the numerous organisations of different kinds of teachers, surveyors, civil servants, accountants, local government officers, etc.

Many professions began as study societies whose object extended no further than discussion and research, and perhaps publication, in a particular field. The next step is to set up standards of competence for the exercise of the particular functions and duties; thereafter the members try to obtain public recognition of the professional status of the new occupation, and the protection of the interests of its practitioners. This has been the usual progress of development in the established professions, and is being followed now by some skilled occupations which are striving for professional status. Such occupations as librarian, dental mechanic, hospital administrator, chiropodist, etc., are seeking professional status and

[13] I have drawn here on the work of A. M. Carr-Saunders and P. A. Wilson, *The Professions* [1933], and also R. Lewis and A. Maude, *Professional People* [1952].

recognition, quite apart from many of the new occupations based on technological advances.

Most professions, whether scientific or not, and whatever their specialised techniques, have certain common character-istics which are significant in the analysis of social organisation. They show the following four distinctive features:

1. The members have a monopoly of function, sometimes legally enforced, based on a specialised technique.[14]

2. The members qualify by examination, usually at a university or college; or, if not, by satisfying standards set by universities.

3. The members are organised within a formal association, often with a hierarchical structure, which protects their interests and regulates their relationships with the public. Some have grades of membership which depend on seniority and experience.

4. Individual members can anticipate an increase in salary, responsibility, and prestige through experience and ability. In other words, they can look forward to a career.

Professional occupations, therefore, are usually organised within associations of similar pattern, and despite the extreme specialisation of their individual techniques, share a similar educational experience over a long period of years. Their educational progress up to and including university equips them with a generic culture and ideology. Even their special techniques are based on principles generally accepted and understood. Their generic culture is based partly on common liberal values with a wide range of diversity, so that it can support a number of sub-cultures without losing a common identity. In other words, professional persons with a university education and an accepted status in society share character-istics which differentiate them from other groups in the com-munity. Most professional persons enter into life-careers of an

[14] For a history of the enforcement of monopoly in the medical profession in the U.S.A., see D. R. Hyde and P. Woolf with A. Gross and E. L. Hoffman, "The American Medical Association: Power, Purpose and Politics in Organized Medicine," [1954], pp. 938-1022.

almost identical pattern, whatever the exact nature of their work and the considerable variation in salaries. This pattern is a progress up the ladder of promotion through competition for higher posts with greater responsibility, and with higher salaries and prestige.

PROFESSIONAL MOBILITY

The opportunities for progressive careers for most professional people are provided by the productive and administrative structures of large-scale enterprises. These industrial and commercial organisations, whether they are publicly or privately owned, tend to have a similar bureaucratic pattern of organisation, usually consisting of hierarchies of managers, technicians, supervisors, accountants, administrators, etc., all of them in various positions of superiority and inferiority to one another.[15] A successful career may take a professional person from a junior position in one such organisation, through intermediate positions in several, to a senior position in yet another. At each new advance in his career, such a man may be obliged to change his place of residence; thus upward mobility may be accompanied by spatial mobility. Some organisations, Imperial Chemicals or Unilevers or the Foreign Service, are so large that they provide opportunities for a career entirely within the same organisational structure.[16] The scale of operation of such organisations is usually national and often international in scope; consequently, a climb up the ladder of promotion even within one such organisation may necessitate considerable residential movements. One obvious example is the movement of a Colonial Service officer from one part of an overseas territory to another, or even from one country to another, as he is promoted in the service. But similar movements can be found among engineers or chemists or administrators in large-scale industry. This residential movement is often held out as an incentive to join the organisation. Even academic persons are now involved in this process, for today an academic career can take a man through several universities in different countries.

[15] See A. W. Gouldner, *Patterns of Industrial Bureaucracy* [1955].
[16] Unilever Ltd. supports an establishment of 22,600 managers, according to a report by the chairman, Lord Heyworth, "The Managers," in *Progress* [1956].

K

In addition to this promotional and residential mobility, professional people may also be occupationally mobile. Among allied professions the demarcation of skills is not yet as rigid as among other occupations;[17] a person who acquires certain key qualifications can move from one professional occupation to an allied one. Perhaps more importantly from a career aspect, every professional qualification carries with it the potentiality of achieving high administrative, managerial, or executive position. An increasing proportion of the recruits to the highest levels of management and policy-direction in industry tends to be drawn from the different groups of specialists.[18] A chemical engineer can leave his specialised department and become a general manager; a university lecturer can become a civil servant; a former army officer can become a bank official; a schoolteacher can become an administrator in the educational system.

At the lower levels of bureaucratic hierarchies, promotion is usually bound up with the exercise of professional skills. But at the higher levels other qualities and a more general ability are needed, and the professional qualification becomes relatively less important. For instance, in academic institutions progress from research assistant to senior lecturer is usually bound up with the exercise of professional skills. Thereafter promotion depends on imponderable factors: "administrative ability," "qualities of leadership," "drive," "personality," "judgment," and so on. Above the status of professor, the higher reaches of the academic world are open to men of many

[17] Carr-Saunders and Wilson (*The Professions*) point out that the history of trade-unionism seems to indicate that the problems of demarcation between the different categories of wage-earners have always been a source of friction. The protective functions of the union tend to dominate, with a consequent search for the strongest bargaining unit. These are problems that so far have scarcely arisen among professional groups, although current disputes concerning professional salaries seem to indicate that the bargaining and protective functions of professional associations are likely to be emphasised in the future.

[18] This does not apply to small-scale industry, which still forms an important sector of the British economy. In this sector, entrants to management may come from the families of the owners, or of shareholders, or through promotion from the workshop. Nevertheless, even in the small firms, some managers may possess professional qualifications, particularly when the industrial process is highly technical. In such small firms, the specialist may leave because he sees that promotion to the top is blocked. See R. V. Clemens, *Managers: A Study of Their Careers in Industry* [1958].

professional qualifications, and the abilities needed for such positions cannot be determined by examination or by measures of strictly professional competence. This appears to apply to most large-scale organisations, whatever their function; the general manager in industry may have begun his career in any one of the specialised departments, so that accountants, engineers, administrators, chemists, etc., are all eligible to compete for the highest executive positions. The highest positions and salaries in industry appear to go to persons who succeed in combining general administrative abilities with intelligent understanding of specialist techniques.[19] Thus top executives can move from the summit of one bureaucratic organisation to another, whatever their initial professional training, and irrespective of the basic functions of the organisations concerned. High-ranking officers move from the services to banks and then to industrial organisations, or a professor may become a civil servant, then an ambassador, then a corporation executive, and so on.

The progressive ascent of the specialists of different skills through a series of higher positions in one or more hierarchical structures, and the concomitant residential mobility through a number of communities at one or more steps during the ascent, forms a characteristic combination of social and spatial mobility which may be called "spiralism." This mobility in career and residence common to many professional people has significant social consequences, for it affects both the organisations for which they work and the communities in which they live.

This does not imply that every professional person has an equal potential of mobility, either in career or residence. The nature of a professional occupation may set definite limits on the possibility of mobility. A civil engineer or a diplomat is likely to be more mobile than a doctor in general practice, or a family solicitor. This is reflected in the way they are paid. Some professions are entirely dependent on large-scale organisations for opportunities to increase their financial rewards, while others are not. Those professions entirely dependent on salaries are likeliest to produce spiralists, while those who still

[19] See K. Gales, in *Journal of the Royal Statistical Society*, [1958], Series A, pp. 438-453.

take fees as part or the whole of their reward are not. Thus 99 per cent of the scientific professions are salaried, and may be said to depend on large-scale organisations and institutions for their careers, whereas only 42 per cent of the legal profession and 51 per cent of the medical profession are salaried, and are thereby less dependent on large-scale organisations. There is a clear tendency away from fees as professional remuneration, and towards salaries (see Appendix). A spiralist's possible range of activity is the total number of fields within which his education qualifies him to compete. Any given professional person's potential mobility, therefore, will be the resultant of a complex of factors: his basic skills, his social background, his educational affiliations, and his personality. Furthermore, the age at which a man achieves successive rungs in the ladder may also affect his chances of moving further up or down. The race is not entirely to the swift.

PROFESSIONAL AND OTHER OCCUPATIONS

Professional people are clearly differentiated, by function, education, and culture, from those skilled and unskilled persons who work for weekly wages and make up the bulk of the population. Although skilled workers employ specialised techniques, some of which take years to acquire, the standard of education demanded from apprentices is not so high as that demanded from an entrant to a profession. Their working careers, too, tend to have a quite different pattern. The worker earns his maximum wage as soon as he completes his training, or very shortly afterwards. He usually continues at more or less the same level throughout his working life, except when the wage of the whole occupation goes up. Promotion for a skilled worker is often restricted to the lowest grades of supervision, such as chargehands and foremen, and the higher levels of management tend more and more to be monopolised by persons with professional qualifications.[20] This also applies to routine clerical workers, even though some of these may be salaried, for their promotion to higher administrative positions is hindered by their lack of formal qualifications in higher education.

[20] See F. H. Harbison and E. W. Burgess, "Modern Management in Western Europe" [1954], pp. 15-23.

In most local communities one other occupational group can be distinguished, *viz.*, the burgesses, that is, shopkeepers, owners and managers of small-scale industries, and other small capitalists, whose limited scale of operations usually restricts them to a specific local community. Such persons may become mobile and change their occupational status, either by developing their businesses or by extending their operations over a wider area. But in general they are tied to a local community, and often share the same local culture as members of the working class.

As stated earlier, these local cultures, each particular and unique, are marked by persistence of residence, limited spatial mobility on the part of the bulk of the population, distinguishing customs, and a local dialect. In this they differ from the spiralists who share the generic spiralist culture acquired through their higher education and prolonged training. Even when a professional person has emerged from a local culture, particularly through the siphoning process of the educational system, this cultural background is of little significance to him in his functional relationships with other professional people, although it may be of very considerable significance in his social relationships with them. The product of Eton and Oxford is a different social person from the product of a grammar school and Redbrick, even though both may pursue the same profession.

Residential mobility on the part of wage-earners and other non-professional people is in the main limited to movement within one town or to a neighbouring town.[21] Such movements arise from a variety of motives: to find suitable accommodation, to seek higher wages, to obtain a supervisory job, to open a new business, to obtain better educational opportunities for children, etc. These movements often result in changes in the social standing of the families concerned, whether they move within the boundaries of their own community or into another. But residential movements for these categories of occupations seldom involve a change from non-professional to professional status. In other words, residential mobility may involve these persons in minor changes in social standing within the social-prestige system of one limited area.

[21] See G. Thomas, "Labour Mobility in Great Britain 1945-1949 [1950]."

The social mobility of spiralists, therefore, differs in quality from that found among persons of non-professional occupation. Professional people have a much greater potential of mobility in their career expectations than others. This potential originates in their superior training and education, which in an increasingly complex society qualifies them to compete for the highest posts in industry and commerce. It is the general awareness of this which helps to increase the severe competition for places for children in the higher levels of secondary education, the main channel through which professional status can be acquired. In addition, spiralist professionals in particular share a common generic culture, and whatever community a spiralist enters, and whatever the local system of rating social prestige, his professional status and education guarantee that he will be judged by values common to the whole society. This high social estimation of professions ensures that professional people are generally at the top, or at least very near the top, of the social scale in most local communities. A residential movement by a spiralist to a post in another community will hardly affect his social position in relation to the majority of the inhabitants, although his position in relation to other professional people may change considerably, because of promotion or demotion or of the number and character of professional people already resident. In most local communities, the social relationships of a spiralist will tend to be conditioned by his membership of functional associations. And because the functional position that a spiralist occupies is part of a regional or national or international hierarchy, the particular occupational skills, social background, educational affiliations, personality and age of an incumbent will all help to determine his social relationships within the local community of residence. A young man in a junior position who expects promotion and a consequent move elsewhere will tend to have a different attitude to, and degree of participation in, community activities than, for instance, an older man still in a junior position who can no longer reasonably expect to be promoted. The hopes and interests of younger spiralists generally extend outside the local community within which they live. On the other hand, a given spiralist may be inhibited by local ties from seeking such further progress in his career as would necessitate a residential move.

The higher levels of large-scale hierarchical organisations are usually to be found within the larger towns, and particularly within the conurbations; as a result, these support a large number of spiralists. In Edinburgh, for instance, the proportion of persons of professional occupations to others is four times greater than that found in the industrial area of which our coal-mining Burgh formed an integral part. These larger communities tend to have socially-distinct residential areas, and many spiralists live together in suburbs and commute to work. These suburbs may be regarded as specialised residential local communities made up entirely of business and professional people with similar incomes and interest. Such residential areas have rarely been studied in Britain. When place of residence and place of work are so closely demarcated and distinct from one another, social relations between varied occupational and economic groups are bound to differ from those that occur in local communities where residence of a wide range of occupational groups is contiguous. The existence of suburban concentrations of occupational groups of all kinds presents analytical problems of social relations and mobility of a different order from those already discussed in the local community.

SPIRALISTS AND ORGANISATION POLICIES

The career and residential movements of spiralists may affect the policies of large-scale organisations. Some firms already guarantee their recruits opportunities of promotion within their own management and administrative structures in order to insure themselves against the loss of men suitable for promotion to the higher echelons. They also seek out those men to whom movement will be congenial. Uniliver advertisements for graduates, for instance, make this quite clear. The qualities needed are described: "*Avis Unileverensis* (*Managerialis*), Plumage: highly variegated, Habits: too varied to list, Habitat: the world, Distinctive Characteristics: a high flyer." Some large firms with international connexions have already adopted a policy of providing free homes, furniture, cars, etc. to executives above a certain level in order to increase their potential mobility within the various branches of the organisation. The argument here appears to be that these men will not be tied by the difficulties of moving their own possessions. On the other hand, some firms forbid their executives to take part in local affairs, for this, too, could tie them to one place and reduce their potential mobility. Some firms distribute shares in the company, both as an incentive to effort and an economic bond of loyalty to the firm. This is analogous to the practice of various Government services, for the share distribution is comparable to the prestige emblems awarded to senior Government officers when they are appointed to certain posts. Other aspects of policy may also be affected. Within bureaucratic structures the operation of informal groups is of importance to the smooth functioning of the organisation. The composition of these informal groups within the formal structure can be influenced by the social background and age of individuals and the different stages they have reached in their careers. Within a university, for instance, a young man may consider that he has opportunities for promotion available to him, or he may consider that it is only likely to achieve promotion by moving somewhere else. He may be prepared to move his family and live elsewhere if promoted. Conversely, he may accept that he can no longer reasonably anticipate promotion, or because of local attachments and interests he is unwilling to move. An older man may have reached the final stage of promotion in his career that he can reasonably expect. It is fair to assume that these factors will affect the attitudes of individuals towards matters of policy concerning the operation and future of the institution, as well as the extent to which they develop informal relationships with others. However, these consequences of mobility in career and residence on the policy and structures of large-scale organisations must await further investigation and research.

EDUCATION AND SOCIAL MOBILITY

Because of the development of professionalism, higher education is evidently of primary importance in achieving certain types of social mobility, and the social system can almost be specified in terms of the educational structure alone. Every local community supports a primary school system which imparts common cultural elements. Above this level, selection divides children into separate educational streams with different occupational expectations and potentialities. Each stream is taught in separate secondary classes whose curricula effectively impose different cultural patterns. From the lower streams are drawn the unskilled and semi-skilled workers of the future. The highest stream runs through the grammar school, and this is the decisive institution for training children for university education and entry to the professions. This is the most important stage in the process of creating a discontinuity of culture between the children of wage-earners and their parents.[22] The majority of children involved in such a discontinuity will probably be drawn away from their local communities of upbringing to live and work elsewhere. Few of them return to settle in their communities of origin when their training is complete.[23] Such children enter their new communities as adults with professional occupations and different standards and therefore with quite different social positions from that of their parents in their own community. As the whole process of selecting and training children for professional careers is in the hands of professional people, it follows that those children are selected who are considered most likely to conform to professional standards. In such selection, the children of professional persons start with a considerable advantage, and the children of wage-earners most likely to be selected are those whose parents' mode of life resembles most closely that of professional people.[24]

Children from professional families who fail to achieve the higher secondary level will tend to fall below the occupational level of their parents. Such children have already absorbed the elements of the generic culture of their parents in their homes, and failure to achieve a comcomitant professional occupation involves them in a discontinuity of another kind. For if they take up non-professional work in a local community, particularly manual work, they will inevitably lack the local culture, and this can have significant social consequences.

The universities set the ultimate standards of achievement

[22] See M. Mead, "Our Educational Emphasis in Primitive Perspective [1943]," pp. 633-639.

[23] See A. H. Birch, *Small-Town Politics* [1959], p. 36.

[24] See *Social Class and Educational Opportunity* [1956], edd. J. E. Floud, A. H. Halsey, and F. M. Martin.

for students who at every stage of their educational careers have been subjected to a progressive standardisation of culture and achievement. The State educational system culminating in the universities provides the main channel for children to rise from a local community and its particular culture into the functional associations of spiralists and their generic culture.

Although Britain has two systems of education, the State system and a private system, both converge on the same universities, and share educational and cultural standards. This is not to say there is no effective difference between the two systems of education. For historical and social reasons, the private system has an important function in that it inculcates patterns of social behaviour in children which later on give them an advantage in competition with children from the State system, an advantage of sufficient importance to ensure that the private system continues to flourish.

Many studies have shown that the children of professional persons have a much greater chance of achieving professional occupations than the children of wage-earners, even when the children of professionals go through the State school system. There is a connexion between a father's occupational level and that attained by his children.[25] The social and cultural factors involved in maintaining this connexion are extremely complicated, irrespective of questions of "innate" ability in children from different occupational groups. It is more common for children of non-professional fathers to rise to the level of professional occupations than for children of professional people to fall below this level. At present the social system permits a great deal of upward occupational mobility. This is not entirely due to the increase in the number of professional occupations in a changing economy. Demographic factors have an effect on patterns of occupational mobility. The two broad groups of "manual" and "non-manual" workers have a differential fertility, and the replacement ratio between sons and fathers in the two groups is different. The ratio of sons to fathers in the "non-manual" group is much lower than that in the "manual" group. Therefore, even if every son from a "non-manual" family achieved this occupational status, opportunities for the sons of "manual" workers to attain professional

[25] See *Social Mobility in Britain* [1954], ed. D. V. Glass.

occupations would still exist. Hence, from the point of view of people in a local community, several factors combine to provide opportunities for their children to achieve upward occupational mobility.

SUMMARY AND CONCLUSION

I have attempted to argue that we can only understand social phenomena within a local community against the changes that have taken place in society as a whole. Because the economy is tending towards centralised enterprises, industrial, manufacturing, commercial, distributing, agricultural, etc., and the extension of Government and administrative services, any given local community will contain one or several branches, workshops, or offices, of such organisations. Existing local industries and other services, too, are tending to become branches or departments of large-scale organisations.

As a result, there are few isolated communities whose economic, social, and political relationships are wholly or almost wholly contained within specific boundaries. There are more multiple communities and conurbations bound together by the complexity of industrial processes and economic and other organisations whose relations extend into the national or international sphere. The particular constellation of occupations found in any community is the basis for its particular system of evaluating social status and prestige. Local communities are distinguished from each other by these particular systems of status and prestige and their unique cultures. They are linked to each other through the hierarchical organisations of industry, commerce, and administrative services, together with national economic, political, and other organisations to which most of the population belongs. These hierarchical organisations are operated and controlled by spiralists who form a series of functional associations, marked by a generic culture depending on a high level of education.

Within this whole system occupational and social mobility are related, but occupational status is not a sufficient criterion by which persons can be ranged on a unilinear social scale. There is a qualitative difference between manual occupations on the one hand, and professional, managerial, and administrative occupations on the other. This difference is represented most clearly by the hurdle of higher education necessary for entry to a professional occupation. The highest levels of the educational system are reserved for the instruction and training of entrants to the professional, managerial, and administrative groups which operate and control large-scale organisations.

There are different fields of social mobility. Individuals can rise and fall in terms of various prestige structures, either of local communities, or of regional or national organisations, not only industrial and productive, but also political, educational, religious, recreational, etc. Many of these interact on one another, but the range of participation and the degree of prestige achieved within them will be affected by an individual's occupation, which helps to determine his cultural equipment and mode of life.

The whole social system may therefore be envisaged as a plurality of prestige structures, some of them interconnected and others quite independent, and each with its own particular standards of evaluation, although all are liable to be affected by the fundamental division of function and culture between members of professional and non-professional occupations.

The "class" position of individuals and groups is explicable only in terms of these sub-structures; in a local community the "class" system will reflect the number and constitution of such sub-structures as are represented; on a national scale, the "class" system can be interpreted only in terms of the plurality of sub-systems which makes up the whole.

Appendix

PROFESSIONAL OCCUPATIONS (CENSUS 1951, ENGLAND AND WALES)

	1951 *as a percentage of* 1921	*Total occupied in* 1951	*Percentage salaried in* 1951
Social Welfare	714	22,151	99
Science	640	109,563	99
Medical Auxiliary Services . .	502	60,643	80
Accountants	445	32,424	68
Engineering, surveying, architectural	400	125,997	92
Industrial designers, draughtsmen .	385	123,912	99
Miscellaneous (librarians, officials of political, industrial and trade associations, others)	378	41,758	97
Nursing	193	235,397	98
Authors, editors, journalists . .	179	23,822	77
Medicine	161	57,234	51
Law	137	23,450	42
Artists (painters, sculptors, engravers)	135	16,548	61
Teaching	114	313,235	96
Religion	93	51,198	92
Actors and musicians . . .	73	29,452	76

7

Ely Devons & Max Gluckman

CONCLUSION:
MODES AND CONSEQUENCES OF
LIMITING A FIELD OF STUDY

RESTRICTING REALITY

Reality is complex, and the first task of any scientist is to delimit specific problems within a restricted field of data. Because the social scientist, like the student of human personality, can only in a few situations isolate the facts he is investigating from the rest of reality, we have collected five essays to show what particular anthropologists and sociologists[1] have done in coping with the consequences of this situation. Here we consider the situation in general terms. After delineating the problems and setting out the procedures which social anthropologists employ to demarcate their fields of study, we apply these to our colleagues' essays; and then we discuss more generally, through specific examples, how other social and human scientists have demarcated their fields of problems and the consequences of this demarcation. At that stage, we shall cite the views of other writers on these topics.

To set these questions in perspective, we have first to describe the nature of our subject-matter. In social anthropology and sociology it was, and in some quarters still is, common for the field of study to be defined as "society" or "culture." We consider that such definitions of the field lead to difficulties, and

---

[1] Lupton and Cunnison were trained as sociologists, but they worked in a department of social anthropology and their research was social anthropological in nature. Hence we feel justified in describing them as "social anthropologists." Both were elected members of the Association of Social Anthropologists of the British Commonwealth.

attempts to delineate "exclusive domains" (in Durkheim's phrase) for the various biological, psychological, and social sciences. When, at the beginning of his *Les Règles de la méthode sociologique*, Durkheim attempted to demarcate the "exclusive domain" of sociology, he had to concede that drinking, sleeping, eating, and reasoning must be allowed to be of interest to biology and psychology, and hence he seems to exclude them from the domain of sociology, though he adds that a society is concerned that these functions be exercised in an orderly manner.[2] This attempt to demarcate a domain of facts leads Durkeim into many difficulties. We start, therefore, with the late Professor A. R. Radcliffe-Brown, from the view that reality, as Whitehead put it, is a "passage of events" in space-time, and that we can observe these events. These events may be of varying duration, as the earth and sun are "long events" while others are "short events," perhaps as "transient" as a spoken sentence. Nevertheless, they are all events which can be observed—and we do not enter into the difficult, but here irrelevant, problem of how agreement is reached on these observations.

Any event which influences how men live together may thus be part of the field which an anthropologist studies—the heavenly bodies and their movements, or rain and soil, as well as books and words and men's feelings. On this view it is not necessary to distinguish an exclusive domain for anthropology or sociology, or psychology, or biology, and many of the difficulties in which Durkheim became involved can thus be avoided.[3]

[2] E. Durkheim, *Règles* [=*Les Règles de la méthode Sociologique:* 9th edn, 1938], p. 5. Later (*op. cit.*, pp. 17 f.). Durkheim has also to exclude such facts as those of topography, communications, habitations, from the domain of "social facts" (French edn., pp. 17 f.). A crucial paragraph on p. 17 seems not to be included in the English translation (pp. 10-11).

[3] This is of course elementary epistemology, but we feel we must set it out since some social and behavioural scientists still work with the view that each science must have its own field of facts, and conceive of these facts, as Durkheim did, as "things" rather than as "events." Gluckman fairly recently lectured on the anthropological analysis of witchcraft, and was challenged by a senior psychologist because he was talking about motives, beliefs, ideas, and feelings, and these were "psychological phenomena." On this clarifying view of reality see the works of A. N. Whitehead, and N. Campbell, *What is Science?* [1921], pp. 36, 167. Gluckman wishes to acknowledge the extent to which the late A. R. Radcliffe-Brown's exposition of this view in social science clarified problems for him, since Radcliffe-Brown did not publish extensively on the theme (see Radcliffe-Brown, *Structure and Function in Primitive Society* [1952], where in the Introduction it i

Furthermore, in this passage of events we observe certain regularities. When we meet an individual we are able to a degree to anticipate his actions and reactions in the light of our knowledge of other individuals; and as we get to know him better, we can anticipate even his idiosyncratic behaviour. Similarly, when an anthropologist enters an exotic society, he can expect certain responses from its members on the basis of his knowledge of other tribal societies; and as he comes to know the new society, he begins to anticipate the actions of its members, where these vary specifically from action in other societies. Regularities in social life and individual behaviour are thus observable; and scientists assume that these regularities depend upon one another in a systematic way.

Different disciplines may study the same events, and even some of the same regularities in those events: but they look for different kinds of interdependencies between the regularities, *i.e.*, for different kinds of relations.[4] Thus a social anthropologist, like a psychologist, may study events of mental and emotional life—the actions and thoughts and feelings of individuals, and (if he has the techniques to collect the necessary information) even "unconscious" thoughts and feelings. The psychologist seeks to find the relations between these events as they occur in the life of single individuals, what Radcliffe-Brown called "individual mental or psychical system." The social anthropologist seeks to find relations between these events as they link together mental systems within a physical environment, *i.e.*, he studies them within social systems. The economist or political scientist or lawyer may study some of the same events, as well as other events, in a different set of interrelations.

The different social and behavioural sciences are in the main distinguished not by the events they study but by the kinds of relations between events which they seek to establish. Events themselves are neutral to the different disciplines. Nevertheless, it makes for brevity to speak of psychological,

---

[4] For a clear statement of this approach in social science, see Homans, *The Human Group*, I-II, and *passim*.

presented in one packed paragraph, pp. 5-6; and his posthumously collected papers in *A Natural Science of Society* [1957], p. 12). For a more detailed application of this thesis to social life, see M. Gluckman, "The Difficulties, Limitations and Achievements of Social Anthropology" [1944].

cultural, social, and economic facts or phenomena, which are events taken into some framework of analysis: but anyone who does so is referring to events brought into relation with one another in a psychical, cultural, social or economic system respectively.

The preceding paragraphs have transposed the statements made in the Introduction about "aspects" of reality into a terminology which distinguishes a number of different kinds of systems. As different people favour each of these terminologies, we re-state this view of the way in which facts can be fitted into various types of system in terms of one system of reality with different aspects, each aspect having apparent regularities and interdependencies between the regularities. For example, economics looks at men as they are concerned with making a living or accumulating and exchanging wealth, political science looks at men when they are mainly concerned with administration and power through the organised machinery of the State or whatsoever other groups and relationships serve these purposes, and psychology looks at the interrelations between the acts of behaviour and the feelings and thoughts of individual men and their reactions to the physical and social environment. These are different ways of looking at aspects of reality—and there are others. Every situation can be viewed from several aspects. Thus the behaviour of workers in a factory has its economic aspect, its political aspect, and its psychological aspect. In a fundamental philosophical sense all these aspects are part of the complex reality of human life, and this is not separable into economic life, political life, social life, psychological life, and so forth. But if one is to succeed in studying society, one must split up reality by isolating a particular aspect which presents certain regularities and is *relatively* autonomous and independent of the other aspects. Having chosen a particular aspect for study, the social or human scientist, who then becomes an economist, sociologist, psychologist, or student of politics, confines himself to that aspect and ignores aspects, and complexities, studied by others.

If the aspects which one thinks are relatively independent, are in fact closely interrelated, then confining one's study to a particular aspect leads nowhere in terms of understanding reality; and if the social scientist concerned is under the illusion

L

that it does, he may be misled in his whole analysis. In our other terms, it is fruitless to demarcate as a relatively autonomous and independent system, a set of regularities which depend essentially on events and relations between events outside that system.

PROCEDURES FOR DEMARCATING A FIELD

Initially, as stated in the Introduction, we thought that we were dealing with two sets of issues. First, since "the passage of events" is "infinite," we asked, "How does an anthropologist decide where to demarcate a field of data, or a set of purposive activities, out of the total flow?" Second, there was the problem of how an anthropologist decides whether or not to take notice of the work of investigators in other social sciences who are studying the same events by other techniques and modes of analysis. And finally, what limitations did these decisions impose on his ability to explain the nature of reality?

In working through the essays in this book, and through other researches in which these issues have arisen, we have come to realise that there are more than two sets of issues, and we now distinguish five procedures by which fields of study are demarcated. These procedures can be usefully distinguished from one another, even though an anthropologist may employ all simultaneously and though it is sometimes difficult to decide which he is using, because they shade into one another.

1. There is delimitation of a field in space and in time. Every anthropologist uses this procedure to isolate a manageable amount of interconnected data, as when he studies social relations in a tribe or in a factory over a certain period. This delimitation may also be of what Fortes calls a "domain" of activities, such as domestic relations, or political relations, or the inter-personal linkages between kinsfolk, or the relation between legal or religious activities and social relationships. This procedure of closing off a field will be called *circumscribing* a field of research. When an anthropologist circumscribes his field, he cuts off a manageable field of reality from the total flow of events, by putting boundaries round it

both in terms of what is relevant to his problems and in terms of how and where he can apply his techniques of observation and analysis. Establishing the boundaries is a major separate procedure, which may involve some of the following procedures, though they have their own logic of application.

2. The anthropologist may take for granted, as "given" facts, some events which exert marked influence in his field. He does not bother about their internal complexity and can completely neglect the disciplines which study them. Thus every anthropological study of a tribal society begins from the fact that rain falls in certain quantities at certain times, and this affects the growth of crops and grazing and therefore social life, but no enquiry is made into what determines the rainfall and the growth of crops. Anthropological studies of factories take for granted that there is machinery, but they do not worry about how it works, though they are concerned with how the technological process affects social relations. We propose to call this procedure by which certain events are taken for granted, as given basic facts, *incorporation*,[5] on the mixed analogy that the anthropology merely *incorporates* them into his field.

3 (*a*). The next procedure has to be applied with greater care. Frequently an anthropologist has to base his analysis on more complex combinations of relations between facts, where these relations are appropriately studied by another discipline. Thus the question of whether a particular tribe has an abundance of land, or is running short of land, is relevant to many anthropological studies,[6] and an anthropologist may even discuss in detail the relative availability of different types of land.[7] Accurate judgment on this point requires considerable ecological and agricultural knowledge and

---

[5] We feel that it is not altogether a satisfactory word, but have failed to find a better.

[6] See, *e.g.*, A. I. Richards, *Land, Labour and Diet in Northern Rhodesia* [1939], an outstanding anthropological report on a people's use of their land.

[7] *E.g.*, G. Wilson, *The Land Rights of Individuals among the Nyakyusa* [1938], another excellent study.

research.[8] Similarly when an anthropologist states that a particular dance, or form of leechcraft, involves "dissociation" or "hysteria," he is making a statement the validity of which can only be tested by skills which are not normally part of the anthropological battery.[9] This kind of statement about a complex of facts falling outside the anthropologist's competence cannot be taken for granted in the same way as facts which we have said can be *incorporated*. Conclusions by other scientists have to be summarised, and often simplified, and we propose therefore to call this procedure by the distinctive term, *abridgement*. If an anthropologist *abridges* research carried out by appropriate specialists on any complex of relations of this type, it is *validated abridgment*. But where, in the absence of research by such a specialist, he nevertheless has to make a judgment on some complex in order to proceed with his analysis, it is *postulated abridgment*, and he should be careful, after trying to "validate" his summary statement as well as he can, that he does not build more of his analysis on it than it can warrantably carry. Thus it is possible for an anthropologist to assess to some extent, though not accurately, the availability of types of land by using the opinions of Africans themselves, and particularly by judging the efficacy of fallowing; but this inexpert judgment sets limits on the extent to which he can judge, for example, immediate developments which depend on this factor.[10]

3 (*b*). Abridgment moves a step further when the anthropologist takes over not only complex combinations of fact appropriate to the investigations of other disciplines but even their postulates and hypotheses. For example, Turner concludes that ". . . the ritual symbol, we may perhaps say, effects an interchange of qualities between

---

[8] For an exposition of how difficult it is to make a judgment on these points see W. Allan, *A.L.U.* [1949], and *African Husbandman* [1964].

[9] These examples are given by S. F. Nadel in *Foundations* [1951], p. 213. We state immediately that we do not accept Nadel's view that there is a hierarchy of sciences (see below, pp. 172-74).

[10] As an example of these difficulties we cite Gluckman's *Essays on Lozi Land and Royal Property* [1943], in a study of an area later investigated by an agriculturist: D. U. Peters, *Land Usage in Barotseland* [1960], ed. N. W. Smyth.

its [ideological and sensory] poles of meaning. Norms and values, on the one hand, become saturated with emotion, while the gross and basic emotions become ennobled through contact with social values" (above, p. 32). This might appear to abridge the psycho-analytic thesis of sublimation: we discuss below (pp. 216-17) whether we believe that it does. It exemplifies a possibility which we classify with abridging the conclusions of another discipline, for though we think it important to distinguish hypotheses from conclusions, for our purposes we do not need another term to cover this distinction. Clearly arguments based on the abridgment of hypotheses must be more carefully scrutinised, since they depend on the validity of the findings in the other discipline.

Later it will be necessary to refer simultaneously to both the procedures of incorporating and abridging, and this will be called *compression*.[11]

4. As against abridging the findings of other disciplines, whether by validated or postulated abridging of conclusions or by abridging of hypotheses, the anthropologist may make *naïve assumptions* about the complexes of events which lie at the boundaries of his circumscribed field, or about the aspects of events which are studied by other disciplines. In doing this, he considers that he is entitled to disregard the researches and conclusions of those other disciplines as irrelevant to his problems. We wish to restrict *naïvety*—artlessness—to this procedure. We believe that most social anthropologists are in this sense naïve about researches into human personality, and that their naïvety is a *justified naïvety*. Political scientists are usually still more naïve about the personalities of individuals in their fields of study, for, unlike anthropologists, they rarely concern themselves even

---

[11] Nadel speaks of both these processes in terms of a science which is higher in the hierarchy of sciences using "shorthand," for reasons of economy, to cover the findings of sciences lower in the hierarchy (*The Foundations of Social Anthropology*, pp. 290 ff.). We have already stated that we do not consider that the sciences are related hierarchically: we also consider, and hope to show, that Nadel's way of formulating this problem obscures the procedures used.

with the possibility of unconscious motivations influencing these persons. When economists assume that individuals are consistently and consciously rational and are motivated by enlightened self-interest, they are plunging still deeper into naïvety. Correspondingly psychologists studying the human personality may be naïve about social, political, and economic aspects of life. We again believe that this naïvety may be justified, if the investigator concerned is to proceed with his own research and analysis.

It is in defining the procedure of starting from naïve assumptions that we go beyond the views of most writers on methodology in the social sciences, though many practitioners use this procedure. Clearly in many instances the making of naïve assumptions is quite distinct from compression, which is a process dealt with by some of these writers on methodology. But since naïvety and compression shade into one another they have not been distinguished. "Naïvety" is not a question of parsimony in research (Parsons),[12] or of economy in phrasing under which an investigator takes over the findings of other disciplines and states them in "shorthand," without spelling them out in detail (Nadel).[13] We consider that if a social scientist is to set himself a manageable aspect or field for study, about which he can say significant things, he may often have to make assumptions which will appear to be distorting or even false to the practitioners of other disciplines. We go so far as to say that he has a duty to be naïve in this way about his "outside" assumptions, and a duty to avoid attempting to deal with aspects of reality which can only be adequately handled by some discipline other than his own. Provided that it is appropriately used, the naïvety will not mar his work. On the contrary, getting entangled in considering, let alone studying, other aspects of reality, tempting though this may often be, might be an impediment to his under-

---

[12] Talcott Parsons, *The Social System* [1952], pp. 9 f. "Parsimony" in scientific method is also used to cover other procedures (see C. S. Hall and G. Lindzey, *Theories of Personality* [1957], p. 14).

[13] See above, note 11, p. 165.

standing of those aspects of reality which are properly the concern of his own discipline. If so, these basic assumptions themselves set limits to what a particular analysis can explain, and the investigator must not draw conclusions beyond those which the assumptions can bear. Leading scientists have sometimes failed in this respect to recognise what we call "the limits of their naïvety," and have in practice gone on to claim that their analysis of some aspect of reality explains a quite different aspect.

5. A social scientist follows a quite different kind of procedure *within* his circumscribed field. There he has to simplify facts and variables; and we propose to specialise the word "simplification" for this procedure. In any complex field under study there is bound to be some simplification of this kind, but the degree of simplification depends both on the nature of the discipline and on the particular problem set. In social science the raw material to be analysed is almost always far too complex to be presented *in toto*, and it has to be simplified to some extent.[14] We consider that on the whole social anthropology does this *relatively* little, since it is concerned with complexity within narrowly circumscribed fields, while economics and political science simplify to a relatively high degree, since they deal with fewer, and more aggregated, variables in wider fields. This process of simplification raises difficult problems with which we are not on the whole concerned in this book, but we draw attention to its importance in relation to the procedures we are discussing, because the rules for the application of incorporation, abridgment, and naïvety, apply also to simplification.[15]

[14] We are specialising the word "simplification" in this context: the same root, in the form of "simplicity", has been used to describe the procedure of choosing between alternative theories (Hall and Lindzey, *Theories of Personality*, p. 14). These authors also use "parsimony" to define this process, though Parsons uses it quite differently. We have searched diligently throughout for words which have not been used in other contexts of discussion of scientific method, as we wished to avoid confusion, but could find no new term to cover what we call "simplification," as we have succeeded in doing for the other procedures.

[15] There is an excellent analysis of this procedure—and of others—in Chs. 1

Since everyone must restrict his field of analysis, these five procedures are of necessity applied by all social and behavioural scientists. As many do not recognise this necessity adequately when considering the work of their colleagues, we again state emphatically that there is a *duty of abstention*, which requires that if we are to solve certain problems we have to abstain from studying other, though apparently related, problems, and leave these to our colleagues, whether in the same or in some other discipline. In research, as in other activities, gluttony can choke one. Properly applied, the duty of abstention involves a *rule of disciplined refusal to trespass* on the fields of others.

In carrying out this duty of abstaining, a social scientist is entitled to perform *warranted* limitation, by using *justified* circumscription, compression (incorporation and abridgment), naïve assumptions, and simplification. For example, naïvety, the procedure which has been most queried, is warranted and justified if the naïve assumptions are not essentially involved in the analysis of the field. A fair test is to ask whether the analysis would stand if different naïve assumptions were adopted. In these circumstances, the investigator must *accept the consequences of his own naïvety* (or circumscription or compression), by recognising *the limits of his accepted naïvety*, and he should not draw conclusions about the relations between events involved in that naïvety. If he does, he commits *the error of ignoring the limits of his own naïvety*. Correspondingly, there is an error in criticism which we call *the error of unjustified allegation of naïvety*. This error is made when an investigator is rebuked because he has accepted naïvety on some point about which the critic believes he should be more sophisticated, when that sophistication is irrelevant to his mode of analysis, though not irrelevant to understanding of the total reality one of whose aspects he is investigating.[16]

[16] For a detailed pointing out of this kind of error in criticism, see M. Gluckman's Introduction to his collected essays, *Order and Rebellion in African Tribal Society* [1963]. Gluckman considers critiques of his analysis of political relations of ritual based on (*a*) the mistaken view that he was making a psychological instead of a sociological analysis, and (*b*) the view that he should make a more sophisticated psychological analysis, in addition to his sociological analysis.

---

and II of G. C. Homans, *The Human Group*. The tendency to construct "models" in social anthropology, as in the work of Lévi-Strauss, Leach, and Needham, falls under this category, and hence is outside the scope of this book.

We emphasise at the outset that the limits of warranted naïvety, and of warranted circumscription, compression, and simplification, cannot be set theoretically. They shift with the problem which is being considered.

Though we are chiefly concerned with circumscription of field and with naïve assumptions, we begin by considering incorporation and abridgment, which appear to be the simplest procedures.

INCORPORATION

None of the essays in this book contains much detailed discussion of incorporation, but Bailey uses the shifting limits of warranted incorporation of facts about the natural environment, in order to argue by analogy his case for a right to incapsulate facts from the history and culture of India in analysing some events in the backwoods of Orissa. He writes: "Some events which intrude into and affect a social system which we are studying, we have no difficulty in treating simply as accidents. . . . If half the population is wiped out by a plague, we do not feel bound to study the medical etiology of the disease. . . . [I]f there is a medical explanation available in terms we can understand, then, by knowing this explanation, we feel we have pushed back the frontiers of our ignorance one degree. But if the explanation happens to involve concepts peculiar to medical science . . . then we are satisfied to say simply that half the population died of a plague, and begin our analysis of the effects of this disaster on the social system. We do not feel naïve in limiting our investigations in medical etiology at this point. The same can be said of a crop failure due to blight, or a drought, or excessive rainfall, or a landslide, or any one of the countless other "acts of God' which change the course of social development" (above, pp. 68-9).

We agree that there is no naïvety here, in our now restricted use of the term. The incidence of rain and the occurrence of plague are clear and definite events which have to be known by the student of social life in a region; and he need not feel ignorant in not pursuing analysis of—or even in not understanding—their internal complexity. As Bailey puts it, ". . . events like a plague or a crop failure have a 'given' quality; they are a starting-point, both for our explanations of their effects on society and for the biological explorations into their cause. If the medical research worker or the agricultural scientist lights on an explanation which subsequently proves to be wrong, then his mistakes do not affect our studies of consequences, any more than a wrong diagnosis of the cause of death alters the fact of death."

Incorporating facts, without analysing their internal complexity, is a procedure persistently and inevitably used in all social science, and it therefore occurs in all the essays. Thus, besides his hypothetical examples, Bailey states that he takes "as given the Hindu concepts of untouchability and Hindu values about the cow and about vegetarianism," because for him "a knowledge of the culture is only the beginning of the effort to understand sociologically why these disputes occurred." In circumscribing his field in time, he considers that he can treat the policies decided upon in the 1935 Act affecting Harijans and Adibasis, or the opening of roads into the Kondmals, "as *given* events affecting the social system which we are studying," and that although "we need to look at their effects . . . we need not be concerned with their historical genesis." He incorporates similarly the 1935 Act and the development of major political and economic systems. Epstein similarly speaks of the Whites bringing the complex machinery of coppermining to Northern Rhodesia, and of the Africans as coming from numerous tribes with different cultures; and he states these as obvious and well-established facts without feeling obliged to prove or to analyse them. He describes equally briefly the provision of welfare services by the mine, the allocation of African labourers to gangs after they have passed through an induction school, and the working of gangs under African boss-boy and European supervisor, without going into the details of the mining process, which are irrelevant for the purpose of his problem. Like Bailey, he treats the forms of administration of mine and central government, and the policy of both on the question of stabilising labour, as facts he can incorporate without analysis. Similarly, he explicitly feels he can neglect, as given facts that do not affect his immediate problem, "the whole question of foreign investment, as well as the complex pattern of relations between the European parties."

We shall suggest that in relating varying forms of political development among the Africans to differences in the forms of organisations outside his field, he is moving towards making naïve assumptions.

In this way quite complex sets of facts can be incorporated, and clearly the more complex they are, the more careful we must be when we treat them as given and capable of simple incorporation. It is easy for Watson to incorporate the existence of schools, universities, factories, and expanding national enterprises. It is more difficult, as they realise explicitly, for Lupton and Cunnison to treat the details of industrial organisation and economic interrelationship in this way, because they build an elaborate hypothesis on these variables. "Here," they admit, "we have made what may seem to some to be shaky generalisations on the basis of unsystematic data." This is in contrast to the certainty with which they incorporate how the manager is placed in the industry, how the machinery works, how garments or transformers are put together, and how the responsibilities of men and women workers for their families differ.

Finally, Turner seems to us to abridge much psychological research, but he does this as if he were incorporating facts. What he does incorporate are such obvious yet important facts as that men feel varying emotions, that they reason, and that they obey and disobey rules. This is not—any more than the examples we have given from the other essays—what we understand by "naïvety." Yet we feel it is important to stress that a process of reducing data is being carried out, even when it appears so simple, because in isolating this process we clarify the relations between the disciplines. Turner incorporates the facts that men reason and feel different emotions: Nadel would put it that the anthropologist does not "bother" to expound these points. Thus Nadel says that he does not "bother to mention the knowledge concerning vision, hearing or memory which psychologists have accumulated, nor the physiologist's knowledge of muscle tensions and innervations, though all these processes must operate in movements and perceptions which go to make up any social action."[17] According to Nadel: "Empirical science is arranged, fortuitously or otherwise, in a hierarchy of disciplines each representing a level of analysis,

[17] *The Foundations of Social Anthropology* [1951], *c.* p. 212.

which proceeds to a certain point and no further. Social enquiry has its place in that hierarchy, being placed above psychology, which in turn is placed above physiology, chemistry, and physics. In this general hierarchy the analytical levels stand in the relationship of progressive inclusiveness so that any phenomenon taken to define a unit on one level may be broken down to components which are the unit phenomena on the next lower level. In every phenomenon visible on the higher level, then, phenomena open to lower-level analysis must be implicit, and all formulations of unit phenomena on the higher level constitute a 'shorthand' as compared with the 'longhand' of lowei-level analysis. Furthermore, any statement of the regularities discovered on the higher level must 'bracket' regularities discovered or discoverable on the lower level; these are taken for granted and assumed to be established (at least potentially) by that deeper-going analysis. I have used the word 'must,' for all this is indeed a basic postulate of our understanding. We cannot conceive of the kind of nature in which, say, physical laws would be inapplicable to chemical processes or the bloodstream of the organism would not obey the laws governing the behaviour of fluids."

He goes on to state that "the human sciences, too, appear at first sight to embrace a homogeneous field, divided fortuitously and conveniently into different levels of analysis: man is the same whether he is studied by sociology, psychology, or physiology, and reveals different aspects of his being only in conformity with the agreed depth of analysis."

We ourselves disagree with the conception of a hierarchy of disciplines, since this implies that one discipline is superordinate to others, even if Nadel did not intend to say so.[18] We do not believe that the relations established by one discipline can necessarily and inevitably be subsumed in, or transposed into, the findings of another.[19] Here we stress that when an anthropologist incorporates facts which are studied intensively by agricultural science, or by psychology, he can do this because they are obvious events, which can be taken for the

---

[18] He appears to intend this. We note that our disagreement here must not be taken as a judgment on Nadel's whole analysis.

[19] We cannot discuss this important issue. Parsons has done this well in *The Social System* [1952], Ch. 1 and *passim*.

purposes of his problem as crude and homogeneous. For the procedure of incorporation may be employed in either direction, which Nadel's phrasing obscures. The economist incorporates workshop behaviour which the anthropologist analyses in detail, and the psychologist may incorporate facts about social life which both economist and anthropologist regard as the complex fields they study. To put Bailey's examples the other way round, the spread of a plague may be due to the form of relationships between the sufferers, and certain kinds of flooding may be connected with soil erosion caused by slash-and-burn agriculture which is deeply rooted in a tribal tradition. In these instances, medical and agricultural research workers incorporate facts about social relationships and tribal tradition into their analyses. By placing the sciences in a hierarchy, Nadel fails to distinguish between incorporation and abridgment, and the situations where these are appropriate procedures.

Nevertheless even in dealing with such obvious facts as these, where internal complexity appears to raise no problems for the anthropologist, it is essential to keep an open mind in case this judgment is mistaken. Thus Bailey in drawing his analogy is careful to stress that plague and flooding due to slash-and-burn agriculture "are not our problems, unless we choose to make them so"; for there may be problems in the analysis of social relations which cannot be solved without determining the connexions between these other events.

ABRIDGMENT

In our view, as against Nadel's, when an anthropologist speaks of men seeing, hearing, and remembering, he is not using a "shorthand" description of psychologists' and physiologists' findings: he is treating as simple facts events which for those other scientists are full of internal complexities. He is justified in doing this so long as these complexities are irrelevant to his problems, and they are probably irrelevant to most anthropological problems. It is enough to incorporate the fact that all normal men see, hear, and remember, and to treat as special deviations those who are blind, who are deaf, or who cannot remember, and examine how they are fitted into social relations without asking why they suffer from these organic defects. It is possible to conceive of situations demanding anthropological analysis of how memory works, because, for example, those things which are remembered in different groups are influenced by social relations and culture: but even this problem is not likely to lead to an investigation of how memory operates within the psyche.

Nadel's other example of "shorthand" is somewhat different. He says,[20] "Occasionally this [external] specialist knowledge requires to be expressed in so many words or at least referred to, as it were, in a footnote. For certain social actions have the result (intended or not) of producing or utilising particular mental states or physiological processes. Think of religious cults or dances inducing mental dissociation and hysteria, of alleged cures of disease, customary ways of securing physical fitness, and the like. As a student of society I wish to be reassured that I have correctly diagnosed these phenomena, which are not really in my field;[21] perhaps, too, I wish to learn more about them since this amplified knowledge might lead me to relevant connexions I should otherwise overlook. This sort of situation poses no problem of method but bears only practical considerations. Nor is it peculiar to the human sciences; the study of electric currents in nerve-physiology or of the surface tension of liquids in chemistry represents the same amplification of knowledge in terms of lower-level analysis."

Leaving aside the question of levels of analysis again, we suggest that conditions like mental dissociation and hysteria, or even physical fitness, are so complex that judgments upon them require specialised training and skills. Even trained clinicians find it difficult to make such judgments, as they would to judge whether an alleged cure influences the course of a disease, and, if so, how. Unless the social anthropologist possesses the relevant skills he should be chary of making judgments of this kind: he may state that a dance appears to produce mental dissociation, but he should beware of building his analysis on that opinion, or, we venture to say, on that guess. If he can state this firmly, either on the basis of his own

---

[20] *The Foundations of Social Anthropology* [1951], pp. 212-13.

[21] We would add "and skilled competence" explicitly, as Nadel presumably intended to imply.

additional skill or of an investigation carried out by an appropriately trained specialist, we consider that he might well not find it necessary to enter into the psychical processes by which mental dissociation is induced, even if he uses the fact of "dissociation" in his analysis. He would then, in our terminology, be "abridging" the findings of another discipline; but an amendment of those findings, in the light of advances in the other discipline, would jeopardise his analysis.

Bailey explicitly separates what we have called "incorporation" from what we have called "abridgment." He says that it is important to distinguish between taking over such an obvious fact as that there is rain at a certain season, and taking over more complicated classifications or combinations of facts which have to be established by another science, or, *a fortiori*, the hypotheses of that science. We can state, without much doubt or anxiety, the régime and variations of rainfall and growth of crops or whether there had been a plague or not, and be sure of our ground. But if the facts are more complex, then we cannot incorporate them, but must go further and abridge judgments which are appropriate to another discipline. In case there has been an error, we must be more careful how much of our argument we found on those facts. We must beware of proceeding beyond the limits set by our abridgment, in case it was not warranted; and we should be stating continually what those limits are, and reminding ourselves and our readers of how significant that abridgment is. Bailey puts this warning thus: "One tries to handle only intrusive *events*; but one may be forced back to allow *hypotheses* to intrude from another science. I think this can only be accepted as a necessity, provided one has exhausted all the possible explanations within the system one is studying (*i.e.*, providing one is not evading sociology), and provided that we recognise the intrusion for what it is: something which one cannot verify, but which is, in theory at least, capable of verification."

Turner uses specific abridgments in his interpretations of ritual symbols and how these function. Thus he abridges Carl Jung's and Sapir's formulations of the difference between a "symbol" and a "sign," and this involves an acceptance, and therefore an abridgment, of the psycho-analytic theory of the rôle of the "unconscious" mind in the human psyche. To the extent that he uses this theory, it seems well enough validated in these general terms for him not to worry about specific interpretations of the rôle of the unconscious, or of how unconscious dispositions influence the conscious: this is warranted abridgment, and Turner keeps within the limits it imposes.

Again, he abridges the psycho-analytic theory of *sublimation* of emotion when he writes that a ritual symbol effects an "interchange of qualities between its ideological and sensory poles of meaning," and that "norms and values, on the one hand, become saturated with emotion, while the gross and basic emotions become ennobled through contact with social values." We shall discuss this argument more fully when we come to consider how social scientists may make "naïve assumptions": here we point out that this statement "fits with," and hence in a sense "abridges," the theory of sublimation, though we consider that Turner's argument stands even without this abridgment. Finally, when Turner found that he could not collect any exegetic statements from Ndembu to "explain" why mother and daughter exchanged clothes during the daughter's nubility ritual, he concluded that in his opinion "it is legitimate to infer . . . that powerful unconscious wishes, of a kind considered illicit by the Ndembu, are expressed in [the exchange]." Here he cites the way mourners wear bits of the deceased's clothing and refers to the Freudian thesis that identification with another involves death-wishes. This is an abridgment, but he uses it only for limited purposes—to explain why exegesis is "blocked."

Every essay in the book abridges certain very important findings of psychology on the marginal importance of differences in innate intelligence between the members of whole ethnic or "class" groups. That differences in technological achievement of groups, or the performance of their members in different activities or on tests, are due rather to cultural and environmental and historical influences than to innate endowment, is accepted by most psychologists and anthropologists, though it is extremely difficult to state dogmatically the negative conclusion, that these innate differences are marginal to our problems. Watson takes over this conclusion most explicitly when he writes: "Many studies have shown that the children of professional persons have a much greater chance of achieving professional occupations than the children of wage-earners, even when the children of professionals go through the State school system. There is a connexion between a father's occupational level and that attained by his children. The social and cultural factors involved in maintaining this connexion are extremely complicated, irrespective of questions of 'innate' ability in children from different occupational groups. . . ."

This statement is cautious enough. In the other essays this particular abridgment is implicit, and not explicit as in Watson's. Turner states his analysis of ritual symbols in terms of a general human psyche, without concerning himself with possible differences in intelligence at all; Bailey does not differentiate untouchables, twice-born Hindus, and Kond tribesmen in respect of intelligence; Lupton and Cunnison do not in this respect distinguish between managers and workers, or between men and women workers; Epstein also regards African miners and White managers, employers and officials, as the same kind of men, and he obviously feels no need to account for their interactions in terms of varying endowments of intelligence. Such abridgment of the conclusions of a substantial body of psychological and other research is basic to all comparative social anthropology, cultural anthropology, and sociology.

We may state this particular abridgment as follows: "By and large all human beings have the same biogenetic and mental equipment though this varies for normal members of all groups within certain limited ranges; as between so-called races, stocks, ethnic groups, tribes, and classes, differences in biogenetic equipment are marginal to the social and cultural differences which we study." Though there is still controversy over this problem, the stated abridgment seems warranted by a whole series of careful studies. Klineberg, who has been a leading authority in this research, has summarised admirably the anatomical, psychological, social-physchological, and anthropological arguments for and against opposite views on this question.[22] He demonstrates that the observable differences

---

[22] O. Klineberg, *Race Differences* [1935]; and even more pithily *Race and Psychology* [1951], in the UNESCO series, "The Race Question in Modern Science." See also A. Barnett, *The Human Species* [1950].

in the culture of various human groups, and the performance of their members in such skills as answering intelligence tests, can more satisfactorily be accounted for by the effects on a plastic organism of variations in physical, social, economic, and cultural environments, through a long period of maturation, as well as by the effects of immediate social situations. Since the plasticity of human beings has been carefully documented both by psychological and cultural-anthropological studies, social anthropologists can take it as established. Economists on the whole have come to a similar conclusion. Myrdal in his *An American Dilemma* wrote that "it is not so much in the simple personality traits—measurable by existing psychological tests—that Negroes differ from Whites, but in the complex traits connected with the cultural differences. Klineberg's recent summary shows that few, if any, psychological studies indicate Negro-White personality differences."[23] In his *The Theory of Economic Growth* W. Arthur Lewis is more cautious; and though he accepts this general abridgment, he particularly reserves judgment on the distribution of superior, ordinary and inferior persons in various groups.[24]

As stated above, it is very difficult to prove the negative conclusion. S. Biesheuwel has carried out substantial research on the relative intelligence of Whites and Africans in South Africa. In a recent broadcast, he began by stating that differences in their intellectual ability, as shown in performance in intelligence and other tests, can be ascribed to differences in familial and general cultural environment, as well as to the incidence and effects of inadequate diet and tropical diseases.[25] He then went on to argue: "And yet we cannot conclude from this that if all environmental inequalities were removed, the intellectual differences between Africans and persons of European descent would be found to have vanished. In practice such differences can never be wholly removed, for Africa can never be Europe, neither climatically nor culturally. . . . The question regarding the abilities of Africans must therefore

[23] P. 148, par. 6, with a reference to "Experimental Studies of Negro Personality," *Characteristics of the American Negro* [1944], ed. O. Klineberg.

[24] [1955] pp. 35-6.

[25] Klineberg in *Race and Psychology*, pp. 20-1, cites evidence to show that the effect of this sort of factor is significant both during very early infancy and, through the mother, during intra-uterine life.

remain an open one. The possibility cannot be ignored that natural selection and isolation have produced strains in Africa that are different, both in respect of the power of the mind, and of the skills that are most readily developed."[26]

Caution thus forbids a definite denial of any difference in biogenetic endowment. But so much evidence has accumulated to relate observable differences with general environmental factors, that we can safely neglect genetic variations between different groups. Nevertheless, it is worth considering how much social anthropology depends on this abridgment of others' work, and therefore how important it is for the anthropologist to watch developments of knowledge about these problems.

Parsons is obviously correct when he says that under the rule of parsimony the sociologist can leave these problems aside: "The soundness of this procedure is confirmed by the knowledge that individual variations are by and large more important than those between large populations and that it is relatively unlikely that the most important differences of large-scale social systems are primarily determined by biological differences in the capacities of their populations. For most sociological purposes [note the warning] the resultant of the genes and life experience is adequate without attempting to segregate out the factors."[27]

Parsons therefore concludes that neither the sociologist, nor the social anthropologist, need study biogenetic problems: not being competent to do so, they leave these problems to colleagues. But they have looked at what their colleagues in the relevant disciplines have found; and in abridging the well-tested and carefully stated conclusions of these disciplines they are not being naïve, in our sense, which describes the way in which economists, for their purposes, make assumptions about the behaviour of consumers or the motivations of businessmen, without paying any attention whatsoever to the work that is done by psychologists.

Social anthropologists and sociologists have to be aware of what psychologists and cultural anthropologists have to say

[26] S. Biesheuwel, "The Abilities of Africans," in *Africa in Transition* [1958], ed. P. Smith, esp. pp. 36-7.
[27] *The Social System* [1952], p. 10.

about the biogenetic endowment of various groups of human beings, for, should the conclusion that this equipment does not vary materially between these groups be disproved, the disproof would call in question the whole manner in which social scientists relate social relationships, institutions, and customs to one another. We have to keep an open mind on this point, because the abridgments are taken as very large "givens." It would, for example, make a big difference to the anthropologists who attempt to explain the wider-spread distribution of witchcraft beliefs in tribal societies than in modern society, or the greater tendency of tribal societies to develop "particularistic" rituals,[28] by reference to economic and social factors, if it could be shown that members of these societies had different emotional constitutions, perhaps based on differences in glandular secretions. In working out his theory of ritual symbolism, Turner clearly assumes that men are sufficiently alike for him not to bother about the particular physiology of the Ndembu.[29] Again, Godfrey Wilson writes that "the institution of polygamy has many other social elements besides the economic, but the economic is not the least important of them: the taking of additional wives is the best capital investment which is open to an ordinary, uneducated Nyakyusa peasant."[30] He proceeds to detail the interconnexion of social and economic elements in the institution of marriage. He does not feel that he has to take any account of ideas that polygamy, as against monogamy, may be accounted for by variations in bodily desires or in the climatic environment of different societies, ideas that are at least theoretically able to explain the occurrence of polygamy.

If variations between the bodily constitutions of individuals in these different types of societies were to be established in such a form as to account for these differences in institutions (as we do not believe is likely to happen), such a finding would not affect the validity of any relations established by the anthro-

[28] See, *e.g.*, G. and M. Wilson, *The Analysis of Social Change* [1945]; C. D. Forde, Introduction to *African Worlds* [1945]; M. Gluckman, *Custom and Conflict in Africa* [1955], Ch. iv and v, and *Essays on the Ritual of Social Relations* [1962].

[29] See also what A. R. Radcliffe-Brown wrote about symbolism of colours in *The Andaman Islanders* [1922], p. 316, on light and dark colours, and p. 318 on "red."

[30] *The Land Rights of Individuals among the Nyakyusa* [1938], p. 11 and *passim*.

pologist between witchcraft beliefs, particularistic rituals, poly-
gyny, and other social and economic institutions in any one
society: but it would materially affect any associations established between their occurrence, and, say, forms of technology
and subsistence economy. Such "explanations" by social
anthropologists therefore continue to depend on the support
which new psychological and biological studies give to the
basic abridgment cited; and if these studies begin to advance
different views, the social anthropologist may have to reconsider
his position. Hence he must keep up to date on this general
point. But under the rule of parsimony it remains unnecessary
for him to try to test the abridgments, fundamental as they are
to his comparative analyses; and indeed, he lacks the competence to do so, even though the evidence he himself provides
from his researches in fact supports these conclusions of other
disciplines. Nor need he enter into the details of evidence and
argument with which his abridged "givens" are established.

This discussion thus raises a general problem which will
recur in other contexts: we shall see that whenever we try to
understand the form of certain phenomena in terms of "why"
they are as they are, rather than "how" they are interconnected
with one another, we are less able to take as given "surrounding" phenomena and interpretations of the relations between
those phenomena. Entry into the nature of surrounding
phenomena is always relative to the problem we set ourselves:
and we have particularly to be open-minded about the need
to take account of and to analyse circumscribing facts when we
engage in comparative and historical studies.

But when studying a single social situation, the anthropologist has to analyse how the varying mental abilities and
temperaments of individuals affect the working of institutions,
without in general concerning himself with the internal relations within the psyches of those individuals.

If intellectual performance and patterns of personality are
at least substantially products of general environmental factors
including upbringing within a particular culture, the social
anthropologist, interested in the interdependencies within a
social system, has to scan facts from another point of view.
The schools of cultural anthropologists, of which Margaret
Mead is the most prominent representative, have in various

ways examined patterns of culture and related them to such
complexes as the structure of social relations and modes of
child-rearing, as well as the biological basis of human nature.
Mead has thus argued that the temperaments[31] of, for example,
men and women, are not determined dominantly in any
society by any inherent tendency which can be described as
"masculine" or "feminine," but are influenced primarily by
certain patterns of expectation which are in turn reinforced by
handling in childhood. There have been many subsequent
developments of the main thesis which she had laid down in
her series of studies.[32] We have not space to quote later developments of her central argument, by Kardiner and Linton, by
the Whitings, by Ericson and Levinson, and others. This
particular kind of anthropological discipline has moved in a
different direction from what is called social anthropology. In
their references to allied studies its practitioners cite psychologists and psychiatrists: but if social anthropologists quote any
"outsiders," they tend to cite sociologists, political scientists,
economists, historians, and lawyers. We merely refer to this
line of research here because we do not think that social
anthropologists have considered how far findings by cultural
anthropologists may affect their own interpretations of, say,
ritual or morals and law. Thus, in considering the symbolism
used in circumcision rituals or in treating a barren woman,
Turner does not refer to work of these cultural anthropologists.
Abridgment and incorporation—compression—of some of
the findings of psychologists is marked in the work of social
anthropologists: they appear to neglect the work of cultural
anthropologists. It would take a whole volume to consider the
implications of this neglect, and whether or not it is justified.
This problem requires to be considered by social anthropologists, but here we leave it aside, since it does not arise in any of
the essays in this book.

As we have already said, the solution to any of these problems of method is relative to the questions investigated. When
a social anthropologist has incorporated a fact, he must con-

[31] Most psychologists would use "personality" where Mead speaks of "temperament."

[32] E.g., *Growing-Up in New Guinea* [1930]; *Coming-of-Age in Samoa* [1928]; *Sex
and Temperament in Three Primitive Societies* [1938]; *Male and Female* [1949]; and
many other writings.

tinually keep a mind open to the possibility that its internal complexities may become relevant to his own analysis; while when he has abridged the findings of another discipline and has used those findings to proceed with his own analysis, he must never let his mind be closed to the possibility that those findings may alter. It is important to keep these two processes of compression separate, since they entail different degrees of dependence on others. On very many problems we can afford to neglect—we need not even "bother" to know, as Nadel puts it—what psychologists and physiologists have discovered, any more than an anthropologist who is analysing tribal life need bother about why rain falls at a certain season and stops six months later, as in Zululand. But knowledge of the work in other disciplines may suddenly become significant. Thus Gluckman[33] has suggested that the coming in of the harvest at a single season in Zululand suddenly provides plenty of food, and above all beer, after some months of dearth, and that this situation *may* produce a surge of energy which contributes to the elaborate first-fruits ceremonies of the Zulu. An argument of this kind should not be woven into any interpretation of these ceremonies unless it is a warranted abridgment from the findings of other specialists, such as physiologists and psychologists.

At different points, a social anthropologist studying tribal life may have to abridge the findings of various kinds of specialists. Lupton and Cunnison, working on factories, may abridge the conclusions of production engineers. The social anthropologist studying tribal life may similarly have to abridge the findings of agriculturists. But here the anthropologist has usually felt it necessary to go into details of agricultural practice far more than the industrial sociologist examines the working of machinery in factories, while frequently there has not been agricultural research on which to depend. Dr Audrey Richards, in *Land, Labour and Diet in Northern Rhodesia*, a masterly study of the Bemba social system in relation to production, distribution, and consumption of food, admits her lack of skilled knowledge about types of soil, agricultural methods, and so forth: but she stresses how important she considered these subjects to be, and

---

[33] M. Gluckman, *Rituals of Rebellion in South East Africa* [1954], reprinted in *Order and Rebellion in Tribal Africa* [1963].

how she therefore carefully recorded the Bemba's knowledge on these subjects. We here draw attention only to her statement (which wisely is vague enough), that ". . . because the land problem is not so acute in this area, as it is in many parts of present-day Africa, we cannot conclude that there are no tribal rights as to its use. . . ."[34] This statement was made not as an abridgment of agricultural findings, but as an assessment by an anthropologist and by the Bemba themselves; and the conception that the Bemba have "plenty" of land must be accepted only in those senses. The Ecological Survey of Northern Rhodesia, published after Richards's book, emphasised that under traditional systems of land usage the area necessary to sustain a family of four in perpetuity might lie between 200 to 470 acres.[35] In this sort of situation, the anthropologist should make clear that such statements as that "there is an abundance of land," or (to quote Richards) that "the land problem is not so acute . . .," are made as statements without foundation in agricultural research. In the light of subsequent ecological and agricultural research, the apparent wide stretches of bush in Bemba country probably concealed growing scarcity in some provinces. Richards in her analysis discusses problems of land tenure as if a real abundance of land prevented disputes arising, and in other ways affected social life: we do not know that her assumption was incorrect, but we cite this example to stress how careful an anthropologist must be before building an argument on a "fact" which needs to be established by another science.

The investigator must thus constantly keep his mind open to the possibility that he may have to amend his analysis, lest his statements of facts, other that those he himself is competent to assess, be wrong. He must be careful of the conclusions he draws on the basis of doubtful incorporation and abridgment; and he must recognise that the limits of his right to incorporate and abridge may continually alter with the problems he sets himself. Nevertheless, as Nadel and others have shown, unless he compresses in this way, he will not be able to proceed with

[34] Pp. 228 f., citation from p. 242.

[35] C. G. Trapnell, *The Soils, Vegetation and Agricultural Systems of North Eastern Rhodesia* [1943]; see also C. G. Trapnell and J. N. Clothier, *The Soils, Vegetation and Agricultural Systems of North Western Rhodesia* [1938]. How difficult it is to work out whether a tribe in fact has plenty of land is shown in W. Allan, *Studies in African Land Usage in Northern Rhodesia* [1948], and *The African Husbandman* [1964].

any analysis at all; and his study will sprawl more and more disconnectedly. Hence it is illegitimate for practitioners in another discipline to criticise anthropological compression, unless they can show that this compression invalidates the social-anthropological analysis itself.

CIRCUMSCRIPTION[36]

In the title of this book, we have set our formula as "closed systems and open minds": to carry out his analysis the investigator must close his system, but he must at the same time keep his mind open to the possibility that in doing so he has excluded significant events and relations between events. Social relations spread out from one area across the world, and only a few island societies are isolated from neighbours. Hence "foreign" relations may affect the working of internal politics even in small tribal polities. External social and economic relations obviously have much more effect on the internal working of factories. From another point of view, if we examine economic relations, these are affected by, and affect, relationships which aim at power, and other sorts of institutional arrangements. The anthropologist, like all other social scientists, is entangled in the web of reality; and if he is to carry out any disciplined analysis, he must at appropriate points decide that he has done enough, first in the way of collecting facts, and then in analysing their connexions. That is, he ceases to follow real connexions, and from them abstracts a set of such connexions as he thinks he can study profitably. He assumes they form a system: he circumscribes and "closes his system." But, since this is only an analytical device, he has to keep his mind open to the possibility that he has made his closure at an inappropriate point, and that the working of the closed-off system he is considering may depend essentially on facts and relations outside the boundaries he has artificially, and to some extent arbitrarily, established. All social and behavioural scientists are bound to follow this procedure. When circumscribing, the anthropologist must be sure that he has demarcated a field of events which are significantly interconnected. He must keep

[36] Homans, *The Human Group* [1951], pp. 86 f., has an excellent analysis of this problem and procedure.

an open mind on whether the way in which he has circumscribed his field is appropriate for his problem, and he must not
forget that in making the limitations involved he is restricting
his ability to apply his findings to fields where the appropriate
limitation would be different.

The same is true in economics. In the recent enthusiastic
efflorescence of theories of economic development, there is a
clear and necessary tendency to construct a closed system with
a limited number of variables. Unless this is done, the whole
subject becomes quite unmanageable, since at present we
cannot investigate either in theory alone, and certainly not
where the theory is related to reality, a system which has a
large number of variables. But the important issue is to make
sure that the crucial variables are included in the closed system,
and to have a sufficiently open mind to recognise that a particular system may not in fact be fruitful in yielding answers to
important questions. It may be that our present knowledge of
what are the crucial variables, or the need to include a larger
number of variables than we can at present handle, makes
present models and theories of economic development largely
irrelevant in relation to problems of reality. Hence the very
frequent complaints about the abstruseness, over-simplicity and
meaninglessness of many current theories. This does not mean
that it is not worth while continuing to explore problems and
theories of economic development in this way, since it is only
by trying that we can discover whether in fact we are likely to
meet with success. Whether particular models and the development of particular lines of research are worth while or not must
in the end be a matter of personal judgment and faith. All that
we can plead for is that those who engage in this activity should
not arrogantly assume that their system is necessarily the best
or that their system will necessarily be relevant to the explanation of reality, or that a model which appears to explain
development in one country will have universal validity and
application.

Almost every essay in this book faces the problem of how
one area of social life within a larger whole can be isolated in
order that it may be studied systematically. Turner is concerned
to study ritual symbolism, which operates in a background of
secular relationships. Bailey deals with incidents in two villages

of India, which are in constant contact with the economic and political and cultural systems of the whole of India. Epstein analyses political developments among Africans in a Northern Rhodesian Copperbelt town, and these developments are affected by many things which happen outside the African population concentrated in that town. The factories studied by Lupton and Cunnison are part of a much wider economic system and the managers and the workers whom they employ occupy specific positions outside the factories. Watson's essay arises from an investigation into the social development of children in a Scottish burgh, a process affected by the occupational and class structure of Britain as a whole. Yet none of these anthropologists could have carried out, completed, and reported on his study, had he not closed off a system of relations susceptible of ordered analysis. The hazard was to avoid omitting anything relevant and important.

When these authors consider how far it is possible for them to effect such a closure, in the light of their own work and its problems and the analyses of other social scientists, they draw different conclusions. These range from Bailey's and Epstein's judgment that they could close off their field of analysis from external events fairly easily, and neglect the complications lying in the events they thus excluded; to Lupton and Cunnison's attempt to sketch, within the space of their essay, a fairly sophisticated view of a clustering of external variables which were shaping the structure of social relations in their workshops; and ultimately to Watson's decision that before he could deal with the social development of children in one burgh, he would have to formulate a theory about the national class-structure and its development which would be more complex than extant theories of class. Hence in his essay, Watson deliberately abandons his original field; and, in practice, he barely reports on the field situation he studied, nor does he discuss the methodological problems involved in his decision. Lupton and Cunnison show some uneasiness about the conditions in which they carried out their field-research, and develop a set of constructs of some complexity (systems of overlap, the notion of inclusion, role-sets or role-clusters) to enable them, as they show with great honesty, to deal with their inevitable ignorance of external factors. Epstein, moving on to slightly different ground, feels that in the study of new African towns anthropologists still have a specific contribution to make, and that though they can to a considerable extent afford to exclude the external world, they must increasingly become aware of the concepts and methods of other relevant disciplines. For the purposes of his immediate problems, Bailey emphasises his right to abstain from involvement in these external analyses and he ends by defining anthropology as the study of those fields of social life where people are linked to one another by relations involving more than a single set of purposes. The problems each of them has set himself, determine where and how he closed his system; and in practice this is a decision for which no rules can be established. Only experience and judgment can help the research-worker in specific circumstances.

We proceed to discuss our colleagues' decisions in the hope that out of their difficulties and achievements we can show the context within which experience and judgment have to operate. Since our colleagues differ in the way they tackle the problems which they set themselves, when they have to decide how far they must go outside their own fields, we feel bound to set out brief abstracts of their reasons. In doing so, we abstract baldly from carefully argued analyses, and cannot do full justice to them. It will appear that these apparently disparate judgments on procedure arise from the problems set, and not from a different approach: unfortunately Watson, who steps out of the social-anthropological frame of reference, has not connected his analysis of the national social structure with the situation which he studied in detail, namely, the manner in which children grow up and are educated in the Burgh.

Circumscription: Bailey

Bailey studied Hindu and Kond villages in Orissa Province in India, and he had already published two books on his research. The first book was on an Oriya Hindu village, Bisipara, and the second on a Kond area, including the village of Baderi. In the second book, he takes into account the conclusions of the first book, so that it moves to becoming a study of a region. Since then he has studied, and has published on, some political problems in Orissa State as a whole. In the essay which he has contributed to this book, he sets himself the problems of analysing the course of two disputes, one in the Hindu village and one in the Kond village. Each dispute started with an assault by a man of the Pan (Untouchable) caste on a clean-caste man, for though the Konds are an "aboriginal tribe" they are of clean caste. Each assault immediately mobilised the clean castes in the village against the Pans: and these castes tried to organise an economic boycott of the Pans. The boycotts failed: but while the whole incident in the Kond village passed over in a few days, in the Hindu village the Pans called on the aid of police and other State officials, and communal tension was high for a long time.

Bailey sets out to explain why these events took such different courses. He emphasises that his villages are not "primitive isolates," as Redfield termed the model areas of analysis of anthropologists, but that they are products of Hindu culture and of Indian history, and are also involved in the modern Indian nation and its economy. We shall later discuss what he says about how much he felt he needed to know about Hindu culture; here we deal with his views on how far he had to enter into analyses of history, economics, and large-scale political relations, to proceed with his limited analysis. He poses for this analysis the questions: "Can these events be understood as aspects of regular behaviour, as social regularities, as parts of a system? Secondly, how can a sociologist explain the differing course of the two disputes, the greater initiative shown by Bisipara Pans [in calling on the officers of the State to support them] and the relative lack of political enterprise apparent among Baderi Pans?"

The whole concept of caste in Hinduism condemns the Pans as an untouchable caste to a position of inferiority, but Bailey shows that there is a contradiction between this conception of caste roles and economic and political realities. Numerically, there are roughly the same proportions of the Pans (one-fifth) and of clean castes (four-fifths) in each village. In both villages there are some Pans who are richer than some members of the clean castes, but, for historical reasons, this is more marked in Bisipara than in Baderi. Bisipara Pans also occupy more skilled positions, such as schoolteacher, and are generally more "advanced" than the Baderi Pans. Under Indian State laws, both sets of Pans are equal citizens of India with the clean castes, and the Pans are also favoured under legislation which lays down special privileges for "Scheduled Castes." This again works more in favour of the Bisipara Pans, since the Kond "superiors" of the Baderi Pans are also favoured as "aboriginals" and therefore share in the privileges granted by the State to their "inferiors." Under this legislation, and the development of the economy and education, a nation-wide "revolution" in the relations of clean and polluting castes is occurring; and the reaction of the clean castes, through meetings in village council from which they excluded Pans, was to mobilise against this revolution. Bailey concludes that "it is obvious, from the course of the two disputes, that the Bisipara Pans wanted a revolution and the Baderi Pans did not. In order to explain this, one has to take into account relationships which the villagers have with persons and groups outside the village, and which are not part of the village structure; and one has also to take into account institutions which do not belong within the village system."

Bailey's essay shows immediately that when an anthropologist is studying the development of social change, as distinct from social relations in a static society or at one period of time in a changing society, then even in a small area external events become more significant and it is more difficult to exclude them. The revolution in the relations of the castes in these Orissa villages arose both within them, and also from the influence of intrusions from outside. But even the internal change in the villages making for a revolutionary situation had arisen from external events which favoured the economic rise of the Bisipara Pans as against their clean-caste superiors. Bailey considered the influence of these external events in three realms: first, in the realm of events conventionally studied by political and economic historians; secondly, in that of systems conventionally studied by economists and political scientists; and thirdly, in that of the actual social ties which the Bisipara Pans have with the Harijan (Untouchable) movement.

After discussing, as a clarifying analogy, his right to take as "given" what he can treat as "accidents" in the natural environment which influence social life (an analogy to which we have already referred), he considers that "this quality of being 'given' belongs also to certain events which are conventionally within disciplines concerned directly with man, particularly within history (when history is considered as a chronicle of what happened). For instance, an historian considering the privileges granted to Harijans [Untouchables] and Adibasis [aboriginals] in Bisipara and Baderi might trace these privileges back and connect them with the Partially-Excluded Areas provisions of the 1935 Act, and, more generally, with the activities of the late Dr Ambedkar and the ambitions of the Congress Party and of the ruling power." Similarly, he says, an economic historian might trace back the events which led to the rise in relative wealth of the Bisipara Pans, and which were thus an "historical cause contributing to the disputes in Bisipara." But he says this development can be taken as "given" for his problem, and again he emphasises his argument thus: "We can take it as a fact that the Bisipara Pans have been able to better themselves; whether, in surveying outside causes, we attribute this (wrongly) to the activities of the missionaries or (correctly) to economic growth and the policy of the Government, is neither here nor there. A wrong diagnosis [sc. a wrong "abridgment"] of anterior causes will not—in the case of these 'given' events—invalidate our analysis of their effects in the social system of the villages," even though (as Bailey states) the social relations in those villages have contributed their quota to these historical developments.

The dispute in Bisipara finally was taken to the Magistrate, whose actions are partly to be explained by the fact that he stands at a certain point in the administrative hierarchy; and Bailey recognises that he might easily be led into examining the hierarchy. But he considers that it would be irrelevant to do so for his problem: "It seems legitimate to take as given the system of administration and the wider economic system, or such historical events as the developments of these systems." Hence Bailey argues that he can afford, for his immediate purposes, to neglect any considerations which influenced the officials who entered from outside to judge the dispute between Bisipara clean castes and Pans—for example, the Magistrate's fears of how the decision might affect his relationships with his superiors. As he puts it, "all the time the material throws up questions, the answers to which seem to lie in systems of relationships outside the one we have chosen to study." But, he insists, the point at which one decides that it is no longer appropriate to circumscribe,[37] and at which external or anterior events have to be investigated more deeply, shifts with the problem posed. If one were studying the whole of village or regional political development, it might become relevant to study whether Harijans, though granted equal citizenship by statute, are able to exercise that right, and, if not, why not. This enquiry might lead into a study of the Government's recruitment policies, of the caste status of officials, of the devolution of administrative and executive powers, and of other problems more commonly tackled by the political scientist. These problems and others certainly would have to be studied in trying to compare how far Indian Harijans, as against Negroes in certain States in the United States, are and are not able to exercise their statutory rights as equal citizens. But Bailey demonstrates convincingly that he can proceed with his systematic analysis in ignorance of the answers to those problems, even though they are the problems which might strike a political scientist as among the most important.

Bailey is the only one of our authors who actually sets out a rule to guide him in determining the restrictions of his circumscription, perhaps because his essay was written late in the series, when problems had become clearer: "As a rule of thumb, I found myself following single-interest relationships to one link only. One would go as far as, for instance, a decision by the Magistrate; or the salary that policemen received; or the rule by which schoolteachers had to work in villages not their own." Out of this experience, he concludes that the field of social anthropology is any area of social life where relationships are "multiplex," a term he takes from Gluckman to define relationships which involve several different kinds of interests (domestic, political, economic, ritual, etc.).[38] Hence he concludes that he had to study the social hinterland of each village, the relation between politics and descent in the "small region, the dispersal of castes through the region and the institution of caste councils, and possibly even the system of extinct, small

---

[37] He calls this "naïve," but we have since specialised this word in a different sense.

[38] Equivalent to Parsons's "diffuse."

Orissa kingdoms." He considers that the Harijan movement must for these reasons be studied by the technique of the social anthropologist since it involves multiplex ties, in addition to the techniques of other specialists. And he suggests that wherever in the development of single-interest relationships there are established areas of activity where multiplex ties are involved, the traditional techniques and modes of analysis of social anthropology become relevant.[39] Conversely, the more outside, single-interest relationships become significant in the life of, say, a village, the less effectively can the social-anthropological tradition be employed. An Indian village thus might come to be, like a London suburb, not susceptible of analysis in this way. In this way he draws certain boundaries round social anthropology.

Bailey also discusses a different kind of limitation and circumscription. Even a tribal society exists in an area where the general form of its culture spreads beyond its own political boundaries; and units like an Indian or a Welsh village, a Scottish burgh and a Lancashire factory, obviously are part of national and regional and class cultures. Some social anthropologists consider with Professor Evans-Pritchard, as quoted in Bailey's essay: "If one has any regard for scholarship one cannot be a student . . . of Indian peasant communities without having some knowledge both of the literature of their language and of Sanskrit, the classical language of their ritual and religious tradition." Bailey cites Redfield's independent support for this statement. In *Peasant Society and Culture*, Redfield argued that "the little tradition" of village culture and "the great tradition" of the wider culture are mutual determinants of one another. Bailey disagrees with both these authorities. He poses not the general problem, but the specific question: ". . . no one would deny that there is some connexion between, for instance, the Siva who appears in sacred texts and the Siva who is worshipped in Bisipara. Does it then follow that I must know what this connexion is, and trace its every link, before I can appreciate the significance of the Bisipara temple in the dispute between the clean castes and the Bisipara Pans? Must I know what is written in the Sanskrit texts about untouchability

[39] See P. Laslett, "The Face to Face Society," in *Philosophy Politics and Society* [1956].

N

before I can understand why the clean castes of the two villages took such a serious view of the assaults?"

Once the question is posed in relation to a specific problem, and not in terms of the general *cachet* of scholarship, Bailey's answer is reasonable: detailed acquaintance with, and scholarship in, Sanskrit and the sacred texts and literature, may not be relevant to a specific social-anthropological analysis. Hindu culture as represented in the sacred texts and in Sanskrit is not the culture of the village: indeed, the fact that villagers are so ignorant about these cultural items may be an essential part of the rôle that these play in the village social system. Bailey agrees that it is most helpful to know the background in Hindu culture to the polluting effects of untouchables, the situation of Brahmins, the avoidance of alcohol, the sinfulness of handling dead cattle and hides, the merit of a vegetarian diet. But, as he suggests, these are pieces of knowledge which could be learnt by the anthropologist in the village he studied: we would go further, and say that if an anthropologist were suddenly landed in an Indian village (as Evans-Pritchard was among the Nuer of the Sudan in 1932), and he had no previous knowledge of Hinduism, he could learn as much of the cultural tradition as would be relevant to his analysis of the village social system. Correspondingly, it would be misplaced scholarship to interpret actions within that system in terms of the great Hindu tradition. Hence, we suggest, that tradition may safely be excluded from a justifiably circumscribed problem. To import too much knowledge of Hinduism would indeed be a dangerous solecism. It might, of course, be relevant to bring in the fact that the villagers believe that they are part of this great tradition, and respect and envy the bearers of that tradition—though their respect might be misplaced. For example, in his full study of Bisipara Bailey shows that the Brahmin priests of the village do not themselves know very much about All-India Hinduism, and in fact know far less than the villagers believe they do.

We are not here asserting that knowledge of Hinduism and Sanskrit might not be extremely useful even for this limited problem of analysing the village system. As Bailey says, it is obvious that any knowledge which might be relevant is helpful in work of this kind; and it may well be possible to incorporate specific items from this knowledge. But we do assert that the social anthropologist who has that knowledge will have carefully to scrutinise his use of it, lest he apply it in the wrong situation. That is, he may have to analyse as if he were as ignorant as his subjects outside the little culture of the village. Bailey himself would not go as far as this, for, in his opinion, "the nuances of social relationships only become apparent to one familiar with the culture in which those relationships are expressed," and "the better one is able to absorb Hindu values and Hindu culture, the more penetrating is likely to be one's insight into social relationships."

Turner similarly suggests that when the social anthropologist is studying the meaning of ritual symbols, his interpretation will be aided if he knows that similar and different symbolic elements are developed to a varying extent in other parts of the "culture-area." This seems to be validated in, for example, Professor Monica Wilson's study of Nyakyusa ritual.[40]

Bailey emphasises (and we would, of course, agree) that he is stating his rule of warranted exclusion of knowledge with reference to a specific problem. He considers that a knowledge of sacred texts might be essential to study a Buddhist monastery, or to study Redfield's problem, the relation between the "great tradition" and the "little tradition." And none of us disputes the legitimacy of studies of Hindu culture or some other "great culture." We are asserting merely that a social anthropologist, concerned with certain problems, need not make a general fetish of scholarship in what Bailey calls (for want of a better term) "Indology"; and beyond that, we assert that even if the anthropologist has that scholarship, he will have to dole it out carefully. If he lacks that scholarship, he may still be able to proceed with his analysis of a village. We would indeed contend that knowledge of South American and European villages might be more useful for the analysis of Indian villages, than is knowledge of Sanskrit. Here, as with the pursuit of social connexions outside the system one has circumscribed, there are certain warranted limits of circumscription, and possibly indeed a duty to abstain from proceeding outside the field. The study of Sanskrit and the sacred texts is a lifetime's work in itself.

[40] M. Wilson, *Rituals of Kinship among the Nyakyusa* [1957] and *Communal Rituals of the Nyakyusa* [1959].

Again, Watson finds it necessary to distinguish between the "generic" culture which has to be inculcated in all who aspire to join the professional class if they are to move freely in national institutions through many local areas, as against the local culture of each local area. Presumably, then, it is important to study the distribution of the traits of this generic culture and therefore to know something about it, in order to see how far it is achieved by various professional persons as well as by various members of the working class. But Watson has posed his problems on a national scale; and in any one local area it may be sufficient to know that the professional class believe they have a widely distributed culture which they share with other educated persons.

Circumscription: Epstein

Epstein at times adopts a point of view similar to Bailey's about his research into political developments among the African population of Luanshya: but because he is concerned with general problems of urbanisation widely treated in the history of sociology, he raises other issues. His problem was why political developments in the two areas of Luanshya, the compound attached to the mine and the municipal location for Africans of the township servicing the mine, took such different courses. For example, he found that, on the mine, there was greater consensus among Africans about who their leaders were; and there was a rapid development of a powerful, almost closed-shop trade union. By contrast, in the location, trade unions were weak and ineffective, and the leaders whose basis of authority lay in tribal systems continued to exert influence long after they had lost authority in the mine compound, even though the miners were as likely to return to their tribal homes as were inhabitants of the municipal location. The hypothesis by which Epstein seeks to explain the difference is that what he calls the "unitary" structure[41] of the mine, which controlled work and wages, housing, feeding, medical and social services of the African miners, produced a response of an equally "unitary" trade union, serving many purposes for the African miners; while the more amorphous, and less organised, dis-

[41] Discussed further below, p. 198.

tribution of employers and authorities for the inhabitants of the municipal location did not do so. Yet he is well aware that there are important cleavages among the African miners and he shows how these cleavages led to the election of a chairman of the local branch of the African Mine Workers Union from the unskilled labourers to replace one of the educated men who had previously supplied leadership. He shows also that important external events were affecting this situation: the high-level discussion of advancement of Africans to new skilled jobs; the development of opinion among African leaders on this issue of new jobs; the relations between the permanent secretary of the local union and the President of the Mine Workers Union serving all the Copperbelt mines; possibly the attitude of the mine management to the likely emergence of an African Salaried Staff Association separate from the main union, if a number of Africans were advanced to a few highly skilled posts; and so forth.

Epstein concludes that he can make a satisfactory study of how political relations among Africans in Luanshya developed, without his knowing in detail about those external events, though he must know about them in general terms. He feels able justifiably to circumscribe as his field the African population of Luanshya. First he incorporates the facts that the mines and the towns around them were established and are controlled by Europeans, who entered the territory with power to control the Africans, with skill and capital to establish the mines, and with a complex series of motivations. But he is well aware that the running of the mine was to a large extent influenced by events far outside Northern Rhodesia. In addition, he realises that decisions taken by Northern Rhodesian Government authorities, as well as decisions taken by the mining companies, about the African population of Luanshya and its developing political relations, culminate from a complex series of events. These two sets of external events are affecting each other; and little academic study of them has yet been made. He is also aware that the African labourers come from many tribes, variously organised, and that these labourers continue to have intimate relations and to share important interests with their fellow-tribesmen and chiefs. Epstein considers that he does not need to go in detail into events in any of these areas in order to analyse his problems. This might seem a counsel of despair as far as events in the European field are concerned, since data were not accessible to him and no one else had studied the field: but he compresses events in the tribal field, where accurate and well-analysed data are available, since there has been considerable study of many tribes by anthropologists. We agree with Epstein that his compressions and circumscriptions —like his naïve assumptions discussed below—are adequate and appropriate for his purposes; and we note that in his earlier published, full study[42] of this situation Epstein accurately predicted events which he describes in this later essay.

Epstein concludes that in presenting his hypothesis to explain political differences in Luanshya, it was sufficient for his purpose if he "set up an extremely simple model of the urban social system." In drawing a comparison between Mine and Government Townships, he felt he was "presented with a crude polarity of forms" of economic and administrative organisations which he was able to take as given: it was unnecessary in the circumstances to make a detailed analysis of them. These are the assumptions in Epstein's analysis which we should categorise as "naïve assumptions" and "simplification." He goes on to say that similarly, when it became necessary to consider the wider system, it was sufficient for his purpose to present an unsophisticated account of the factors which entered into the analysis of the working of that system: this is the procedure which we call compression of external factors.

Nevertheless, Epstein remains unhappy about his ignorance of some of the fields which lie outside his circumscribed area. He suggests that as soon as different urban communities are compared, it becomes more important to take account of the complexity of these external factors; and he thinks such comparison with other African towns "might very well demand the modification of the hypothesis . . . proposed earlier and the development of another in terms of a cluster of external variables of the type suggested by Lupton and Cunnison. In this event it might become necessary to undertake analysis of those factors which in Luanshya [he] was able to accept as given—a task which would necessarily involve the use of tools and concepts which are not part of the standard equipment of

[42] *Politics in an Urban African Community* [1958].

the social anthropologist." Hence he draws his final conclusion, that "in the field of urban studies the anthropologist will have to become increasingly aware of the importance of external factors and accordingly of the concepts and methods by which these are handled by other disciplines impinging on his field."

Epstein, then, seems to be less satisfied than Bailey about the risks of ignoring the complexity of external factors. We think that part of this dissatisfaction may arise from the fact that he introduces the quite different problem, whether it is worth doing studies of "local communities," as against studies of social relations on a far wider canvas. Early in his essay he quotes C. Wright Mills, who wrote: "most local community studies [of prestige], so often the unit of sociological study, are merely of local interest. One cannot even say that they are of interest beyond that because of the methodological innovations they make possible, for in truth most of these methodological advancements are suitable only for what they have been worked out for—local community studies."[43] We do not know whether Mills would therefore have said that studies of local communities, and other small social units or networks, are not worth making at all. If so, Epstein's essay itself demonstrates that this view is unjustified. But we feel that Epstein, in too modest appreciation of his own achievement, is still not content to have shown how the internal structure of Luanshya influenced political developments there, and presumably therefore influenced Central African national politics. Ultimately, like other anthropologists, he may be worried because his specific expertise does not specially qualify him to discuss national problems.[44] But he shows that a study of problems which occur throughout the world can lead to serious error unless local variables are taken into account. He argues that for comparative study these local variables must be considered: if the micro-sociologist, the social anthropologist, cannot compress at the point where he circumscribes his narrow field when he enters into comparison, the macro-sociologist must also

---

[43] Cp. Watson's much more penetrating treatment of national and local scales of prestige and the relation between them.

[44] One of us, Gluckman, has always felt that his expertise on tribes did not give him special skills to discuss territorial developments in Africa, save in so far as it aided his general understanding of political problems.

watch his modes of compression at his own boundaries when he too tries to compare.

Clearly the more one reduces the area or restricts the types of relations under examination, the more significant do "localised" internal factors become, and the less significant are the external variables.[45] Thus Epstein asks why, if world conditions primarily determine the course of events in Central Africa, as the late Godfrey Wilson[46] and possibly Wright Mills seemed to suggest, were Africans in the Katanga copper-mining region of the then Belgian Congo slower to develop trade unions and political parties than Africans in Northern Rhodesia? The answer, he suggests, must lie largely in the local structures of the two areas. Since his essay was written, there has been extremely rapid political change and development of political organisation in the Congo, which suggests that their seeds were there, though not observed, in earlier years. But the effects of this comparatively rapid development may be felt for a long time in that tribal divisions in the Congo may prove to be more significant in national politics than they are likely to be in Northern Rhodesia.[47]

We recognise that what we have written in the preceding pages considerably underestimates the practical difficulties in making comparative and historical studies—difficulties which we emphasised in our brief references to theories of economic development. In theory, our procedures of abstention, of warranted naïvety (which will be discussed presently), of compression, and of circumscription, apply in these contexts, as in straightforward systematic studies; and they set definite limits on the scope of analysis. But as soon as one poses questions in the form "Why are the structures of these two fields different?"

[45] See the discussion of this problem for an analysis of Zulu social system and history in M. Gluckman, *Analysis of a Social Situation in Modern Zululand* [1958], pp. 61-2.

[46] G. Wilson, *An Essay on the Economics of Detribalization in Northern Rhodesia* [1941-42].

[47] See J. C. Mitchell, *Tribalism and the Plural Society* [1960]; and M. Gluckman, "Tribalism in Modern British Central Africa," in *Cahiers d'études africaines* [1960], and "Anthropological Problems arising from the African Industrial Revolution," in *Social Change in Modern Africa* [1961], ed. A. W. Southall, pp. 67-82; and "Tribe and Town," in *The Nation* [1960], on Northern Rhodesia, in addition to Epstein's works. For a contrasting situation in the Republic of South Africa, see P. Mayer, *Townsmen or Tribesmen* [1961]. On the Congo, see D. Biebuyck and M. Douglas, *Congo Tribes and Parties* [1961].

or "Why did developments here go this way, while there they went that way?" we tend to become involved in "historical" rather than in "scientific" analysis. When analysing the regularities within a system whose variable components are limited, social scientists can at least discuss their problems in terms of accuracy and value and comprehensiveness of data, of logic, and of validity of proof. Different social scientists ought to be able to agree on the analysis to be drawn from the data, or at least to narrow their range of disagreement to particular issues which can then be further investigated and checked. And it is for this reason that we call their method "scientific." But in dealing with complex comparative and historical problems, a different kind of judgment and evaluation is required. In our present state of knowledge, at any rate, we are likely to have many apparently conflicting but equally convincing interpretations, and there is no clearly agreed way by which one can decide which is the "right" answer. This is not to deny that studies of this kind can be made in a highly "disciplined" way: but the issues raised are very complex and difficult, and we cannot explore them fully here. These issues come out markedly in Lupton and Cunnison's essay.

Circumscription: Lupton and Cunnison

Lupton and Cunnison's attitude to the limits they must set themselves is strikingly different from Bailey's and Epstein's. They had studied workshops within factories in a large conurbation, and they take the view that they cannot explain the working of social groups and relationships within the workshops without bringing in the wider economic and social systems. They feel that they have also to consider the systems of social relations outside the workshop in which managers and workers are involved, and the history and organisation of the industries of which the workshops are part. Indeed they go so far as to suggest, as they themselves admit on not entirely adequate evidence, that they can in fact provide an explanation which embraces both the internal and the external system.

Lupton and Cunnison set out to investigate the influence of social factors on workers' output. In the light of previous studies of this problem, particularly in America, they had expected to find that workers set themselves a target of production lower than that to which management aspired, and that this "norm" of output would be supported by sanctions, in that pressure would be brought to bear by workers against anyone who exceeded or fell far below the "norm." That is, they set out to study the social context of so-called "restriction of output." To their surprise, in the first workshop each studied, there were no such norms. They found a norm of output in a workshop in the engineering industry. Accordingly they began trying to analyse two quite separate problems: first, how do informal groups form and work inside the factory, and in particular by what procedures and methods do such groups effectively impose norms of output, or operate in the absence of such norms; and, second, why are norms of output imposed in some factories, and not in others?

Both from their essay in this book and from the more detailed publication of their results elsewhere,[48] it seems quite clear that in answering the first set of questions Lupton and Cunnison can, and in fact largely do, deal with each workshop as a social system in isolation. It is in dealing with the second issue that they feel the need to extend the field of their observation to the wider system which includes important variables outside the factory. As soon as they do so, they meet the problem, as they recognise, of having to deal with various aspects of reality, such as economic monopoly and competition, which are not traditionally the subject-matter of social anthropology and sociology. They courageously suggest a hypothesis that in industries with certain clusters of variables such as high degree of competition, easy entry of new units of production, high labour cost, and weak unionism, "collective control over output by workers is less likely to be found than in industries where the reverse is true." They qualify this statement in the light of general and sometimes untested knowledge about workers' control of output in various industries, and they stress that the hypothesis is stated in terms of *"clusters of variables."* Yet they believe these clusters are systematically interconnected, for they state that "for example . . . [they] can think of few industries

---

[48] We had seen full reports by them on three workshops, and these are now published T. Lupton, *On the Shop Floor* [1963], and S. Cunnison, *Wages and Work Allocation* [1965].

with a constantly fluctuating market, where one finds strong trade unions, large productive units, and high capitalisation."

It is not our province to discuss here whether this hypothesis is likely to be sustained by further research; it certainly suggests important lines of investigation. We are concerned with Lupton and Cunnison's reluctance to come to the conclusion that they can state the hypothesis—which is stimulating and worth stating—and then leave it to colleagues in the appropriate disciplines to examine the interrelations within the suggested clustering of variables, while they as "social anthropologists" carry out further intensive and extensive investigation of other workshops. Since the hypothesis is important in the context of a problem which had previously been analysed largely in terms of internal problems, we sympathise with this reluctance. It is akin to Epstein's reluctance to be content, in the end, with a study of local urban communities, while major developments are occurring on a larger scale. Lupton and Cunnison themselves consider that no one else is likely to study the cluster of variables in which they are interested. Nevertheless we doubt whether sociologists or social anthropologists can successfully pursue the investigation of Lupton's and Cunnison's hypothesis without great expertise in other social sciences, particularly economics. For the variables which they suggest are significant —for example, the degree of competition in the industry, or the proportion of labour costs to total costs—are mainly economic variables. We think it is at least doubtful whether one can usefully pursue this subject in terms of rather crude measures of these variables, variables which specialist economists have found it by no means easy to handle. Therefore we ourselves judge that, for the present at least, pursuing research on the basis of a simple model of the kind they postulate is not likely to yield as much enlightenment as the less ambitious, but possibly wiser as well as more prudent, course of studying more factories before attempting to test the all-embracing hypothesis by which they seek to explain what they recognise is a highly complex phenomenon.

This is a matter on which opinions may well differ, and the research which Lupton is continuing to direct may prove highly successful. Nevertheless, we feel that it would have been wiser had the two problems involved been treated separately, so that the analysis of each workshop as a circumscribed system, affected by the presence or absence of a norm of output, had been kept separate from the presentation of the wider hypothesis. This hypothesis is, in practice, involved in the analysis of each workshop. The essay presented in this book was written after Lupton had begun to formulate the hypothesis about external variables, and in fact it begins with the last of the three studies that he and his associates had so far made.

We are told that this workshop made garments for a fluctuating market, so that it was uncertain how long orders for garments would continue. Hence both management and workers were insecure, in that the manager was aware that he was in danger of being forced out of business[49] and the workers were aware that they might go on to short-time working, or even lose their jobs. In this situation, it is stated that the manager had to allocate work as best would serve his firm's interests, which were that the work available should be got out, while the manager, as economically as possible, kept on as many employees as he could in hope of new orders coming in unexpectedly. He needed a reserve of workers, because speedy delivery might be essential to get an order. He ended therefore by tending to give work, when orders were short, to those workers who were more likely to leave; and this might mean that he favoured unskilled, short-service workers, mainly women, as against skilled, long-service workers, among whom were men as well as women, since it was difficult for the latter category of workers, who were also older, to move with their skill into other trades. The general situation produced great hostility between small, informal groups of workers; and this situation is skilfully analysed by Lupton and Cunnison. But in so far as the analysis involves and is referred to the external variables, it is difficult to get clear what the evidence on these points is: are they deductions by the research workers from their knowledge, admittedly limited, of the external variables, or are they statements by the parties about their own and others' motives? How far do the parties understand what is happening? On these and other points we consider that the use of the "external" hypothesis has complicated analysis of the internal functioning of the workshop.

[49] The firm went bankrupt some years after the essay was written.

Clearly in circumscribing a field of study, the investigator is bound to compress events at the boundaries. Thus Bailey states that he looks at only the actions of magistrate and other officials without considering what led to those actions; and Epstein does not enter into the pressures operating on Location Superintendent and District Commissioner, or consider the sorts of persons recruited to these posts. Some such procedure of "internalisation" of persons and factors which have important connexions outside the area of circumscription is probably always necessary. But one must not overstep the limits of one's circumscription, and believe that observation of the internalised elements gives accurate information, let alone analysis, of the external relations of those elements. Indeed, the persons concerned may be most unsatisfactory reporters on those external relations. The procedure of "internalisation" here is akin to the "introjection" of social factors into the psychical system in Freudian theory; and no psycho-analyst would assume that his subject reports correctly and objectively on them. It is in admiration of Lupton and Cunnison's treatment of the internal system of each workshop that we think it would have been wiser for them to stick to their last, and tell us more about the internal system, rather than get involved—and involve their analyses—in the clustering of external variables. We consider this to be in itself a difficult problem and one largely in the field of economics.

We would make the same comments on Lupton and Cunnison's anxiety about their relative ignorance of the social characteristics which managers and workers bring in from outside the workshop: their class status and the attitudes that go with it, the different financial and domestic responsibilities of men and women, the traditions of religious and ethnic groups. They do not accept that it is sufficient to say that workers arrive in the workshop with certain motives and patterns of action apparently derived from their roles in external systems, where age, sex, domestic status, ethnic affiliation, may be more directly significant.[50] They do in fact handle the relations dependent on these internalised variables adequately and illuminatingly without accepting that the

[50] Cp. Homans's abstention at this point of his re-analysis of a workshop (*The Human Group* [1951], pp. 89 f.).

information obtained in the workshop faithfully reflects the reality outside the workshop. That is, we are not certain that the ingenious sets of concepts about overlapping systems, role-clusters, and articulation of several systems of roles (above, pp. 125 f.) are necessary to analyse the workshop itself. For these concepts still leave unanswered the problem: at what point in analysing the "situational relationship of elements within the social context" where the demands of various rôles are adjusted, does one stop following up facts and their interconnexions? And how, otherwise than by compression at boundaries, does one circumscribe a manageable field of study? Do we not do this when we regard workers "as bearers of values and expectations *typical* of such systems" [our italics]?

Lupton and Cunnison answer this recurrent problem by saying that we need to know the work of other disciplines, and they also support the idea of inter-disciplinary research. We suggest that they had to come to this conclusion because they originally set out "to *explain*" [our italics] the behaviour they observed (p. 103), and did not limit what "explaining" would cover. To account for all aspects of behaviour in workshops, one may have to go further and further afield: to answer the problem, what systematic regularities are present in workshops where workers exercise control and by contrast in those where they do not, one can be more abstemious, and compress the immediately relevant external factors at the boundaries of a circumscribed field.

This judgment applies to the wider *social* context of the workshops. Lupton and Cunnison have undoubtedly raised most important question about these contexts. But most of the crucial variables in the hypothesis are economic, such as degrees of competition and proportions of capital as against labour costs. Economists indeed have tried to develop ways of measuring these variables without marked success. We do not believe that persons without great expertise in economics will be able to classify firms on the basis proposed, with any refined degree of measurement. If Lupton and Cunnison were to acquire that expertise, they might solve the difficulties that have blocked other economists. They would then be able to test the hypothesis: but they would be working as economists and not as sociologists or social anthropologists, and they would have to employ the appropriate techniques and competence, and work within the limits these impose. Alternatively, they might persuade an economist to tackle these problems again, with their hypothesis in mind.

Were they to work with an economist, Lupton and Cunnison would be entering on the inter-disciplinary team research which they advocate. This kind of research may contribute to a wider explanation. Yet it does not solve for each of the members of the team the problem of defining his context of relevance and competence, nor does it avoid the dangers of breaking the rule of disciplined refusal to trespass on the fields of others. Indeed, it may increase the difficulties, even while providing further stimulus within each field. Should the economist solve his problem, and should he be able to classify firms along a scale in terms of the hypothesis, Lupton and Cunnison would have to develop some means of measuring degrees of workers' control over output, to bring out any association.

These problems of inter-disciplinary research cannot here be discussed in detail. For fuller understanding of a particular situation, research of this kind may be required. It raises a series of problems which we can only list. First, putting the results of each section of the research together cannot be done by a procedure of summation: one or more specialists in the team will have to acquire sufficient expertise in the other disciplines to apply a combined analysis to the total situation. Second, such a combined analysis will run into difficulties involved in specialisation itself. It has yet to be shown that the concepts and relations established by one discipline can be transposed into those of another discipline.[51] Correspondingly, to allow the concepts of one science to become involved in the analysis of a field appropriate to another may lead to hazards in handling of data themselves. We have suggested some of the hazards which affected Lupton and Cunnison, and shall describe below how they affected Kluckhohn's analysis of Navaho witchcraft. Third, it may well be that the existing division of labour between the specialised social and economic sciences is, in Nadel's phrase, "fortuitous," and that to solve certain important problems about social and human life we

[51] See above, p. 172.

need new disciplines entirely. We believe that if this should prove necessary, the conclusions of the new disciplines will not be a summation of the conclusions of older disciplines, and that the difficulties of transposing conclusions between them will remain. The problems raised in this book will continue to be relevant; and it is with these problems only, and not with all the problems of social science, that we are here concerned.

In short, as Epstein and Bailey found, so too when Lupton and Cunnison begin to state their problem as why a smaller sub-system within a larger system is as it is, and not otherwise, they find that external variables are important determinants and have to be stated in some way. They cannot internalise these variables in the sub-system by using conceptions such as those of Homans and Warner whom they quote. And to go beyond the circumscribed field of the workshops with which they started they need the techniques of other disciplines— though this does not apply to all comparative work in social anthropology. Hence their paper raises in an acute form the issue of what can and cannot be done in the process of circum-scribing a field. As always, we do not think it possible to formulate rules to show when one has limited the field in a fruitful or in a sterilising manner. It makes clear indeed that the issue cannot be discussed in absolute terms, but only in relation to the questions and problems one is trying to answer. We consider that in attempting to explain how informal groups work within the factories, Lupton and Cunnison can proceed successfully in the traditional method of anthropology and isolate workshops as distinct and relatively self-contained social systems, with the wider society taken for granted. But when they try to answer the question why some factories develop informal groups which impose norms of output while others do not, they find that they have to break out of the limits of their circumscriptions. This does not mean that social scientists should never pose, or try to answer, this kind of problem. Indeed, the feeling that one is pursuing a major problem, which is difficult to grasp, may generate the enthusiasm that carries one through the ardours of research, as undoubtedly happened with Lupton and his team. The wise and prudent course may dry up the springs of research: the problem, which we shall discuss again below, is to retain this enthusiasm but to discipline it in order to keep one's answers to distinctive types of problems, tackled by techniques themselves distinct and appropriate.

Circumscription: Watson

We pass now to an essay in which the social anthropologist considered, after many years' reflexion, that his initial analysis of the limited field he had investigated was inadequate, because current theories about the structure of national systems were unsatisfactory. He therefore decided that he had to produce a more satisfactory theory in this larger field, before he could analyse the smaller system within it. This is Watson's essay on "social mobility and social class in industrial communities." Some parts of his theory have recently been advanced in similar terms by Whyte in *The Organisation Man* (1957), and by others, so we repeat that Watson's essay was first read at a meeting of the Association of Social Anthropologists of the British Commonwealth in 1957; and he had begun to develop the argument in 1956.

Watson's essay arose "out of field work carried out some years ago [around 1950] in a Scottish coal-mining community." The "object of the research was to investigate the connexion between the educational achievements of children and the occupational and social standing of their families." The more successful children were selected for a kind of education different from that accorded their less successful fellows: the former's education was literary, and led to a professional career on leaving school. Since most of the propulation of the Burgh were working-class, "this success presaged the possibility of a discontinuity in occupational and social status between these children and their parents. Most of the successful children would eventually leave the community altogether and take up careers and residence elsewhere. . . . The educational institutions within the Burgh, which were the main channel for occupational and social mobility, were part of a national system." For these and similar reasons Watson found that "any analysis of the Burgh's internal social system based only on such data as could be collected while working in the community soon turned out to be quite inadequate. The external system had to be taken into account, and the connexions between it

o

and the Burgh examined. But a review of the sociological literature on social class and on occupational and social mobility failed to provide a satisfactory conceptual framework within which to trace these wider connexions. The concepts of social class current in sociological theory appeared to be too blunt an instrument for a satisfactory comprehension of the different prestige systems involved, and the connexion between them, particularly as there is a good deal of occupational and social mobility in the Burgh. In these circumstances the external system could not be accepted as given: it was necessary to attempt to construct a more serviceable picture of the wider and inclusive society and to formulate a theory about the national system as a whole."

We have quoted Watson's own statement on why he decided he could not "compress" the external system of the Burgh, a procedure to which he clearly did not object in principle. Indeed, in his study of an African tribe's adaptation to labour migration, and its reaction to a political crisis, he has readily taken over the results of other researches, and compressed external political and economic events.[52]

He considers that any theories which see the classes of modern industrial societies as layers of persons with common interests in the productive system, or varying prestige and different skills, are inadequate. "Industrial society may be regarded as composed of a large number of local residential communities, which differ in the number and character of the occupational groups to be found within each one." Each local community has a local culture and local standards of prestige. These various communities are linked together by large national administrative and industrial and servicing hierarchies, the growth of which has been marked for a long time. Linked with this growth is the development of more and more professional skills, whose practitioners are increasingly grouped in specialist associations. Watson illustrates the development of this situation with two field studies of local communities. He defines "class" in relation to the extent to which people participate in the national hierarchies or in local communities. He distinguishes various modes of life associated with these categories. Some professional people, whose careers lie in the large-scale

[52] W. Watson, *Tribal Cohesion in a Money Economy* [1958].

hierarchies, are very mobile and they have to have a "culture" which makes such mobility possible. Other professionals, by virtue of their skills, settle in local communities. Workers, who have a different career in front of them, move generally within regions, but not upwards in occupation. Watson discusses the rôles which these different kinds of persons play in the policies and life of organisations and communities. The children of workers who become professionals are likely to move out of their natal communities. The analysis is presented more tentatively than in this bare summary, but Watson concludes: "The whole social system may therefore be envisaged as a plurality of prestige structures, some of them interconnected and others quite independent, and each with its own particular standard of evaluation, although all are liable to be affected by the fundamental division of function and culture between members of professional and non-professional occupations.

"The 'class' position of individuals and groups is explicable only in terms of these sub-structures; in a local community the 'class' system will reflect the number and constitution of such sub-structures as are represented; on a national scale, the 'class' system can be interpreted only in terms of the plurality of sub-systems which make up the whole."

That is, Watson decided that in order to understand what was happening to his Scottish children, he could not abridge any current theory in another discipline—sociology or political science—and treat its findings as factors influencing what was happening in the social field he had himself studied. In short, he ceased to be a social anthropologist and became himself a sociologist. In the present essay he uses the data from his field study, in general terms, to illustrate his main thesis. In other words, if we look at the methodological problems set out in this book, we can take Watson's essay as an example of a macroscopic theory which then has to compress the internal relations of sections of the major system which is it analysing. This is in essence the result that Epstein thought would follow from a survey of urbanisation and industrialisation in several towns of Africa. The local details which are significant for local developments become less significant when the wider system is surveyed.

We have considered Watson's essay only very briefly: this is not because we think it less important than the others. But he has not discussed the problem we have set ourselves, beyond stating that without a more sophisticated theory about the national structure, he could not begin to analyse his local community and the "connexion between the educational achievements of children and the occupational and social standing of their families." He chose to extend his field rather than to set himself less ambitious problems. Nor do we here evaluate his theory. What he shows is that, for the solution of a particular set of problems, a social anthropologist or other social scientist may find that circumscribing his field and compressing external events stultifies his analysis. He then has three choices: (1) he can change his field till some colleague in another discipline solves his problem; or (2) he can produce an analysis of more limited problems; or (3) he must himself tackle the complexity of the external variables. If he chooses the last course, he may have to shift into another discipline. This is what Watson has done; and he could do it because social anthropology and sociology are closely related subjects, with similar concepts and problems. It might well be more difficult for Lupton and Cunnison, who ran into a similar problem about the influence of external variables on the structure of a sub-system, to shift to test their hypothesis about those external variables and the interconnexions between them. Lupton and Cunnison ran into problems involving measurements which have proved difficult for economists, and into problems in the theory of economics. To step from sociology and anthropology into economics is to move into a realm of different conceptions.

NAÏVETY

We have confined the procedure of naïvety to the situation where the anthropologist disregards the researches and conclusions of other disciplines about aspects of the events he is studying, as irrelevant to his problems. He is indifferent to these conclusions, and is even quite artless about them: he may indeed make assumptions about these aspects which he himself knows to be very much over-simplified and indeed largely false. This is deliberate naïvety. Such naïvety occurs not only in social anthropology but also in all social sciences, and indeed, we suspect, in all sciences.

Naïvety: Turner

Without considering the manner in which Turner limits his field of study, we concentrate on the extent to which he makes naïve assumptions about other aspects of the events which he studied, and how far his naïvety is justified within the limitations he set himself.

Turner explicitly asks himself how sophisticated does he, as a social anthropologist, have to be about psycho-analytic interpretations of rituals and ritual symbols, since he considers that this kind of interpretation is an important and valid contribution to our understanding these phenomena. In fact, he begins by pointing out that those social anthropologists who consider associations of symbols which are not fully known to the performers to be irrelevant for their analyses, are cutting themselves off from valuable interpretations. Nevertheless, he criticises those psycho-analysts who believe that they can "explain" rituals and ritual symbols as products of unconscious dispositions, and who argue that because the compulsive actions and fantasies of severely ill neurotics resemble, in some respects, the rites and beliefs of so-called primitive society, they are the same kind of phenomena, and can be interpreted in the same kind of way. He cites Bettelheim, who, after studying the "secret society" formed by four schizoid children, inferred "that one of the (unconscious) purposes of male initiation rites may be to assert that men too can bear children, and that [quoting Bettelheim himself] 'through such operations as subincision men may try to acquire sexual apparatus and functions equal to women's.' " Turner resumes: "Womb-envy, and an unconscious infantile identification with the mother, in Bettelheim's opinion, were powerful formative factors, both in the *ad hoc* ritual of his four schizoids, and in male circumcision rituals all over the world" (above, pp. 38-9). Turner points out that this view is "in important respects opposed to that of many orthodox Freudians, who hold that the symbolic events comprising these rituals result principally from the fathers' jealousy of their sons, and that their purpose is to create sexual (castration) anxiety and to make the incest taboo secure." And Turner pertinently asks: "Where psycho-analysts disagree, by what criterion can the hapless anthropologist judge between their interpretations, in a field of enquiry in which he has neither received systematic training nor obtained thorough practical experience?"

Turner asserts that psycho-analysts who attempt to make individual unconscious motivations the main source—even in the qualified phrase "powerful formative factors"—of rituals like circumcision ceremonies, are ignoring the limits of their naïvety about social and cultural facts, and unwarrantably transferring interpretations which may be valid in one dimension of facts, to another dimension of the same facts. He stresses that ceremonies of this kind are highly complex cultural and social phenomena, developing through a long history during which some rites have been added, others dropped, others amended. Turner does not question that psychological drives and dispositions have contributed to these developments. What he insists is that a social-anthropological analysis of these rites can be carried out independently of the psychological analysis of the same rites, by relating them to other facts in the socio-cultural system—the point that Durkheim and many others have emphasised. Turner then goes on to relate the rituals to different domains of social life and shows that they have to be understood as rites in terms of their connexions within the web of co-operation and competition established by custom and interest in the affiliations of the Ndembu.

In the light of his analysis, and of other similar analyses, the origin of rituals cannot be "explained" by psycho-analytic theory, which is a theory about the structure of the circum-scribed fields of individual human personalities, within which ritual action has certain effects that can be studied. As Turner shows within the brief space of his essay, psycho-analytic inter-pretations of unconscious complexes as the determining cause, or even principal powerful formative factors, of types of ritual cannot stand up to even the barest comparative assessment. He does not suggest that the psycho-analytic study of ritual tells us nothing important about ritual: some form of such theory is essential to analyse, in any illuminating way, the significance of particular rituals for particular individuals (and here both Bettelheim's and the opposed theory may be valid for different persons); to analyse the regular significance of these rituals for various psychological types of participants; and ultimately to analyse the role of ritual in individual psychical life. Doubtless, out of these kinds of dispositions individuals have contributed to the historical development of the rites. But to use data on individuals and analysis of these data, or data on a chance group of four children, to interpret the significance of particular rituals in a system of social relations or in a particular culture pattern, is to commit the error of ignoring the limits of one's own naïvety.

Turner is naïve in our terms even though he has read some relevant books on psycho-analysis to see what help he can get from that subject for his own work; and he has not considered depth-psychology irrelevant *ab initio* to his problem. That is, he decides that he can, for his purposes, ignore the theories which psycho-analysts might advance to interpret the significance of what undergoing a circumcision ritual effects in an Ndembu boy's personality, or what organising such rituls and performing the operation effects in Ndembu men's and women's personalities. He implies that for this kind of interpretation it would be necessary to collect data by the techniques of depth-psychology: reports on overt behaviour at ceremonies cannot provide data susceptible of psycho-analytic interpretation. Turner thus accepts the limits imposed by his own lack of competence, which even prevents him from choosing between alternative psycho-analytic interpretations. But he goes further. He asserts—and we endorse his judgment—that for his problems these interpretations are irrelevant. In other words, he is not making the best of a bad job because he cannot even "abridge" and judge between the complex theories of psycho-analysis: he can afford to be naïve about them. He deliberately eschews involvement in these theories. He maintains that the sociological relations of ritual symbols form a sufficiently autonomous system to be analysed independently of their psychological aspects. His essay itself validates this contention: sociological analysis of symbols is penetrating on its own.

From this position, he can turn, occasionally and within clearly defined limits, to psycho-analysis for help in handling some of his data. When he studied the rite in which a nubile girl during her initiation ceremony is apparently identified through an exchange of clothing with her own mother, his informants could not give any interpretation of this action. Turner suggests that it symbolises a strong conflict between mother and daughter, involving death-wishes against one another: ". . . it is legitimate to infer, in my opinion," he says, "that powerful unconscious wishes of a kind considered illicit by Ndembu, are expressed in it [the rite]" (see above, p. 25). The "blocking" of exegesis here is situational only, particular and appropriate to the girl's nubility ritual, for the Ndembu are well aware that mothers and daughters quarrel and that there are standing causes of hostility between them. But Turner realises that this kind of suggestion has to be proved by the techniques of depth-psychology, and does not do more than put it forward as a tentative suggestion.

Mainly he works with a naïve, and fairly crude, view of the human personality, though he takes account of unconscious feelings and motivations, age-old ideas which have been developed and refined by psycho-analysis. For example, he accepts that there are illicit wishes and drives to commit crimes among the best adapted, and that symbols, as against signs, proliferate meanings in the unconscious rather than in the conscious mind. That this is naïve, rather than sophisticated, is shown by his argument that in the context of his problem the social anthropologist "cannot, with his present skills, discriminate between the *precise sources* of unconscious feeling and wishing, which shape much of the outward form of the symbol; select some natural objects rather than others to serve as symbols; and account for certain aspects of the behaviour associated with symbols. For him, it is enough that the symbol should evoke 'emotion.' He is interested in the fact that emotion is evoked and not the specific quality of its constituents. He may indeed find it situationally relevant for his analysis to distinguish whether the emotion evoked by a specific symbol possesses the gross character, say, of aggression, fear, friendliness, anxiety or sexual pleasure. But he need go no further than this." With this in mind, Turner leads to one of his principal conclusions, namely, that " . . . the ritual symbol, we may perhaps say, effects an interchange of qualities between its [ideological and sensory] poles of meaning. Norms and values, on the one hand, become saturated with emotion, while the gross and basic emotions become ennobled through contact with social values. The irksomeness of moral constraint is transformed into the 'love of virtue' " (above, pp. 31-32). This conclusion is obviously consistent with the psycho-analytical thesis of sublimation, as Freud himself states it: "The relations of an instinct to its aim and to its object are also susceptible to alterations; both can be exchanged for others, but the relation to the object is the more easily loosened of the two. There is a particular kind of modification of aim and change of object, *with regard to which our social values come into the picture* [our italics]; to this we give the name of *sublimation*."[53] It is gratifying when the conclusions of two sciences working on the same phenomena are consistent with one another: but it is not essential that they be so. In this case we consider that Turner's sociological analysis of symbols would stand without this consistency: he does apparently abridge some findings of psychoanalysis, though he does not in fact use the word "sublimate." His theory attempts to explain the significance of ritual symbols in social life: how those symbols stimulate sublimation in individual Ndembu is another type of problem, irrelevant for his purpose. Nor would he contend that his analysis throws light on that problem: for here, as elsewhere, he accepts the limits of his naïvety.

To both depth-psychologists and those anthropologists who are concerned with psycho-analytic types of interpretation of rituals, Turner's views may seem to be too crude. Yet Freud himself often adopted this kind of reasoning. For example, when he introduced the concept of sublimation he wrote: "Whether the relation of a somatic source gives the instinct any specific characters, and if so which, is not at all clear. The evidence of analytic experience proves conclusively that instinctual impulses from one source can join on to instinctual impulses from another and share their further vicissitudes, and that in general the satisfaction of one instinct can be substituted for the satisfaction of another. It must be freely admitted, however, that we are not very clear about the explanation of this."[54] Freud proceeded with his own theorising, despite acknowledged lack of clarity—and hence crudity of formulation and, as we shall argue below, naïvety—on this among other facts of somatology.

[53] *New Introductory Lectures on Psycho-Analysis* [1933], p. 126.
[54] *Ibid.* Freud's position is more fully discussed below (pp. 222 ff.); he took many years to arrive at this point.

Whatever the validity of Turner's theory—and it is not our concern to assess it—we consider that he has been warrantably naïve about psychological relations which touch his problems, and that he has kept within the limits of his naïvety—and of his competence.

Naïvety: Epstein

Epstein is the only contributor, besides Turner, whose essay provides a clear example of naïvety, in our modified sense. Most of his essay is concerned with the problem of the consequences which follow on circumscribing political developments among Africans in Luanshya from the whole of Luanshya life and from political developments outside Luanshya. But he also deals explicitly with the extent to which he treats, in a naïve way, certain complexes of facts in trying to understand the situation, and with the effect that this naïvety has on his analysis. As already quoted, he asks two major questions: first, why is the social organisation of the mine compound so different from that of the municipal location, and, second, how have the divergent interests of different groups of Africans in these situations affected trade union development? He makes a convincing case for arguing that, in answering these questions, the town of Luanshya can be treated as a distinct social system which can be examined separately from the wider world with which it is connected, as discussed under "circumscription." But this isolation and limitation severely restrict the issues with which he can deal. He makes a "naïve" assumption that the actions of the copper-mining company and its policy of looking after all aspects of the African workers' life, both during and after working hours, can be treated as uncomplicated. He does not explore the reasons for this policy, but we agree with him that for the limited questions he sets himself, he is wise to make this naïve assumption.

Much of Epstein's analysis of internal struggles among Africans in the compound, and of their effects on trade-union development, raises issues frequently discussed in studies of industrial relations in economically more advanced Western societies. This is a field of study which is not normally relevant in the work of classical British social anthropology,[55] and if urban studies of the kind undertaken by Epstein are to be a common feature of anthropology, some familiarity with the academic work on industrial relations in the West would be an advantage. Ignorance of this work may indeed imperil conclusions: for example, behaviour of African workers is often ascribed to tribal culture, or the specific situation of migrating labourers, when in fact it shows close parallels with the kind of behaviour of British workers discussed in Lupton and Cunnison's essay. Here the anthropologist may not be looking at the phenomena of industrial relations from exactly the same viewpoint as that adopted by the specialist on industrial relations, but the difference is not very marked. It seems to us, therefore, that this is a case where an extension into another academic discipline is necessary and important: for to study many relevant questions and problems one must be familiar with the techniques and ideas of both anthropology and industrial relations. Fortunately, this should not be too difficult for the anthropologist, since the academic study of industrial relations does not involve any esoteric technique which would take another social scientist years to learn.

Epstein also makes naïve assumptions about industrial relations in the compound, and by implication about industrial relations generally. He does not refer to these explicitly in his essay, but there is an implication that the Company and the workers are two opposed parties, each battling, more or less subtly or crudely, for its own objectives. This no doubt is a naïve assumption in relation to the complex motivation behind the behaviour of the Company and the various organised groups of Africans. But it seems to us to be a reasonably naïve assumption to make in the circumstances, and one which does not seriously affect the issues in which Epstein is immediately interested—the development of trade unions and political groupings. For other issues and problems this naïve assumption might be inappropriate and therefore a dangerous one on which to base analysis. Epstein recognises this explicitly when discussing what would probably be involved in making a wider

[55] We note correspondingly that in our view students of industrial relations could get many valuable leads on the relation of co-operation and competition in society from the work of such social anthropology.

study of the emergence of an African Salaried Staff Association.

Naïvety: Economics

We hope that this commentary on the essays in this book has demonstrated how important it is to distinguish the procedures which are employed in circumscribing a field of study. The methodological problems are present in all disciplined research: they are particularly difficult to solve in the human sciences. We argue that it would be helpful if all practitioners of these sciences were to make explicit the procedures they employ to demarcate a manageable field of study. It would be still more helpful if their critics would distinguish incorrect abridgment from deliberately adopted naïvety, and would indicate how they consider such naïvety invalidates the conclusions arrived at within the discipline involved.[56]

In economic theory assumptions are often made about individual psychology and motivations, and the validity of these assumptions has been the subject of great controversy both among economists and outsiders. It is quite common for psychologists and sociologists to criticise economists on the grounds that they use basic assumptions about human motivations which are quite unreal and unjustifiably naïve. Yet it is uncommon to find any analysis of how these assumptions may affect the validity of the conclusions reached by economists. Usually these critics implicitly assume that, if the assumptions are "wrong" or "unreal," then it necessarily follows that the theory based on them will be mistaken and misleading. This may seem a reasonable view to take, but it is an essential part of our argument that it is an erroneous view. Whether this kind of naïvety has such consequences or not must depend, as we see the procedure, on how far the conclusions are related to the particular assumptions, and in what ways, if any, the conclusions would be altered if different assumptions were made.

The basic assumptions which are most frequently attacked

---

[56] The best explicit defence of such naïvety that we know is Gluckman's reply to the allegation that he needs a more sophisticated psycho-dynamic theory to validate certain of his social-anthropological analyses of political rituals: see his Introduction to *Order and Rebellion in Tribal Africa* [1963].

are those which are used in the classical theory of price, in particular that individuals in the economic system—workers, consumers, and businessmen—are motivated by self-interest, and attempt to maximise their real income, utility, or profits. It is true that such assumptions, and others of a rigorous and "unreal" kind, are used in the economic theory of price to construct a theoretical system showing the determinants of prices of commodities and factors of production, and how these prices are interrelated. If we want to know how far the naïvety of the assumptions affects the validity of the theory, we must, in our opinion, ask what it is that we learn from the theory and whether this would be affected by altering the assumptions.

To discuss at length what we learn from the economic theory of price would be inappropriate here, and would in any case itself raise controversial issues. We are prepared to assert that the main, if not the sole, value of the theory is to show how prices are interrelated in a consistent system, and how changes at any one point will have determinate consequences throughout the system. This enables us to view economic reality as a system of this kind, instead of viewing it as a series of apparently disconnected phenomena which can only be reported descriptively. How far does this conclusion of the theory depend on the particular assumptions about human motivation? Would the conclusions be quite different if, instead of assuming that human beings were motivated by self-interest, we assumed that they were always concerned with the interests of others: *i.e.*, if instead of the assumption of "perfect selfishness" we made the assumption of "perfect altruism."[57] There is a story that a Russian mathematical economist in the nineteenth century worked out a mathematical theory of price, in which he assumed perfect altruism to govern human motivation. The story relates that the price system that emerged from this analysis did not differ in essentials from the classical one which makes the reverse assumptions. Unfortunately, this story is an apocryphal one, but we are assured by colleagues in mathematical economics that the point of the story is valid, for one could construct a formal system of interrelated prices for commodities and

[57] Homans has an illuminating discussion on how—in our terminology— "compression" makes motives self-interested, which in another sub-system are altruistic (*The Human Group* [1951], p. 95).

factors along Walrasian lines if one assumed that altruism was the main motive in human behaviour. This would then give the same lesson as the Walrasian one, by demonstrating how economic phenomena are interrelated and interconnected in a systematic way. The solutions for prices of particular commodities and factors would be different, but the general conclusion that the prices were interrelated in a determinate way, that is the general notion of a price system, would remain. It is part of our general argument that the outstanding value of price theory is to demonstrate this general point about a price system and that it is of much less value in explaining what determines particular prices. It follows, therefore, that the main lesson of the theory would be the same, whether we assume perfectly "selfish" or perfectly "altruistic" behaviour; and attacks on the theory on the grounds that the assumption of "selfishness" is unjustifiably naïve, are misplaced.

It may be, of course, that while the general conclusions of a consistent price system are not affected by the assumption of "selfishness" or "altruism," they would be affected by changes of a different kind in the assumptions made about human behaviour and motivations. If, for example, one assumed that human behaviour was erratic in a quite random fashion from day to day, the notion of a general price system might be completely upset. If this is so, then it does become important in assessing the value of the theory to know to what extent motivations and behaviour are consistent, rational, and stable, and to what extent they are erratic, irrational and random. But we return once again to our main point that it is important to know this not just to check whether the assumptions are "valid" or not, but because completely random behaviour by buyers and sellers might appreciably affect the validity and usefulness of conclusions which we draw from general price theory.

Naïvety: Freud

That the methodological problem is general to the human sciences is shown by a statement that Hall and Lindzey make in their *Theories of Personality*: "Related to the question of hereditary determination and cultural determination is the more general question of how explicitly the personality theorist attempts to relate this theory to the theorising and empirical findings in neighbouring disciplines. This might be referred to as a question of *interdisciplinary anchoring*. Some personality theorists are relatively content to deal with behavioural phenomena in terms of psychological concepts and findings with little or no attention to what is going on in neighbouring disciplines. Others feel that psychological theorising should lean heavily upon the formulations and finds of other disciplines. The 'other-oriented' personality psychologists can be neatly divided into two types: those who look towards the natural sciences (biology, physiology, neurology, genetics) for guidance and those who look towards the social sciences (sociology, anthropology, economics, history) for guidance."[58] The problems which we have so far considered from the point of view of the anthropologist can be looked at in reverse, from the viewpoint of the psychologist.

We have been considering mainly situations in which, even if the anthropologist thought it necessary for deeper understanding of his problem, he usually had not the training to venture into a different type of analysis. Some anthropologists have brought to their profession other types of training, in economics, psychology, history, and law. None of them has stated that he had to forget what he had learnt in one of these disciplines, in order to pursue problems in his newly chosen field of social anthropology.[59] We could strengthen our justification of deliberately assumed naïvety if we could cite an anthropologist who had reported that he did so. Since we cannot do this, we have decided to examine the way in which Freud slowly dropped his attempt to relate his psychological analysis of personality to bodily constitution and processes, until he ended by making naïve assumptions about anatomy and physiology. Our examination of Freud for this purpose is also relevant to our main theme because many have argued that

---

[58] *Op. cit.*, p. 26.

[59] Fortes points out the psychological concomitants of Tallensi religious taboos and beliefs in *The Dynamics of Clanship among the Tallensi*, especially pp. 142 and 146, but states that he was not competent to provide a psycho-analytic investigation (p. 146) [though he carried out important research in academic psychology]. See also his statements opening a discussion of "Tensions in the Parent-Child Relationship," in *The Web of Kinship among the Tallensi* [1944], Ch. VIII, p. 222.

psychological and social anthropological and sociological analyses are incomplete without each other. Freud himself ventured into this controversy, because although he came to accept that he could neglect (be naïve about) physiology and allied sciences in order to pursue his problems, he did not recognise that he was naïve in the social sciences, and he produced analyses which he believed "explained" aspects of social life. This led to controversy between anthropologists and Freudian psychologists. Notably Malinowski, on the basis of data collected for a social-anthropological study of the matrilineal Trobrianders, ignored the limits of his own naïvety in criticising part of Freud's theory of the development of the personality; and Jones demonstrated this, but in turn trespassed beyond his own limits of naïvety. Thus beyond using Freud as a cogent example of the value of naïvety, we can clarify the whole of this perennial controversy, and can indicate where similar trespasses with inappropriate techniques and data continue to lead to muddle between the subjects.

Freud had already won a high reputation as a physiologist and neurologist when he began to evolve his theories about the neurotic, and later the normal, personality.[60] It has taken Jones three volumes to trace the development of Freud's ideas on the relation of psychological processes to bodily processes on the one hand, and to society and culture on the other hand. Here we can only draw attention to a few significant statements in Jones's biography. Jones (1. 283 f.) says that Freud, to begin with, had cherished the hope of establishing a physiological basis for mental functioning, and during the years 1888-89 "he passed through a severe struggle before he decided to relinquish the idea of correlating somatic and psychical activity." Jones summarises the development of Freud's ideas on anxiety neurosis, and his attempts to relate it to an accumulation of physical tension, and concludes: "In all this the bias of Freud's early training is evident. He was on the brink of deserting physiology and enunciating the findings and theories of his clinical observations in purely psychological language." To make this break was difficult in the face of external pressure and his own training in physiology, so that Jones reports (1.

---

[60] This brief summary of Freud's development is culled from E. Jones, *Sigmund Freud: Life and Work*, 3 vols. [1953-7].

285): "A remark he [Freud] made to me years later dates from this attitude. It was a half-serious prediction that in time to come it would be possible to cure hysteria (*sic*) by administering a chemical drug without any psychological treatment. On the other hand, he [Freud] used to insist that one should explore psychology to its limits, while waiting patiently for the suitable advance in biochemistry, and would warn his pupils against what he called 'flirting with endocrinology.' "

We cannot here summarise the course of Freud's development, in this respect, nor indeed have we competence to disentangle the issues where "circumscription" of the psyche was necessary for his theoretical formulations, from the issues where bodily factors had to be considered for clinical purposes. A few references suffice to validate our argument. Jones describes (1.406 f.) how Freud's contact with France "must have helped him to emancipate himself from neurology, although he was dilatory in availing himself of it—evidently from an unwillingness to forsake what he felt to be a secure and 'scientific' basis." Freud continued to share what Jones calls "the illusion" that the most promising approach was through brain physiology (1.416), and clung "to the safety of brain anatomy" (1.421).[61] Eventually Freud reached a point where he could write in 1917: "Psycho-Analysis hopes to discover the common ground on which the coming together of bodily and mental disturbances will become intelligible. To do so it must keep free of any alien preconceptions of an anatomical, chemical or physiological nature, and work throughout with purely psychological auxiliary hypotheses" (cited Jones, 1.433). At some point, not clearly denoted, he even adopted the view (in Jones's words) (1.404) that: ". . . not only was the nature of both mind and matter quite unknown, but they were so intrinsically different in kind as to make it a logical error to translate a description of processes in one into terms of the other. Nor was there any clue for elucidating the direct relationship of one to the other. How an excitation of the retina could be followed by a perception of light or form was an unapproachable mystery. Of course, like all doctors and many other people, Freud could often use loose language incompatible with what has just been

[61] Hall and Lindzey, *Theories of Personality*, p. 31, speak of Freud's "abortive attempt to account for psychological phenomena in terms of cerebral anatomy. . . ."

P

expounded: bodily, *e.g.*, sexual, changes would *produce* anxiety, or an emotion would *produce* paralysis of a limb. Clearly, however, these are shorthand expressions not meant to be taken as literal exactitude. Psychosomatic medicine, for example, is replete with phraseology of this kind." We would speak of *incorporating* sexual changes or emotions into the psycho-analytical frame of analysis.

Some time after Freud delivered his three courses of *Introductory Lectures on Psycho-Analysis* in the medical school in the University of Vienna in 1915-17, he began to delineate "the anatomy of the mental personality"[62] in a manner which, from the point of view of neurology, was completely naïve: it paid no attention whatsover to the anatomy and physiology of the brain, the nervous system, the somatic basis of emotions, and so forth. While the images and metaphors we quote below may have helped him to explain his theses to a relatively untrained audience, the central concepts are essential to his theory; and Jones states of the view of conscious, preconscious and unconscious[63] that "in this topographical discussion he [Freud] was careful to avoid, indeed to deny, any connection with the anatomy of the brain, a former love he had long forsaken, and he was more than sceptical about any attempt to correlate consciousness with the cerebral cortex and the unconscious with lower centres of the brain."[64]

Freud's delineation of "the anatomy of the mental personality"[65] involved the procedure we call naïve simplification, as well as naïve circumscription. We are not concerned with how he simplified, or whether his theory is adequate here: this falls outside the scope of this book. But the spatial diagram in which he illustrated "areas" of the personality is naïve.[66] He distinguished the regions of the perceptual conscious, from the pre-conscious and the unconscious, while showing how ego, super-ego, and id, and the area of repression, overlay this major demarcation. He constantly used territorial and geographical

---

[62] The title of the third chapter of *New Introductory Lectures on Psycho-Analysis* [1933].

[63] *Sigmund Freud*, Vol. II, pp. 360-1. The reference is to *The Unconscious*, first published in German in 1915.

[64] Jones adds: "It may prove that he [Freud] was over-sceptical in this."

[65] Freud, *New Introductory Lectures on Psycho-Analysis* [1933], p. 105.

[66] *Op. cit.*

metaphors and analogies to expound the relations between them, though he said "analogies prove nothing, that is quite true, but they can make one feel more at home" (p. 97).

We do not try to summarise how Freud delineated each of these domains and each of what he called "structural entities" of the mental personality. Only the full text itself can bring out his qualifications, and his references to his own ignorance, or his full awareness that his audience might "ask scornfully whether our ego-psychology amounts to no more than taking everyday abstractions literally, magnifying them and turning them from concepts into things—which would not be of much assistance" (p. 82)—*i.e.*, his awareness of the dangers of false reification. But clearly his account of the mental personality was much more than a compression and simplification of the anatomical and physiological findings of students of nervous and endocrinological systems, even at the time when he first formulated his theory; and he was aware that there were problems for other disciplines in his "compressions." For example, when he first presented his theory in lectures he said that in his opinion "the question of how far the quite justifiable distinction between sexual and self-preservation instincts is to be carried has not much importance for psycho-analysis, nor is psycho-analysis competent to deal with it. From the biological point of view there are certainly various indications that the distinction is important. . . ."[67]

Freud expressly warned his audience that in "dividing up the personality into ego, super-ego and id, you must not imagine sharp dividing lines such as are artificially drawn in the field of political geography. We cannot do justice to the characteristics of the mind by means of linear contours, such as occur in a drawing or in a primitive painting, but we need rather the areas of colour shading off into one another that are to be found in modern pictures. After we have made our separations, we must allow what we have separated to merge again. Do not judge too harshly of a first attempt at picturing a thing so elusive as the human mind."[68]

In our sense of the terms this picture of the personality *is* "naïve" and simple; it is far more than an abridgment of

[67] *Introductory Lectures on Psycho-Analysis* [1933], p. 345.
[68] *New Introductory Lectures on Psycho-Analysis* [1933], p. 105.

knowledge of the human organism established by other sciences studying that organism and its behaviour. The naïvety appears clearly in Freud's constant use of metaphors and poetic analogies. For example, he wrote that the therapeutic efforts of psycho-analysis tried "to strengthen the ego, to make it more independent of the super-ego, to widen its field of vision, and so to extend its organisation that it can take over new portions of the id. Where id was, there shall ego be.

"It is reclamation work, like the draining of the Zuyder Zee."[69]

Freud was well aware that his use of poetic imagery was extreme simplification of very complex problems. Yet he felt he could overlook these problems in order to proceed to investigate the questions which arose for him from his study of slips in behaviour, of dreams, and of neurosis. This appears in his introductory account of the id: "You must not expect me to tell you much that is new about the id, except its name. It is the obscure inaccessible part of our personality; the little we know about it we have learnt from the study of dream-work and the formation of neurotic symptoms, and most of that is of a negative character, and can only be described as being all that the ego is not. We can come nearer to the id with images, and call it a chaos, a cauldron of seething excitement. We suppose that it is somewhere in contact with somatic processes, and takes over from them instinctual needs and give them mental expression, but we cannot say in what substratum this contact is made. These instincts fill it with energy, but it has no organisation and no unified will, only an impulsion to obtain satisfaction for the instinctual needs, in accordance with the pleasure-principle. . . ."[70]

We are here citing Freud's theory as an outstanding example of the method we are describing: we do not require to—and could not—evaluate the theory itself, save that we accept, what

[69] Op. cit., p. 106.

[70] *Op. cit.*, pp. 98 f. Freud uses other types of imagery, as when he compares the ego with a rider of the horse which is the id, in a situation where "all too often . . . the rider is obliged to guide his horse in the direction in which it itself wants to go." On the same page he described the "poor ego" as serving three harsh masters and having to do its best to reconcile their always divergent and often seemingly quite incompatible demands, so it is "no wonder that the ego so frequently gives way under its task. The three tyrants are the external world, the super-ego, and the id" (*op. cit.*, p. 103).

few would deny, that he threw brilliant light on the inner workings of the human personality. Nor, for our purposes, need we examine his own, and others', developments of his main theory, or alternative theories of depth-psychology. We are quoting him because he produced what we call a "naïve" as well as simplified picture of the anatomy of the mental personality, although he knew how complicated was the structure of the nervous system, since only in that way could he proceed to tackle his problems.

The form of Freud's conceptual scheme has been criticised because it is reified and poetical. As early as 1918, for example, W. H. R. Rivers, himself a neurologist and psychologist, and an anthropologist, wrote an essay in which he tried to cast "Freud's Concept of the 'Censorship' "[71] in terms more acceptable to neurology. He did so after stating that "this concept of a censorship, acting as a guardian of a person against such elements of unconscious experience as would disturb the harmony of his life, is one which helps us to understand many of the more mysterious aspects of the mind," and he went on generally to praise Freud. Though he implied that he was prepared "to go far" in adherence to Freud's scheme of psychology, Rivers found it difficult "to accept a concept which involves the working within the unconscious of an agency so wholly in the pattern of the conscious as is the case with Freud's censorship. The concept is based on analogy with a highly complex and specialised social institution, the endo-psychic censorship being supposed to act in the same way as the official whose business it is to control the press and allow nothing to reach the community which in his opinion will disturb the harmony of its existence . . . it would be more satisfactory if the controlling agency which the facts need could be expressed in some other form. Since the process which has to be explained takes place within the region of unconscious experience, or at least on its confines, we might expect to find the appropriate mode of expression in a physiological rather than a sociological parallel. It is to physiology rather than to sociology that we should look for the clue to the nature of

[71] *The Psychoanalytic Review*, vii, No. 3 [1930]. Rivers receives three laudatory mentions in Jones's account of Freud's life and work, but there is no reference to this article (see Vol. iii).

the process by which a person is guarded from such elements of his unconscious experience as might disturb the harmony of his existence." Rivers then argued that neurological investigations had established that, "in so far as function is concerned," the nervous system "is arranged in a number of levels, one above another, forming a hierarchy in which each level controls those beneath it and is itself controlled by those above. If we assume a similar organisation of unconscious experience, we should have a number of levels in which experience belonging to adult life would occupy a position higher than that taken by the experience of youth, and this again would stand above the experience of childhood and infancy." If any level became active in sleep or in waking, it would retain the special characteristics appropriate to its type of experience. Hence he considered that the slips of tongue and pen and action, and the fantasies of dreams, which according to Freud were disguised forms of prohibited desires allowed to pass into consciousness by the censor, would be better seen as the re-emergence of earlier forms of activity and thought breaking through the layers of later experience when the individual was tired or under emotional stress.

Rivers's formulation may have been an advance in the detailed analysis of how the "censorship" functions physiologically. Yet it fails to take account of at least three important things on which Freud insisted. First, "in the id there is nothing corresponding to the idea of time, no recognition of the passage of time, and (a thing which is very remarkable and awaits adequate attention in philosophic thought) no alteration of mental processes by the passage of time. Conative impulses which have never got beyond the id, and even impressions which have been pushed down into the id by repression, are virtually immortal and are preserved for whole decades as though they had recently occurred." Second, Rivers neglected the selection and distortion which Freud argued occurred during dreams "under the influence of the censorship." Third, he overlooked Freud's view that "dream-censorship" was part of "the special criticising and forbidding function which we call the super-ego"—it was purposeful.[72] Rivers did not deal with these points in his essay. We suggest that Rivers here

[72] *New Introductory Lectures on Psycho-Analysis* [1933], pp. 99, 33, 42.

mistook the methodological procedure which Freud used in formulating his concept of the censorship, and the related concepts of ego, id and super-ego, on which the censorship depends. Rivers mistook Freud's deliberate naïvety (as we would call it) for abridgment. It does not follow that because endopsychical processes are involved, a physiological parallel is more satisfactory than a sociological parallel (and it might be argued that the essence of the "censorship" is that it is social). Rather, as Freud penetrated further into his research on the behaviour of neurotics, and as this led him to apply his findings to the "normal" personality, he left on one side the highly complex physiological problems in which he was well versed, and began to work with what was a naïve and simple, indeed metaphorical, view of the psyche, in using which view he neglected much work in physiology and neurology. (Of course this applies to the theory of psycho-analysis, not to Freud's clinical practice.) We suggest that if he had continued to try to embrace neurological processes in his study, he would never have been able to make his epoch-making contribution to the understanding of the human personality. He would instead have been perpetually held up by his involvement in a quite different set of problems, observations, experiments, and interpretations. This is indeed confirmed by the complex developments which have in fact taken place in neurology during the last half-century.

We have taken Freud's theory as an example, though it is in a field in which we are inexpert, because his poetic personification, when viewed in the light of his early ability as a neurologist, is the best case we know of a behavioural scientist simplifying phenomena to the point where he worked with "naïve" assumptions, though he was skilled in the internal complexity of those phenomena, so that he might proceed with analysis of the problems he considered important. And it follows therefore that on methodological grounds alone, we consider invalid any criticism of his theory based on the argument that his fundamental concepts to draw the anatomy of the personality are so naïve and metaphorical. It appears to us that Freud was here following a wise course, and that his wisdom, which should be taken as a model, establishes graphically two important rules:

1. *The Rule of Abstention*: "If we are to solve certain problems we have to abstain from studying other, though apparently related, problems, and leave these to our colleagues (whether in the same or in some other discipline)."

2. *The Rule of Accepted Naïvety*: "If we wish to progress in our research, we may have at some points to make assumptions which are naïve in that they pay no attention to the complexity which other disciplines have demonstrated to exist in other aspects of the facts we are studying."

As we stated in our summary introduction, a consequence of the rule of "accepted naïvety" is that there is a corresponding error in criticism of unjustified allegation of naïvety. We consider that Rivers commits this error when he tries to reformulate Freud's concept of the censorship in neurological terms, since he ends by not dealing with Freud's problems. This error among critics is balanced, on the side of the investigator, by the error of ignoring the limits of his own naïvety, which Freud might have committed had he drawn conclusions about neurological processes from his analysis. We consider that a psychoanalyst, who to solve his problems may be rightly naïve about social and cultural and economic interconnexions, commits this error if he moves from his work to interpretations of those interconnexions. Turner criticised Bettelheim for ignoring the limits of his naïvety in this way.

Ignoring the Limits of Naïvety: Freud

If one works with naïve assumptions, it is essential to remember, therefore, that one is able to analyse only those problems which fall within the limits of one's deliberately accepted abstention and naïvety. We consider that Freud ignored the limits imposed by his own naïvety about sociology and economics when he discussed the Bolshevik revolution in Russia, and other historical events. He judged that "sociology, which deals with the behaviour of men in society, can be nothing other than applied psychology. Strictly speaking, indeed, there are only two sciences—psychology, pure and applied, and natural science."[73]

---

[73] *New Introductory Lectures on Psycho-Analysis* [1933], Lecture xxxv, p. 229. For

Every prediction Freud made about the Russian Revolution has turned out to be wrong, and his discussion of the complex situation which he aimed to analyse was shallow in the extreme in the light of historical analyses. His *Totem and Tabu*,[74] in so far as it attempts to explain the origin of religion in historical terms, was described as a "Just-So story" by the great American anthropologist Kroeber, though he later felt it was significant if re-interpreted in terms of individual psychology. For we do not agree that sociology can ever be reduced to applied psychology: the dynamics of social life are quite different from those of individual life. But we must note with Fortes that Freud himself surrounded his thesis with careful qualifications, even if he did not always heed his own warnings.[75] Turner in his essay demonstrates how psycho-analysts ignore the limits of their naïvety if they attempt to "explain the origin" of rituals by reference to conflicts in the psyche, simply on the grounds that there are some similarities, which also attracted Freud's attention, between the religious and magical beliefs and rites of so-called primitive society and the compulsive actions and fantasies of neurotics.

We are arguing that while Freud and many of his followers acted as if they could largely ignore (what we call "be naïve about") neurological and some physiological processes, many of them did not recognise that they were equally "naïve" about social, cultural and economic processes, whose complexity they may not have recognised.[76] Had they been aware of their own naïvety in these fields of knowledge, and in others such as the complex history of Europe, they might have abstained from producing theories such as the one which explains the structure

[74] *Totem und Tabu* [1913].

[75] See M. Fortes, "Malinowski and the Study of Kinship," in *Man in Culture*, ed. R. Firth [1957], pp. 157 ff.

[76] Since they did not always discuss these methodological problems it is difficult sometimes to say how far they did this deliberately, or were aware of its implications. Psycho-analysts inevitably discuss somatic processes and socio-cultural facts in their clinical analyses; and the distinctive problems of logic involved appear then usually to be irrelevant to them. We do not state this as a criticism.

many similar references to Freud's error here, though it is not perceived as such, see Jones, *Sigmund Freud*, Vol. ii, pp. 240-4, 305, 328, 336, 380, 393-404, 415. See also E. Fromm, *The Fear of Freedom* [1942], for a similar kind of discussion.

of the Wehrmacht and the Germans' determined attempt to avoid battle on their own soil, by psychological analyses of individual Germans and the authoritarian structure of the German family dominated by the husband/father.[77] This stricture does not apply to all psycho-analysts.

We are not therefore arguing that psycho-analysts should become sociologists, social and cultural anthropologists, and historians, to give a new dimension to their interpretations. We do not believe that their theories can deal, even with sophisticated knowledge of other disciplines, with those kinds of facts and thus operate in other dimensions.[78] They should accept in

---

[77] We select this example at random, to illustrate how easy it is to step over the limits of naïvety, from H. V. Dicks, "Personality Traits and National Socialist Ideology," in *Human Relations*, III, No. 2 [1950], pp. 111-54. Dr Dicks made a psychiatric examination of a number of German prisoners-of-war. He makes careful safeguarding statements such as: "nothing in this paper must be taken to imply that the economic and historico-political forces are in any way under-rated by the writer" (p. 112), and "the temptation to enter fully into the relationship of German culture, institutions and character with the Nazi movement [will have to be] resisted" (p. 137). Nevertheless (p. 139) he concludes that "hierarchial pyramidal patterns for social institutions and the Army as the model and apex were created as the most appropriate to meet the needs of such a character structure" [worked out by psychological methods]. Again, "Germany took the utmost pains to keep the enemy at arm's length and away from the homeland. This would seem to be an effort at warding off assault and castration fears from the self" (p. 142). We do not criticise Dicks's psychological analysis, save to suggest that he might have divided his subjects by age to see if those who grew up under Nazi power were influenced differently from older Germans. But we note similar attempts to account for Soviet history and institutions in psychological terms in Dicks' "Observations on Contemporary Behaviour," in *Human Relations*, V, No. 2 (1952), pp. 111-75.

[78] It is impossible to enter fully, in terms of our methodological problems, into later developments in theories of the personality which attempt to take greater account of social factors, such as those of A. Adler, H. A. Murray, H. S. Sullivan, K. Horney, or E. Fromm, or into the "field-theory" of K. Lewin (see Hall and Lindzey, *Theories of Personality*). The most elaborate of these theories in many ways is that of H. A. Murray, with his multiple classification of needs and of social "press." In the theory, if not the practice, all the "press" are what we would call "incorporated" (cp. Freudian "introjected") elements from the social environment with no deep analysis of the relations between the elements (H. A. Murray and others, *Explorations in Personality* [1938]). This appears also in C. Kluckhohn and H. A. Murray, *Personality in Nature, Society and Culture* [1949]. The argument that an individual's behaviour is a "product" of biological, psychological, and various kinds of social forces, as well as of a history full of accidents, does not solve the problem of isolating systems for analysis. Freud operated with introjection and other mechanisms by which social facts are internalised in the psychical system: Homans in effect thus internalises elements of the external system in the small-group system. None of the theories of the scholars cited at the beginning of this footnote solve the problem: Is it possible to analyse systems of physiological,

every respect the consequences of their abstention and the limits of their naïvety. Correspondingly, we do not consider that it is valid to criticise the psycho-analytic theory because, as is sometimes said, Freud's clinical experience was among *bourgeois*, largely Jewish, Viennese.[79] He was studying how individual personalities were formed, on a biophysical basis, from infancy into adulthood, and how adult personalities functioned.[80] He could take the social relationships and the cultural patterns within which these individuals lived as "given": *i.e.*, he could simplify, indeed over-simplify, them, and be naïve about them, as they were introduced into the psychical system. Whether his theory is valid for the individual personality in all societies and varied cultural patterns must be decided on the basis of data of the same type as he collected from his patients in Austria—data on errors in behaviour, on dreams, on neuroses, and so on. But if psycho-analysts are justified in claiming the right to be naïve about the social and cultural aspects of life, and in demanding that their own theories should be tested by appropriate and equivalent data, they should conversely have accepted that their own naïvety sets limits on their capacity to make statements about society and culture. Anyone who makes naïve assumptions about certain types of relations in a field of complex events is thereby precluded from producing theories of any value to explain those relations. This caution Freud and some of his followers did not always observe.

An investigator's naïve assumptions thus set limits to the kind of analysis he can hope to make and, therefore, to the kind of questions to which he can hope to give answers. These questions are necessarily limited: the problem of how a "complete" explanation of reality is achieved lies outside our brief.

---

[79] We have frequently heard this stated, but not found it in print, save for a rather differently slanted statement by B. Malinowski in *Sex and Repression in Savage Society* [1927], p. 15.

[80] We are not of course competent to assess its general validity, or its strengths and weaknesses. We are using it to illustrate the general methodological problem, since it is a type of theory that has been important for anthropology.

---

psychological, and social relations simultaneously in terms of the same concepts? Our comment does not touch on problems of handling individuals in the context of social fields (see Homans, *The Human Group*, for one demonstration of how this should be done, as well as K. Lewin, *Field Theory in Social Science*).

The Importance of Clarifying the Limits of Naïvety:
Malinowski and the Freudian Theory

Unless different scientists who are involved in any such situations are clear about the limits of one another's naïvety, disputes are only too apt to arise. The fruitlessness of these disputes can best be illustrated by reference to Ernest Jones's well-known controversy with Malinowski concerning his criticism of the Freudian theory of the Oedipus complex. This controversy still persists in anthropology and psychology, and has therefore to be considered.[81]

Malinowski showed that in the Trobriands the role of authority, and of the main provider of material necessities and inheritance, was taken by the mother's brother, and not by the father, as with Freud's patients. He showed further that in this situation myths and beliefs emphasised antagonism between mother's brother and sister's son, and not antagonism between father and son. This also appeared in Trobriand dreams, and many other aspects of Trobriand life. Hence, he argued, Freud's theory of the Oedipus complex could not be applied to the Trobriand Islanders, and that it was applicable only to "the Aryan, patriarchal society." We have not space to set out the intricacies of Malinowski's careful documentation of his argument, or of Jones's criticism of it. What is relevant here is that Jones argued that in the Trobriands the boy's initial hostility and hatred of his father, emotions arising from jealousy of the father's access to his mother, were later "displaced" on to the authoritative figure of the mother's brother. He also went further, and argued that Trobriand ignorance of the rôle of semen in impregnation was "repudiation of the father's part in coitus and procreation, and consequently softening and deflection of the hatred against him." Thus there was a "decomposition of the primal father into a kind and lenient actual father on the one hand and a stern and moral uncle on the other." As Malinowski put Jones's argument (p. 138), "the

---

[81] Malinowski, *Sex and Repression in Savage Society, passim*; Ernest Jones, "Mother-right and the Sexual Ignorance of Savages," in *International Journal of Psycho-Analysis*, VI, No. 2 [1925], criticising two preliminary articles of Malinowski (for references see Malinowski, *op. cit.*, p. 136). For an illuminating discussion of the controversy see M. Fortes, "Malinowski and the Study of Kinship," in *Man and Culture*, ed. R. Firth, pp. 157 f.

combination of mother-right and ignorance [of the physiology of impregnation] protects both father and son from their maternal rivalry and hostility. For Dr Jones, then, the Oedipus complex is fundamental; and the 'matrilineal system with its avunculate complex arose . . . as a mode of defence against the primordial[82] Oedipus tendencies.' " Malinoswki accepted the hypothesis that hatred was deflected from father on to maternal uncle as "a daring and original extension" of his own conclusions, "that in mother-right the family complex must be different from the Oedipus complex; that in the matrilineal conditions the hate is removed from the father and placed upon the maternal uncle; that any incestuous temptations are directed towards the sister rather than towards the mother" (p. 139). But he still denied that the Oedipus complex would be found in matrilineal societies; and he argued cogently—in the terms that Turner has followed—against the thesis that matriliny evolved as a protective device against the hatred involved in the Oedipus complex, which he said Jones regarded as "the *cause*, and the whole sociological structure as the *effect*."

Clearly the protagonists in this controversy are at cross-purposes, and it illustrates well the great difficulties that arise in the borderland between different disciplines. Malinowski accepts the thesis of displacement of hostility from father to maternal uncle, but he does not seem to be clear about how this displacement occurs. Malinowski had misunderstood the main implications of this part of the Freudian theory, and he did not realise precisely what kind of data would be required to test it. For he was dealing with cultural data in myths and folk-tales, reflecting Trobriand rules of authority and succession, and with "the manifest contents" rather than "the latent thoughts" of dreams. According to the Freudian theory, the Oedipus complex is effectively established in infancy and early childhood; and as Malinowski himself described,[83] at this period of his life a boy associates with his mother and father (or a later husband of his mother after divorce or widow-

---

[82] The reference is to the original parricide depicted in Freud's *Totem und Tabu*.

[83] *The Sexual Life of Savages* [1929], *passim*. On this discussion see M. Fortes, "Malinowski and the Study of Kinship," in *Man and Culture*, ed. R. Firth, pp. 170-1.

hood), and not at all with his mother's brother. Indeed, during his infancy it is difficult for him to have any close relationship with his mother's brother, who is under taboo not to approach his sister, the boy's mother. On the other hand, the father sleeps with the mother, apparently in the same hut as the child, and he is "considered to be the master for he is in his own village and the house belongs to him."[84] He helps with the nursing and disciplining of the boy, not only petting and fondling him but also cleaning, washing, and feeding him.[85] We have quoted enough to show that, if there is anything in Freud's theory of the development of the Oedipus complex, it might be expected to develop among Trobriand boys. At that stage of his life, the boy is not likely to be aware of how dominant a role his mother's brother will play in his life and career, and surely an infant or even a young boy cannot understand the significance of rules of succession, inheritance, and ultimate authority, though these may induce the father to take a gentle role and try to win the boy to him.[86] Malinowski himself thus describes clearly the situation in which the Oedipus complex is said by Freudians to arise. Indeed, as he skips over the details of how the child is handled, and does not even explicitly state where the child is when its mother has intercourse with its father (facts which are crucial in the Freudian theory), he is overstepping the limits imposed by his own competence and its techniques when he uses his data to deny the development of the complex among Trobriand males.

Jones's hypothesis that, within the triangle of parents and child, hostility was engendered in the unconscious of the boy against his father, may therefore be psychologically correct: Malinowski gave no data by which this could be validated, and it lay outside his competence. But when Jones, on the basis of this ontogenetic hypothesis, erects a phylogenetic hypothesis of the origin of matriliny, he ignores the limits of his naïvety: his theory cannot deal with Malinowski's problems[87] (the

[84] *The Sexual Life of Savages*, p. 14.

[85] *Op. cit.*, p. 16.

[86] This kind of fatherly gentleness does not necessarily distinguish matrilineal from patrilineal societies: cp. R. Firth, *We, the Tikopia* [1936], pp. 138 f., and M. Fortes, *The Web of Kinship among the Tallensi*, pp. 187 f.

[87] The imperviousness to mutual understanding which develops through failure to appreciate this fact is shown by the following passage in Jones on *Sigmund*

relations between myths and dreams and ritual and social relationships among Trobriand Islanders) any more than Malinowski's theory and data can deal with psycho-analytic problems.[88] Both had ignored what we call "the rule of disciplined refusal to trespass" on each other's fields, and in result they could not meet in discussion. Only awareness of one's own naïvety, and hence of its limits, can produce mutual respect for specialised competence.

We may further ask, would it made any difference to Malinowski's analysis of Trobriand domestic and interpersonal life, of myth and cultural interpretation of dreams, whether or not Jones's thesis that hostility is displaced from father on to maternal uncle is correct? The answer must be, as always, that it may or may not, depending on the problem set. For, as Turner argues in the context of his article, "the *precise sources* of unconscious feeling and wishing" may be irrelevant to the social anthropologist. "He is interested in the fact that emotion is evoked and not in the specific quality of its constituents. He may indeed find it situationally relevant for his analysis to distinguish whether the emotion evoked by a specific symbol possesses the gross character, say, of aggression, fear, friendliness, anxiety, or sexual pleasure. But he need go no further than this" (above, p. 39). It was irrelevant for Malinowski's sociological analysis if the sources of the patent hostility directed by a young Trobriander against his mother's brother lay in the Oedipus complex, with its early resentment against the father: it was sufficient to note that there is hostility against the mother's brother, and that it is standardised in myth and belief and story, while the pattern of relations between father and son is loving and indulgent in later life, even though the father reared and trained the boy, a process which must have

[88] For the complexity of factors surrounding matriliny, see *Matrilineal Kinship*, edd. D. M. Schneider and K. Gough [1961].

Freud, Vol. II, p. 404: "Freud was right in his prediction that the book [*Totem und Tabu*] would be badly received. Outside analytical circles it met with complete disbelief as one more personal phantasy of Freud's. Anthropologists united in discounting his conclusions and in maintaining that he had misunderstood the evidence. I [Jones, writing just before 1955] have, however, not come across any of their criticisms that contained serious arguments; mere expressions of disbelief to them seemed as adequate as similar expression seemed to psychologists when Freud published his *Interpretation of Dreams*."

involved some early disciplining. Fortes has argued that, while Malinowski's study of kinship was greatly stimulated by Freud, his failure to distinguish between the two fields of study prevented him from developing a systematic sociological theory of kinship;[89] and Singh Uberoi has shown that Malinowski's attempt to relate his analysis of the triangle of father, young man, mother's brother, to psychological problems seriously distorted his sociological analysis of kinship and political relations.[90]

In contrast to Malinowski, Turner's essay demonstrates the irrelevance of psycho-analytical theory for at least one anthropological analysis of ritual symbols, since it makes no difference to Turner which of different psycho-analytical theories is correct. As he considers himself "hapless" in attempting to consider theories, it is fortunate that they are thus irrelevant. He rightly abstains from trespassing on the field of psychoanalysis, and he deliberately and explicitly, after carefully considering the position, abstains from becoming involved in the structure of the human personality, though he knows that the full study of ritual symbols raises many problems in this field. His psychology is naïve: and even if it is informedly naïve, in that he has sharpened his mind by seeing if he need use psycho-analytic doctrine, most of the concepts he uses were part of commonsense knowledge of men about one another. The results show that he was wise to proceed in this manner.

Naïvety: Studies of Witchcraft

We have already alluded to the enthusiasm that is engendered by the feeling that one is solving vast problems, and the danger that being restricted within the limits of one's competence may prevent one from pursuing new discoveries. It is likely that this enthusiasm led Freud to generalise inadequately about social problems on the basis of his psychological studies, but nevertheless inspired him in those latter

[89] "Malinowski and the Study of Kinship," in *Man and Culture*, ed. R. Firth, *passim*.

[90] J. P. Singh Uberoi, *Politics of the Kula Ring* [1962]. For a similar corrective to this type of error in Malinowski's analyses, see E. R. Leach, "Concerning Trobriand Clans and the Kinship Category *Tabu*," in *The Development Cycle of Domestic Groups*, ed. J. Goody [1958].

studies. He obviously felt he was working on an insight and a technique that would solve major problems of mankind. Correspondingly, Malinowski was inspired to feel that his study of the Trobriand matrilineal system of succession contributed substantial amendments to Freud's startling theory. Without this inspiration he might not have been emboldened to write either *The Father in Primitive Psychology*,[91] or *Sex and Repression in Savage Society*,[92] which are both books of great importance in anthropology, as Fortes has shown.[93] They also contributed to the development of psycho-analysis, in that they influenced anthropologists who in turn directed the attention of depth-pyschologists to the importance of socio-cultural factors. Confusion and mistake may not prevent, and may occasionally advance, scientific understanding. Yet it remains doubtful whether the same advances could not have been made without the confusion and the mistake, and perhaps more quickly.[94] Fortes and Talcott Parsons have shown how Malinowski's unwarranted trespass into psychological fields prevented him from advancing his analysis of kinship systems in particular, and of social systems generally.[95] When he tried to produce a general theory of culture, he ended with a not very skilled, or illuminating, kind of behaviourism.[96]

We ourselves believe—and this must be a matter of judgment—that confusion of this kind, arising from undisciplined trespass on fields one is not competent to traverse, in the end produces more obscurity than it does creative inspiration. Freud stirred up misplaced hostility to, and futile controversy about, his psychological insight, by his statements on historical problems, and this is not only among Marxists.[97] Malinowski was inspired to write two important studies by his drive to test Freud's hypotheses, but he stultified the develop-

[91] Psyche Miniatures, London 1927.

[92] London 1927.

[93] In *Man and Culture*, ed. R. Firth.

[94] *E.g.*, M. Polanyi, *Personal Knowledge* [1958], pp. 107 f.; and pp. 308 ff., on "commitment."

[95] Fortes, "Malinowski and the Study of Kinship," and Parsons, "Malinowski and the Theory of Social Systems," both in *Man and Culture*, ed. R. Firth.

[96] See M. Gluckman, *The Sociological Theories of Bronislaw Malinowski* [1948]; reprinted in *Order and Rebellion in Tribal Africa* [1963].

[97] For a typical Marxist criticism of Freud see C. Caudwell, *Studies in a Dying Culture* [1938]. R. Osborn attempted to reconcile *Freud and Marx* [1937].

Q

ment of his own ideas, and left a legacy of barren argument to
anthropology and to psycho-analysis—though Jones does not
mention Malinowski's criticisms in his biography of Freud.
Hence we ourselves incline towards insisting on recognising
the limits of one's own competence, even if this means one must
accept that one produces limited answers to limited problems.
Otherwise one is liable either to remain in confusion and to
lose the opportunity to develop, or one is liable to produce
sweeping and unsubstantiated, though plausible, explanations.
We propose to illustrate these dangers by contrasting the
"psycho-analytical" explanation which Kluckhohn produced
of *Navaho Witchcraft*[98] with the less sweeping, but much more
penetrating, analysis by Evans-Pritchard of *Witchcraft, Oracles
and Magic among the Azande of the Anglo-Egyptian Sudan.*[99]

In view of the published summaries of Evans-Pritchard's
analysis, we can state this briefly. He eschews all psychological
interpretation of witchcraft. He analyses how the Azande
perceive fully the empirical causes of the misfortunes that befall
them, but they explain "why" a particular man suffers a
particular misfortune at a particular time and place by ascrib-
ing it to the malevolence of a witch. Beliefs in witchcraft thus
are used to explain the particularity of misfortunes. The
sufferer seeks the responsible witch by putting the names of
those whom he considers to be his personal enemies to oracular
devices or persons. He seeks the witch among his enemies
because the Azande believe that, though witchcraft is a constitutional, inherited quality, its evil "soul" is set to work by
anti-social feelings like envy, spite, jealousy, anger, and hatred.
A man may have witchcraft in him, but if he does not have
these feelings, the witchcraft remains "cool" and harms no one.
Witchcraft beliefs thus contain a philosophy of morality, as
well as a theory of "causation," and this involves the beliefs in
the total system of social control.

[98] Papers of the Peabody Museum [1944].

[99] Evans-Pritchard's analysis [1937] and some later work based on that
analysis have been summarised in Gluckman, "The Logic of African Science and
Witchcraft," in *Rhodes-Livingstone Journal*, I [1944], which has been published in
some American *Readers* in Anthropology, and "Social Beliefs and Individual
Thinking in Primitive Society," in *Transactions of the Manchester Literary and Philosophical Society*, XCI [1949-50], and finally in Ch. IV of *Custom and Conflict in Africa*
[1958].

Evans-Pritchard shows that when a man accuses a personal enemy of harming him, he is not "cheating," but is acting by a logic arising from a system of beliefs and from a system of social relationships. He states that witchcraft accusations are not made within the Azande vengeance-group of agnates, since witchcraft is inherited within this group. Accusations are made against other neighbours with whom a man has relations provoking the anti-social feelings, but accusations are also excluded against social superiors. He discusses the manner in which a man charges another with witchcraft, and how the accused reacts. He has a full analysis of how oracles and witch-doctors operate, and he shows how magical procedures to protect a man against witchcraft or to punish a witch close the circle. In the course of this analysis, Evans-Pritchard considers the relation of witchcraft to other types of mystical causes of misfortunes while all these causes are excluded as explanations of moral misdemeanours. He considers also how individuals operate the system of beliefs, and how the system itself is so constructed that it appears to accord with reality and is insulated against apparently contradicting evidence by secondary elaborations of belief and the limited perspective which any one man has on the setting of witchcraft accusations and magical operations.

Evans-Pritchard's analysis of how Azande beliefs in witchcraft, oracles and magic operate as a self-sealing and self-supporting system is so acute that Polanyi used it as a model to examine "the stability of beliefs" in science.[100]

Evans-Pritchard's study has been taken over substantially by all later British investigators of the problem. They have assumed a large part of his analysis, and have then proceeded to investigate more fully a new range of problems, which fall directly within the field of social relations: who is and who is not accused of witchcraft in relation to the ascription of misfortune to other mystical agents, and how the incidence of accusations in a particular society is related to other constituents of the social system.[101] This brief series of references

[100] *Personal Knowledge*, pp. 287-94, 318.
[101] *E.g.*, by E. J. and J. D. Krige, *The Realm of a Rain-Queen: The Pattern of Lovedu Society* [1943]; M. G. Marwick, "The Social Context of Cewa Witchcraft Beliefs," in *Africa*, XXII [1952]; P. Mayer, *Witchcraft* [1954]; J. Middleton, *Lugbara Religion* [1960]; J. C. Mitchell, *The Yao Village* [1957]; S. F. Nadel, *Nupe Religion* [1954], and "Witchcraft in Four African Societies: An Essay in Comparison," in

shows how the problems set by Evans-Pritchard have been fruitful in stimulating both further observation and analysis, and how his solutions have been applied in other fields of social life.

Though Evans-Pritchard is concerned with acts of perception, with modes of thought, and with ostensible and alleged feelings, these are always examined in their relations within a social system. The acts and feelings of individuals are facts which can be examined in relation both to events in social systems and in individual psychical systems; and their value differs accordingly. For example, Evans-Pritchard shows that it is irrelevant whether in practice an accused witch felt the alleged envy or hatred: when he is accused, he must act as if he did, blowing water over the wing of a chicken which died when his name was put to the oracle—"poison" administered to the chicken. He does this while stating that if it was his witchcraft which injured the sufferer, he was ignorant of this, and by his conciliatory gesture he "cools" his witchcraft. He has to do this whether or not he credits the accusation: if he refuses, this refusal itself will demonstrate his malice. Hence Evans-Pritchard's analysis on this point does not involve him in making a judgment on the precise internal emotions of individuals; he can content himself with saying what their actions, and their stated feelings, are, and these observations are clearly within the competence of a social anthropologist. This point is emphasised when he discusses situations in which a man accuses as a witch not a man who hates him, but someone whom he hates, a situation of which the Azande are fully aware.[102] Evans-Pritchard is able to discuss this type of accusation without concerning himself with whether this has to be interpreted in terms of the psychological mechanism of "projection," which it would require depth-analysis to establish.[103] Throughout his book, he abstained from trespassing into another

[102] Cp. Gluckman's citation of how clearly a Zulu diviner saw this kind of process to be operating, in *Custom and Conflict in Africa*, pp. 89-90.

[103] Cp. M. Fortes's abstention from psychological speculation in his treatment of animal taboos, in *The Dynamics of Clanship among the Tallensi*, p. 142.

American Anthropologist, LIV [1952]; V. W. Turner, *Schism and Continuity in an African Society* [1959]; M. Wilson, "Witch Beliefs and Social Structure," *American Journal of Sociology*, LVI [1951]. There is a general discussion both of these problems, and of variations in belief, in Gluckman, *Custom and Conflict in Africa*, Ch. IV.

discipline, but nevertheless he was able to go on to fruitful investigation of many problems, and stimulate others to further enquiry.

What a man actually feels—in all its complexity—both when he accuses a particular person of bewitching him, or when he is thus accused of bewitching another, is on the other hand essential to a psychological analysis. This problem is central to Kluckhohn's attempt at a social-psychological analysis of Navaho witchcraft, though he had no data indicating the precise nature of men's feelings; and we shall argue that though his discussion is plausible, it is completely unsubstantiated. More than this, it fails to account for most of the quite different kind of data which he himself cites.[104]

Kluckhohn describes four kinds of "witchcraft" in which the Navaho believe, including beliefs in were-animals. He also describes protective devices against witchcraft, and observed behaviour of Navaho relating to witchcraft. He carefully cites his evidence—and gives texts and descriptions in full appendices —before interpreting this evidence. He distinguishes between the "manifest" and the "latent" functions[105] of witchcraft for individual Navaho; and his list of "latent" functions contains his main argument (p. 48):

1. The individual can capitalise on the credence of his fellows to gain the centre of the stage for himself.

2. Witchcraft lore allows expression for the culturally disallowed, so that incestuous and necrophilic wishes can be described in fantasies of how witches behave, while the lore disapproves of these alleged practices; therefore a witchcraft tale involving alleged occurrences of incest and necrophilia through "the psychological mechanisms of identification or projection" allows an "outlet in phantasy without conflict."

3. "Quantitatively more significant as adjustive responses are the ways in which witchcraft beliefs and practices

[104] Marwick ("The Social Context of Cewa Witch Beliefs") summarises Kluckhohn's analysis, among others, without, it seems to us, considering at all the problem of substantiating data for social-psychological analysis.

[105] Following the well-known distinction made by R. Merton in *Social Theory and Social Structure* [1949], pp. 19 f.

allow the expression of direct and displaced aggression . . .: the objectification and alleviation of displaced
anxieties arising from the general situation of the Navaho
or from the particular situation of a particular Navaho at
a particular time."

This third latent function is the one on which Kluckhohn lays
most emphasis.

Kluckhohn describes the hazards of life for the Navaho in
general and for particular Navaho: they live under constant
threat of environmental and economic misfortunes. Stress is
accentuated by the impact of Whites on their culture. With
their inability to cope with all these hazards, their fears are
converted to anxieties. The hostility and aggression involved
are projected on to ghosts and witches, a projection which
Kluckhohn places in the more general category of "scapegoat
patterns." Some Navaho aggression is turned against the self
in hypochondria, in alcoholism, and in peyotism, and there may
also be withdrawal from one's fellows. Passivity is marked.
When two Navaho quarrel, conciliation is attempted, but it
has limited utility.

All these mechanisms are insufficient to enable Navaho to
cope with their aggression. This is because the "consumption
units" in which Navaho dwell enforce co-operation in geo-
graphically "isolated" settings (the isolation ranges from one
to ten miles). Contact with "outsiders" to whom to "let off
steam about grudges, suspicions, and jealousies" is limited.
People tend to be involved "in a morbid nexus of emotional
sensitivities from which there is little escape through socially
approved patterns." Drinking can lead to fights: most of those
recorded are of husbands against wives; sons-in-law against
fathers-in-law; between brothers, own and classificatory; and
uterine nephew against own maternal uncle (the Navaho are
matrilineal and often uxorilocal). American authority has
prevented the displacement of aggression in warfare, which
was important in the indigenous culture pattern. In this
situation, the aggression which is felt (*e.g.*, against a stingy
father-in-law) but which cannot be expressed directly for fear
of economic reprisals and social disapproval, is displaced
"against a totally unrelated witch in the community." Accord-

ing to Kluckhohn, "This displaced aggression does not expose one to punishment so long as one is discreet in the choice of intimates to whom one talks. And if one rages against a witch who isn't even in the locality but lives over the mountain a safe hundred miles away one is perfectly assured against reprisals.

"The fact that a high proportion of witchcraft gossip refers to *distant* witches makes Navaho witchcraft much more adaptive than most patterns which centre witch activity within the group" (p. 55).

But Kluckhohn adds that in "some circumstances, witchcraft provides a means for attack upon the actual targets of my personal feelings"—as when, for example, a singer ascribes his rival's greater success to witchcraft, or when a jealous husband explains the fact that his wife has been unfaithful to him by alleging that her lover has used "frenzy witchcraft."

There are similar discussions of how witchcraft handles the anxiety problem and acts as a technique of social control, some of them in similar strain: but enough has been cited to show how Kluckhohn's analysis runs.

All this analysis is plausible, once the psychological mechanisms of displacement, identification, projection, aggression release, are assumed. But one would have expected that Kluckhohn would cite some data to show that these mechanisms are operating, and are in some sense effective. In fact he cites none at all. The appendices contain no material which gives any indication of the working of the Navaho unconscious psyche in relation to conscious action. Against Kluckhohn's whole argument, out of a total of "222 cases of persons accused of witchcraft where some other information was available . . .," in 103 cases persons accused, or repeated accusations against, their own relatives. Of these, 14 were directed against a maternal uncle, and 81 against affinal relatives, mostly sons-in-law against father-in-law (p. 34). Some of the others, judging by cases cited, were against close neighbours[106]. And we should note that to become a witch a person is believed to have to kill a full sibling, and commit incest with a full sibling. Gossip may be against distant Navaho: accusations are often against those with whom people are closely involved.

[106] Cp. how D. F. Aberle draws attention to these cases in *Matrilineal Kinship*, edd. Schneider and Gough, pp. 117 and 170.

The allegations in "gossip" of the intensive practice of witchcraft are made against two Navaho groups which are "in some sense aliens." One of these groups has a large admixture of Pueblo Indians. The other is a group of "Navaho who are not quite Navaho," since its members were partially missionised by the Spanish during the eighteenth century. In the wars between Navaho and Spanish, "this group of Navaho often aided the Spanish. Hence, they are commonly referred to by reservation Navaho as 'enemy people,' and expressions of hostility towards them are not infrequent." Kluckhohn suggests other Navaho may believe that these people got witchcraft from the powerful Spanish: and he states that "finally, the fact that Navaho witches who were expelled from their own communities took refuge among . . . [this] group has doubtless intensified the conviction that witches were especially to be dreaded in this region" (pp. 43-4). The belief that foreigners are supernaturally powerful is common enough; and hostility against renegades and heretics, and the ascription of incest and other sexual sins as well as horrible murder to them, are intelligible on principles stated by Simmel and Coser.[107]

Kluckhohn does not attempt to reconcile his theory of displaced aggression with the actual incidence of accusations against relatives: he could, of course, argue that the displacement of aggression is not always effective. He does not consider other types of accusation. He does not consider the difference between gossip against distant witches, and actual accusations which are made against specific persons. He does not consider the different rôles of gossip against distant witches and of gossip against relatives. He does not relate modes of treatment to diagnoses of treatment in terms of the people involved in the treatment. An anthropologist as acute as Kluckhohn necessarily says many penetrating things. Yet because he has tried to make a psycho-analytic interpretation of Navaho witchcraft beliefs, and behaviour in relation to those beliefs, he failed to take full account of the data he had collected so well at the conscious level, while he has not the data to substantiate his thesis that aggression is displaced in the gossip about witchcraft

---

[107] G. Simmel, *Conflict and the Web of Group Affiliations*, trans. K. H. Wolff and R. Bendix [1955], pp. 43 *f*; and L. A. Coser, *The Functions of Social Conflict* [1956], pp. 67 f.

from inside the consumption unit on to outsiders. We suggest that an interpretation of this kind should attempt to analyse the emotional and intellectual life of a Navaho who operates with such a system of beliefs. It may well be that witchcraft beliefs create anxiety—as indeed Kluckhon shows in describing how children are taught to be anxious about how they dispose of their faeces—and that this anxiety is periodically discharged both in gossip and in accusations. This anxiety and its discharge may involve suppressed aggression arising from relations in the consumption unit, and also the anxiety created by the hazards of life in a hard environment. The emotional life of a man believing in witchcraft may consist of a wave-like surge and fall of anxiety, and in this be different from the emotional life of a man reared in a society which does not have such beliefs. These appear to us to be the sort of problems that are proper for psycho-analytic investigation; and clearly they require the same sort of data to be collected as psycho-analysts have collected on European patients.[108]

Despite its plausibility, Kluckhohn's main thesis adds little to our understanding of either Navaho social or Navaho individual life, and as it applies psycho-analytic theories mechanically and without the appropriate data, it can add little to psycho-analytic theory. Hence his study well illustrates the danger, and the sterility, of incompetent trespass into the field of another discipline, particularly when its results are compared with the fruitful results of Evans-Pritchard's disciplined refusal to trespass thus.

By contrast, anthropologists who have followed Evans-Pritchard's line of analysis, on the whole have avoided becoming involved in psychological interpretations without appropriate data. For example, Marwick carefully separates the two kinds of interpretation, and poses a purely sociological hypothesis: ". . . (*a*) competition will tend to occur between persons in a social relation if their relative statuses are not

---

[108] For an example, see W. Sachs, *Black Anger* [1947], who knew little of Shona society, but was able to give us a study of a Shona individual. G. Devereux had this background knowledge for his *Reality and Dream: Psychotherapy of a Plains Indian* [1951]; D. F. Aberle for *The Psychosocial Analysis of a Hopi Life History* [1951]; G. P. Stead for "Notes on Approach to the Study of Personality Formation in a Hindu Village in Gujerat," in *Village India*, ed. M. Marriott [1955]; and G. M. Carstairs for *The Twice-Born* [1957].

ascribed by the social structure, and . . . this competition will develop into tension and conflict if (i) the desire for the object or status competed for is intense and-or (ii) social structure does not eliminate or regulate the competition; and (*b*) . . . this tension will tend to be projected into witch beliefs and subsequent conflict if there are no other adequate institutionalised outlets for it."[109] It is unfortunate that he used the word "projected," which has acquired psycho-analytical connotations, even though it is a word in everyday use. Any implication that he is discussing unconscious psychical processes could have been avoided by saying "expressed" instead of "projected." However, he proceeds to discuss the conditions and social contexts in which competition is aggravated into conflict, so that believers can no longer apply the rationality of judicial procedures to their disputes and struggles, but invoke divination to validate accusations of witchcraft which facilitate and justify[110] the rupturing of valued social relationships. By posing a social-anthropological problem, Marwick is able to make a considerable advance on parts of Evans-Pritchard's analysis: he adds to our understanding of witchcraft as a social phenomenon, to our insight into situations of conflict in general, and to our study of various mechanisms of social redress. In total, he makes a substantial contribution to the general theory of social anthropology.

Turner advances this theory even further, in his fuller analysis of the role of judicial action, ritual practices, and accusations of witchcraft in the "on-going" process of Ndembu life. He concludes: "judicial mechanisms tend to be invoked to redress conflict, where the conflict is overt, and these judicial mechanisms involve rational investigation into the motives and behaviour of the contending parties. Ritual mechanisms tend to be utilised at a deeper level. Here conflict expressed itself through projection—that is, in the collective association of misfortune with ill-feeling and the working of mystical beings and forces, with dreams, and with answers to divination. The conflict is between norm and impulse in each individual member of the group, but since in a tightly-knit group similar

    [109] Marwick, "The Social Context of Cewa Witch Beliefs," in *Africa*, xxii [1952].
    [110] Points well made by J. C. Mitchell in *The Yao Village* [1957].

impulses assail common norms in situations which embrace the whole of its membership, this conflict attains recognition through repetition down the years, and ultimately cultural techniques are devised to handle it. It appears to the members of the society as though mysterious forces are attacking the very foundations of the moral and social order, not from within, but by projection from without, in the form of witches, spirits and mystical powers which penetrate individual members or some representative individual in the group in the form of dreams, illness, infertility, madness, etc."[111] The use of the word "projected" is again unfortunate, even more so than in Marwick's statement, for it appears to lead Turner through the word "devised" into appearing to explain the origin of practices and beliefs by a conflict which is not clearly located anywhere, the error for which he criticised Bettelheim in his essay above. This distracts attention from the otherwise clear sociological statement that ritual mechanisms are invoked when the occurrence of illness or other misfortune is ascribed to mysterious forces and to disturbances in social relationships, so that judicial mechanisms are not applicable. These disturbances in social relationships, he states elsewhere, arise from situations where there is conflict between two or more valued social principles,[112] so that rational enquiry cannot adjust the disturbances. The desire of individuals to "assail common norms" must be seen in terms of this situation, and not in psychological terms, if the analysis is to stand.

Nadel also becomes involved in sterile guessing when his explanation of Nupe beliefs that women are the evil witches shifts from an analysis of overt behaviour to an interpretation in terms of unconscious motivations. He argues: "It is, I think, true to say that man surrenders to woman his virility in the sex-act and his independence and self-containedness in the love relationship; the fulfilment of his desires is thus bought with the sacrifice of Ego-completeness. If we take this sacrifice to be unconsciously hateful, as I think we must, and accept this ambivalence of love-hatred as the source of an inescapable

---

[111] *Schism and Continuity in an African Society* [1958], pp. 126 f. Turner also uses the word "projection," but not in a psychological sense. See also on this whole problem, Gluckman, *Custom and Conflict in Africa*, p. 98, and "African Jurisprudence," pp. 12-13.

[112] Cp. the formulation of Marwick's above, in terms of lack of clear ascription.

antagonism having no normal or legitimate outlet, then the belief in female witches (of the Nupe or any other people) represents a 'displacement' and licensed expression of the repressed hatred. Different cultures fashion the normal social relationship between the sexes in widely diverse ways, as has been amply demonstrated in the work of Margaret Mead. But few societies can by this means resolve the conflict of sex antagonism. If the society makes the men the socially dominant sex, it is able to compensate for the surrender of virility but fails to express the importance of woman as sexual partner and procreatrix, and hence invites male fears of female revenge; and if the social dominance of men is reduced, whether by design (as in some societies) or in consequence of uncontrollable social processes (as in Nupe),[113] this produces the kind of situation we have been discussing. There is some evidence that a carefully balanced relationship between the sexes can avoid this impasse. But where it does not, the psychological mechanism of projection, with its offer of vicarious or fantasy hatreds, comes into play." Nupe men, Nadel goes on to say, fear that too much sexual intercourse is weakening, and they comment on the sexual voraciousness of women. Women, unlike men, are known to practise homosexuality: hence (Nadel says) woman is "more 'complete' in herself than the man and her sex less vulnerable; above all her satisfaction, more insatiable than the man's, threatens his virility. . . ." He argues that all this appears, appropriately rephrased, in Nupe witchcraft fantasies: "Witches feed on the life and strength of a man, as women do on his virility; and his anxieties are allayed or compensated in a wish-fulfilment which sees the female witch incomplete, possessed only of half her power without a help she must beg of men [witches] if she is to kill."

But ". . . admittedly," Nadel continues, "the witchcraft legends fail to corroborate this view, containing nothing that could be construed into a reference to the sexual dominance of women. Rather the contrary . . ."[114] In other words, Nadel

---

[113] Nadel examines the operation of these processes against social norms in his sociological analysis of the belief that evil witches are female. Note how this general thesis here agrees with Turner's and Marwick's and Gluckman's analyses.

[114] Nadel, *Nupe Religion* [1954], pp. 180-1. Antagonism between the sexes can be handled in its significance within the social system, as Nadel does in passages

finds that on this part of his thesis the evidence he collected from observation and statement of Nupe contradicted a psychological analysis, which, with all respect, was guesswork, unsupported by any evidence from the "unconscious" of Nupe individuals. Thus Nadel commits the fallacy against which Turner warns in his discussion of Bettleheim's explanation of the origin of circumcision rites. For in all societies there may well be many men who feel about sexual intercourse as he describes: they do not therefore produce beliefs that women are witches, in any African sense, though they may speak of women as "bewitching." Here again a competent psychological analysis would examine the emotional concomitants of a man's sexual life in a society which believes in female witches, in contrast with the emotional life of men in societies where there is no such belief.

Unlike Kluckhohn, Nadel does analyse beliefs in witchcraft in their relations within the social system, as well as making a psychological interpretation. He specifically states that his varied interpretations refer to "different aspects or elements. . . ." But he gives evidence of how the independence of women traders, and their relative riches and consequent dominance over husband and son, as well as their refusal to have many children, conflict with social norms about women's role *vis-à-vis* men; and he carefully links this evidence with details of witchcraft and anti-witchcraft beliefs and practices. His psychological interpretation, on the other hand, as we have seen, is based on assumptions validated only by the phrases, ". . . *It is, I think, true to say* that man surrenders to woman his virility in the sex-act . . ."; and ". . . If we take this sacrifice to be unconsciously hateful, *as I think we must.* . . ." These are the self-justifying phrases of a man who has moved outside the field of his competence, and is unsure of his evidence and his argument.

---

preceding this argument. See also M. Gluckman, "The Role of the Sexes in Wiko Circumcision Ceremonies, Northern Rhodesia," in *Social Structure: Essays Presented to A. R. Radcliffe-Brown*, ed. M. Fortes [1949], and V. W. Turner, "The Significance of Colour in Ndembu Circumcision Ceremonies," in *Essays on the Ritual of Social Relations*, ed. M. Gluckman, for social-anthropological analyses of sexual antagonism in ritual beliefs. On beliefs in female witches, see Gluckman, *Custom and Conflict in Africa*, pp. 98 f.

SOCIAL ANTHROPOLOGY: CUSTOM AND THE LOGIC
   OF THE IRRATIONAL

When we designed this book, we expected that to define
what is characteristic of social anthropology, we would have to
distinguish it from those branches of anthropology which deal
with variations in culture patterns and in the personalities of
the bearers of these patterns, from the psychology of personality, and finally from studies of small groups by sociologists
like Homans. We have dealt with the relations of social
anthropology with other branches of anthropology and with
personality psychology; and we took the opportunity to consider Freud's methodological position in relation to our
problems, because he provided an example of a man who made
naïve assumptions, and simplified greatly, in fields in which
he had expertise. We are compelled to pass over briefly, for
lack of space, the relations of social anthropology to other types
of "micro-sociology."

According to Firth,[115] social anthropology involves the
"concentrated observation of small-unit behaviour . . .," an
intensive detailed and systematic observation of people in
group-relations, and an attempt to look at all aspects of a
group's life, with a comparative emphasis. All the criteria,
except perhaps the attempt to look at all aspects of a group's
life, apply to the analysis carried out by Homans in *The Human
Group*. Indeed, the groups studied in the essays in our book are
not very different from those he selected for his examples:
Turner's Ndembu are like Firth's Tikopia, Homans considered
a factory "workshop" as did Lupton and Cunnison, and while
Epstein analysed a developing town Homans cited a study of a
declining town. Homans drew not only on Firth's anthropological study of Tikopia, but also on Arensberg and Kimball's
anthropological study of County Clare smallholders. Yet the
kind of analysis which Homans makes of these groups is very
different from the analyses made by anthropologists.

Homans tries to work out a new sociological synthesis of
principles involved in the structure of small groups: ". . . group
behaviour will be analysed into a number of mutually dependent elements. Second, the group will be studied as an organic

[115] Cited above, p. 14.

whole, or social system, surviving in an environment. Third, the relations of the elements to one another in the system will be found to bring about the evolution of the system with the passage of time."[116] The first mutually dependent elements which he considers are: activity, interaction, sentiment; and later he adds others, like norms, values, and rank.

Each of these elements may occur in an anthropological analysis, but the overall weighting is very different. Correspondingly, many of the elements which are present in anthropological analysis, are used by Homans in his work. In studying tribes anthropologists have considered specialised political functionaries, have analysed religious and other beliefs, and have dealt with a number of activities and institutions which do not fall in the scheme of inter-personal relations, and the culture of those relations, which are Homans's central field of analysis. This becomes clear if we examine Homans's analysis of the links of the Irish smallholding family with the external world, of the social disintegration of Hilltown, or of clan relationships in Tikopia. We glance only at the last. Homans[117] states: "Moreover the close association of brothers is the basis for the appearance of larger kinship units, the house and the clan. Our contention is that society is always producing a surplus, so to speak, of interaction, sentiment, and activity, and then finding a use for the surplus." This appears to us to be dangerously close to ignoring the limits of his own naïvety, which Homans recognises in his introductory chapter, for though he uses different terms he clearly has this form of procedure in mind. For a theory of inter-personal relationships within small groups, or between individuals, cannot account for stabilised social institutions which persist for generations. The sum of the parts cannot account for the whole.[118] Later Homans redressed this error (as we would call it) by stressing that "kinship is more widely extended in Tikopia because it is

[116] *The Human Group* [1951], p. 6.
[117] *Op. cit.*, pp. 242 f.
[118] Homans seems to make a few other "slips" of this kind, but in general he is extremely careful to define his procedures of compression and simplification (to put them in our terms): *e.g.*, on the complexity of sentiment in psychological analysis, as against his use of it, see his pp. 38-9, 42, 100, 233 f., 248; and the whole discussion of the Bank Wiring Room within its environment, pp. 86 f., especially at the top of p. 87, and p. 94.

more widely used than it is in our society, where tasks beyond the capacity of the nuclear family are carried out by organisations not based on kinship."[119] That is, he implies that the existence of the Tikopia clan, and in general of Tikopia extended kinship, have to be referred to productive and other types of activities and institutions, and not to the interaction of the elements on which he concentrates. We would prefer to say that the existence of these institutions may involve brothers, when they occupy stabilised position in the clan structure, in activities which reanimate the sentiments of friendship formed in boyhood.

If we compare Homans's system of interdependent variables in inter-personal relationships with the work of social anthropologists, the latter is largely differentiated by its emphasis on custom and institution. We suggest that this is the specific characteristic which social anthropologists derive from their tradition and which distinguishes their investigations and analyses from those of other social and human scientists.[120] Indeed, this is also the traditional interest of anthropologists who analyse patterns of culture and cultural values, and those who analyse variations of personality with culture.

The emphasis on custom is characteristic of all the essays in this book, as of most social anthropology. It shows, for example, in Epstein's treatment of the rise of trade-unionism on the Copperbelt and Watson's study of social mobility, and it illuminates Lupton and Cunnison's analysis of workshop behaviour. This is what differentiates these essays from the work of sociologists, political scientists, and others. The emphasis on custom is even more marked in Turner and Bailey's essays.

In social anthropology the emphasis is on the significance of custom in the relations between persons: hence social anthropology is more closely akin to sociology and political science than it is to psychology or cultural anthropology. Yet social

[119] *Op. cit.*, p. 265.

[120] Gluckman wishes here to acknowledge gratefully how much he has gained from Professor Meyer Fortes's insistence on this point. Fortes makes it pungently in his commentary on S. N. Eisenstadt's "Anthropological Studies of Complex Societies," in *Current Anthropology*, June 1961. Eisenstadt himself does not use the word "custom" but clearly subsumes it under the "norms" which he emphasises are important in the social-anthropological contribution.

anthropologists still treat customs as having some kind of systematic interdependence among themselves, independently of relations between persons; and, in our judgment, it is through insistence on this interdependence that anthropologists make a specific contribution within the social sciences. In their attempt to establish this systematic interdependence of customs, anthropologists have had to demonstrate the "function" of each custom, both in relation to other customs and to the whole of social life. Some of their most striking studies have demonstrated "the logic of the irrational,"[121] as Evans-Pritchard did on witchcraft, Radcliffe-Brown and Malinowski on myth, Malinowski on ritual exchange, Radcliffe-Brown on joking relations, Firth and Fortes on family taboos, Turner on ritual, Gluckman on civil war and conflicts in rules of succession, Colson on gossip and scandal.[122]

How far is this approach of the social anthropologist, evolved in studying small-scale tribal communities, relevant in studying large-scale modern communities? On the whole, when anthropologists began to study modern industrialised societies they sought situations akin—at least in scale—to those of tribal societies. Hence Firth spoke of "micro-sociology." In his essay Bailey suggests that the skill of anthropologists lies in analysing relationships involving many interests, while the skill of political scientists and economists lies in analysing "specialised, or single-interest, relations." When he was following the course of events in his field of study, "as a rule of thumb [he] found [himself] following single-interest relationships to one link

---

[121] Hence perhaps much of the mutual interest of anthropology and psychoanalysis, which shows the logic in the irrational elements of a person's behaviour and belief. Freud saw the analogies between primitive ritual and the behaviour of neurotics, and mistook these analogies for analogues. The surface similarities have to be related to the operation of different types of processes in different systems.

[122] Serially: E. E. Evans-Pritchard, *Witchcraft . . . among the Azande*; A. R. Radcliffe-Brown, *The Andaman Islanders*; B. Malinowski, *Myth in Primitive Psychology* [1926]; Malinowski, *Argonauts of the Western Pacific* [1922]; R. Firth, *We, the Tikopia* [1936]; Radcliffe-Brown in *Structure and Function in Primitive Society*; M. Fortes, *The Web of Kinship among the Tallensi*; V. Turner, *Schism and Continuity*; M. Gluckman, *Order and Rebellion in Tribal Africa*; E. Colson, *The Makah Indians* [1953]. The same emphasis on custom appears in the works of Kroeber, Sapir, Kluckhohn, Linton, Mead, and many other American anthropologists who fall outside our field.

R

only . . ." (above, p. 73).[123] This seems obviously a rule of thumb which, in terms of the development of anthropology through the study of tribal societies, is likely to be a useful guide. Bailey adds that whenever relations with many interests emerge in the midst of specialised relations, the anthropologist will again find a field of study. We suggest that, in addition, anthropology may also make an important contribution to the study of specialised, single-interest relations, through its emphasis on the role, the rationale, and the interdependence of customs.[124]

We agree that social anthropologists would be ignoring the limits imposed by their circumscriptions, and perhaps their naïvety, if they concluded that, because they have developed analyses of "all aspects of a group's life" (Firth) in societies dominated by relationships involving many interests, they can apply their techniques and findings to large-scale segmental societies.[125] Yet their analyses may stimulate an examination of the role of apparently irrational institutions, as well as of

[123] Cp. P. Laslett, "The Face to Face Society," in *Philosophy, Politics and Society,* ed. P. Laslett [1956], for a discussion of the widespread occurrence of these fields of relations in modern society, and his statement (p. 183) that political scientists must learn from social anthropologists, as well as psychologists and sociologists, how to study these fields.

[124] From many examples to illustrate this we cite only: E. Bott on the rôles of spouses in *Family and Social Network* [1957]; C. M. Arensberg and S. T. Kimball on debt in *Family and Community in Ireland* [1940]; R. J. Frankenberg on village recreations in *Village on the Border* [1957]; T. Burns, on embarrassment in "The Reference of Conduct in Small Groups: Cliques and Cabals in Occupational Milieux," in *Human Relations,* VIII, No. 4 [1956], pp. 467-86; E. Goffman on social ceremonials in *The Presentation of the Self in Everyday Society* [1956], and *Encounters* [1951]; T. Lupton on restriction of output in *On the Shop Floor*; and generally Homans, *The Human Group.* We refer also in general terms to the work of cultural anthropologists on national character: details of this work are outside the scope of this book.

[125] Cp. A. S. Bennell in a review (*The Cambridge Review,* 19 Apr. 1958, pp. 459-61) of D. Emmet's *Function, Purpose and Powers* [1957]; "It is a testimony to the quality of this book that it raises the widest questions. One may well question the premise that notions drawn from relatively uncomplicated societies can be applied to the modern society. . . . Are the differences between smaller communities and the giants of our world simply those of scale? Or cannot scale itself bring a difference of kind? There may be parallels between the feuding pattern of the Nuer and the variations in Washington foreign policy, but are these not almost of trivial significance beside the difference in kind symbolised by the megaton bomber?" Radcliffe-Brown did not note this kind of limitation when he spoke of social anthropology as "the theoretical natural science of society. . . . I am quite willing to call the subject 'comparative sociology' . . .": "On Social Structure," in *Structure and Function,* p. 189.

apparent social "breakdowns" in modern life. Little work on these lines has as yet been done in Britain: but we draw attention to the manner in which Devons was stimulated by his reading in anthropology to see a "magic of statistics" in economic analysis and policy.[126] The role of myth and the seemingly irrational, and the power of custom, are of outstanding importance in political life, markedly in England. Here also there is a substantial scope for the expert versed in the concepts of social anthropology. In social and business life too these elements play their part. But here we are only at the beginning of work beyond traditional analysis, which deals mainly in sociological models and in statistical and institutional description. This book is not about the social sciences as a whole, but mainly about social anthropology, and we are merely hinting at, rather than explaining in full, our ideas about the application of social anthropological analysis to modern society.

EPILOGUE

Throughout the introduction and the conclusion we have emphasised the need to simplify, to circumscribe, to be naïve, and so on, in analysis in the social sciences. We have argued that these procedures are necessary, but that out of this necessity comes limitation to the problems and questions that can be answered. This implies caution and modesty in research. Yet we recognise that this is not a prescription to be followed in all circumstances. What we have written should not be interpreted as a set of rules about how to do research. We have tried to clarify the issues rather than provide guides to study.

For the great revolutionary innovator in the social sciences there are no rules. The genius with a new breakthrough in ideas is not likely to pursue his ideas with the passion and enthusiasm needed to shrug off opposition and scepticism from his traditionalist colleagues unless he feels that the new model he has

[126] E. Devons, "Statistics as a Basis for Policy," in *Essays in Economics* [1961], pp. 134 f.; "The Role of the Myth in Politics," in *The Listener*, 21 June [1956]; "Government on the Inner Circle," in *The Listener*, 27 Mar. [1958]. We do not suggest that political scientists have not been aware of these problems and have not studied them fruitfully; but we do suggest that the social-anthropological focus can sharpen our view of them.

R*

evolved is a great new truth. If he were cautious and open-minded at every stage, he would probably never reach his path-breaking innovation. We accept that the model of the genius will not merely be "closed," but that his mind too will be closed by his enthusiasm and excitement. Had Marx, Freud, and Keynes listened at every stage to the caution, hesitation, and doubts, in some cases vilification, of their colleagues working along traditional paths, they would never have arrived at their brilliant new ideas.

Yet this enthusiasm inevitably has its dangerous consequences. A genius convinced that he has at last discovered the truth, previously hidden from the rest of humanity, is tempted to apply that "truth" to aspects of life for which his model is quite inappropriate. Every phenomenon of life comes to be explained by Marxist or Freudian theory. Even more dangerous is the enthusiasm of those who become disciples, spreading the gospel. Some of them are more Marxian than Marx, more Freudian than Freud, more Keynesian than Keynes. And for a time—sometimes unfortunately for a long time—they do not merely lead their subjects into cul-de-sacs, but they also arouse a reaction which brings discredit on the major innovating ideas which were originally so fruitful in their master's work.

We are not arrogant enough to suggest that we know the answer to this difficult issue in the development of the social sciences. But what we have written is for ordinary mortals, not for the revolutionary geniuses. We say of the social and human sciences what Quiller-Couch said of poetry and prose: "They are different realms, but between them lies a debatable land which a De Quincey or a Whitman or a Paul Fort or a Marinetti may attempt. I advise you who are beginners to keep well one side or the other of the frontier, remembering that there is plenty of room and what happened to Tupper."[127] Similarly,

---

[127] In *The Art of Writing*, Guild Books edn. [1946], p. 43, following a discussion of how Burke wrote—or orated—blank verse in his prose. The allusion is presumably to Martin Farquhar Tupper (1810-1889) whose *Proverbial Philosophy* (1838) was taken up by many fairly educated middle-class people with genuine enthusiasm: they thought he eclipsed Solomon. The book was a best-seller. His style with its queer inversions resembles the English of an erudite German, and he was parodied cleverly and criticised savagely: "in due time 'Martin Tupper' became a synonym for contemptible commonplace" (*Dictionary of National Biography* [1899], pp. 318 f.). Although his philosophical writing was regarded as "contemptible commonplace," he was not only a genial fellow, but also a man of

the different social and human sciences may be different realms, in whose borderlands trespass is dangerous save for the genius.

But we do not advise that a writer in prose should not read poetry, or a poet prose: and a social or human scientist may profit by studying disciplines other than his own. It is dangerous to practise them without training and appropriate skills.

---

parts. He was an outstanding radical liberal, who as an inventor was made a Fellow of the Royal Society [1845] and was awarded many British and foreign distinctions.

BIBLIOGRAPHY

ABERLE, D. F. *The Psychological Analysis of a Hopi Life History*. Comparative Psychology Monographs, Berkeley (University of California Press), XXI, 1 (Dec. 1951), Ser. No. 107.

ALLAN, W. *Studies of African Land Usage in Northern Rhodesia*. Rhodes-Livingstone Paper No. 15 (O.U.P., Cape Town) (1949).

—— *The African Husbandman*. Edinburgh 1964.

ARENSBERG, C. *The Irish Countryman*. Cambridge, Mass. 1937.

ARENSBERG, C. M., and S. T. KIMBALL. *Family and Community in Ireland*. Cambridge, Mass. 1940.

BAILEY, F. G. *Caste and the Economic Frontier*. Manchester 1957.

—— *Tribe, Caste and Nation*. Manchester 1960.

BARNETT, A. *The Human Species*. London 1950, and Harmondsworth (Penguin Books) 1957.

BENNELL, A. S. Review in *The Cambridge Review*, 19 Apr., 1958, of D. Emmet (reference below).

BETTELHEIM, B. *Symbolic Wounds: Puberty Rites and the Envious Male*, Glencoe, Illinois 1954.

BIEBUYCK, D., and M. DOUGLAS. *Congo Tribes and Parties*, London (Royal Anthropological Institute) 1961.

BIESHEUWEL, S. "The Abilities of Africans," in *Africa in Transition*, ed. P. Smith. London 1958.

BIRCH, A. M. *Small-Town Politics*, Oxford 1959.

BOTT, E. *Family and Social Network*, London 1957.

BURNS, T. "The Reference of Conduct in Small Groups: Cliques and Cabals in Occupational Milieux," *Human Relations*, VIII (1956), pp. 467-86.

CAMPBELL, N. *What is Science?*, London 1921.

CAPLOW, T. *The Sociology of Work*, Minneapolis 1954.

CARR-SAUNDERS, A. M., and P. A. WILSON. *The Professions*, Oxford 1933.

CARSTAIRS, G. M. *The Twice-Born*. London 1957.

CAUDWELL, C. *Studies in a Dying Culture*. London 1938.

CHESTER, T. E., and G. FORSYTH. "Sociological Aspects of Management Development," a paper presented to the International Congress of Sociology, 1959.

CLEMENTS, R. V. *Managers: A Study of Their Careers in Industry*. London 1958.

COLLINS, O., M. DALTON, and D. ROY. "The Industrial Ratebuster, a Characterisation," *Applied Anthropology* VII (1948), pp. 5-18.

COLSON, E. *The Makah Indians.* Manchester 1953.

COSER, L. A. *The Functions of Social Conflict.* London 1956.

CUNNISON, S. *Wages and Work Allocation.* London 1965.

DEVONS, E. *Essays in Economics.* London 1961.
—— "The Role of the Myth in Politics," in *The Listener*, 21 June, 1960.
—— "Government on the Inner Circle," in *The Listener*, 27 March, 1958.

DEVEREUX, G. *Reality and Dream: Psychotherapy of a Plains Indian.* New York 1951.

DICKS, H. V. "Personality Traits and National Socialist Ideology," in *Human Relations*, III (1950), pp. 111-54.
—— "Observations in Contemporary Russian Behaviour," *Human Relations*, V (1950), pp. 111-75.

DICTIONARY OF NATIONAL BIOGRAPHY, ed. S. Lee, Vol. LVII. London 1899.

DURKHEIM, E. *Les Règles de la méthode sociologique*, 9th edn., Paris 1938. *The Rules of Sociological Method*, tr. S. A. Solovay and J. H. Mueller, Glencoe, Ill., 1938.
—— *Elementary Forms of Religious Life.* London 1954.

EISENSTADT, S. N. "Anthropological Studies of Complex Societies," *Current Anthropology*, June 1961, pp. 201-20.

EMMET, D. *Function, Purpose and Powers.* London 1957.

EPSTEIN, A. L. *Politics in an Urban African Community.* Manchester 1958.

EVANS-PRITCHARD, E. E. *Witchcraft, Oracles and Magic among the Azande of the Anglo-Egyptian Sudan.* Oxford 1937.
—— *Social Anthropology.* London 1951.

FENICHEL, I. *The Psycho-analytic Theory of Neuroses.* London 1946.

FIRTH, R. *We, the Tikopia.* London 1936.
—— *Elements of Social Organization.* London 1951.
—— "The Future of Social Anthropology," *Man*, XLIV, No. 8 (1944).

FLOUD, J. (editor), A. H. HALSEY, and F. M. MARTIN. *Social Class and Educational Opportunity.* London 1956.

FORDE, C. D. (editor). *African Worlds.* London 1954.

FORTES, M. *The Dynamics of Clanship among the Tallensi.* London 1945.
—— *The Web of Kinship among the Tallensi.* London 1949.
—— "Malinowski and the Study of Kinship," in *Man and Culture*, ed. R. Firth. London 1957.
—— Comment on S. N. Eisenstadt, *Current Anthropology*, June 1961.

FRANKENBERG, R. *Village on the Border.* London 1957.

FREUD, S. *Introductory Lectures on Psycho-Analysis* (tr. by J. Riviere). London 1922.
—— *New Introductory Lectures in Psycho-Analysis* (tr. by W. J. H. Sprott). London 1933.

—— *Totem und Tabu.* Vienna (1913). English trs. London 1933.
—— *The Question of Lay Analysis. Works* xx, pp. 183-258. London 1959.
GALES, K. "A Survey of Fellows," in *Journal of the Royal Statistical Society,* Series A, Vol. cxxi, Pt. 4 (1958).
GLASS, D. V. (ed.). *Social Mobility in Britain.* London 1954.
GLUCKMAN, M. *Custom and Conflict in Africa.* Oxford 1955.
—— *Order and Rebellion in Tribal Africa.* London 1963.
—— *Analysis of a Social Situation in Modern Zululand,* Rhodes-Livingstone Paper No. 28, 1958; reprinted from *Bantu Studies,* 1940, and *African Studies,* 1942.
—— *Essays on Lozi Land and Royal Property,* Rhodes-Livingstone Paper No. 10, Livingstone (1943).
—— "The Difficulties, Limitations and Achievements of Social Anthropology," 1 *Rhodes-Livingstone Journal,* (1944), pp. 22-48.
—— "The Logic of African Science and Witchcraft," *Rhodes-Livingstone Journal,* 1 (1944).
—— "The Role of the Sexes in Wiko Circumsion Ritual" in *Social Structure: Essays Presented to A. R. Radcliffe-Brown* (1949] ed. M. Fortes.
—— "Social Beliefs and Individual Thinking in Primitive Society," *Transactions of the Manchester Literary and Philosophical Society,* xvi (1949-50).
—— *The Sociological Theories of Bronislaw Malinowski.* Rhodes-Livingstone Paper No. 16 (1948); reprinted in *Order and Rebellion in Tribal Africa;* originally from *Africa* and *African Studies.*
—— *Rituals of Rebellion in South-East Africa.* Manchester 1954; reprinted in *Order and Rebellion in Tribal Africa.*
—— "Tribalism in Modern British Central Africa." *Cahiers d'etudes africaines* (1960).
—— "Anthropological Problems arising from the African Industrial Revolution," in Southall, A. S., *Social Change in Africa,* London 1961.
—— "Town and Tribe," *Nation,* Sydney, Australia: No. 53, 1960.
—— (editor). *Essays on the Ritual of Social Relations,* Manchester 1962.
GOFFMAN, E. *The Presentation of the Self in Everyday Society.* Edinburgh 1956· New York 1959.
—— *Encounters,* Indianapolis 1961.
GOLDSCHMIDT, W. "Social Class in America," *American Anthropologist,* New York 1951.
GOULDNER, A. W. *Patterns of Industrial Bureaucracy.* London 1955.
HALL, C. S., and G. LINDZEY. *Theories of Personality.* London 1957.
HALL, J., and D. C. JONES. "Social Grading of Occupations," *British Journal of Sociology,* i, No. 1 (1950).
HARBISON, F. H., and E. W. BURGESS. "Modern Management in Western Europe," *American Journal of Sociology,* lx, No. 1 (1954).
HEYWORTH, LORD. "The Managers," in *Progress,* London 1956.
HOMANS, G. C. *The Human Group.* New York 1950; London 1951.

266   *Bibliography*

HYDE, D. R., and P. WOLFF, with A. GROSS and E. L. HOFFMAN. "The American Medical Association: Power, Purpose and Politics in Organised Medicine," *Yale Law Journal*, LXIII, No. 7 (1954).

JONES, E. *Sigmund Freud: Life and Works*. Vol. I, "The Young Freud 1856-1900 ; Vol. II, "Years of Maturity 1901-1919"; Vol. III, "The Last Phase 1919-1939", London 1953, 1955, 1957.

—— "Mother-right and the Sexual Ignorance of Savages," *International Journal of Psycho-analysis*, vi, No. 2 (1925).

JUNG, C. *Psychological Types*. London 1949.

KLINEBERG, O. *Race Differences*. New York 1935.

—— *Race and Psychology*, in "The Race Question in Modern Science" series, Paris 1951.

—— (ed.) *Characteristics of the American Negro*. Carnegie Corporation of New York, Vol. IV, New York 1944.

KLUCKHOHN, C. *Navaho Witchcraft*. Papers of the Peabody Museum of American Archaeology and Ethnology, Harvard University. XXII, No. 2 (1944).

KLUCKHOHN, C., and H. A. MURRAY. *Personality in Nature, Society and Culture*. London 1949.

KRIGE, E. J. and J. D. *The Realm of a Rain-Queen: The Pattern of Lovedu Society*. London 1943.

LASLETT, P. "The Face to Face Society," in *Philosophy, Politics and Society*, ed. P. Laslett. Oxford 1956.

LEACH, E. R. "Concerning Trobriand Clans and the Kinship Category *Tabu*," in *The Developmental Cycle of Domestic Groups*, ed. J. Goody. Cambridge Papers in Social Anthropology, No. 1 (1958).

LEWIN, K. *Field Theory in Social Science*. London 1952.

LEWIS, R, and A. MAUDE. *Professional People*. London 1952.

LEWIS, W. A. *The Theory of Economic Growth*. London 1955.

LUPTON, T. *On the Shop Floor*. Oxford 1962.

LYDALL, K. "The Life Cycle in Income, Saving and Asset Ownership," *Econometrica*, XXIII, No. 2 (1955).

LYND, R. S. and H. *Middletown*. New York 1929.

MALINOWSKI, B. *Argonauts of the Western Pacific*. London 1922.

—— *Myth in Primitive Psychology*, Psyche Miniatures. London 1926; reprinted in *Magic, Science and Religion*, Glencoe, Ill. 1948.

—— *The Father in Primitive Psychology*, Psyche Miniatures. London 1927.

—— *Sex and Repression in Savage Society*. London 1927.

—— *The Sexual Life of Savages*. London 1929.

MARRIOTT, M. (editor). *Village India*. Chicago 1955.

MARSH, D. C. *The Changing Structure of England and Wales*. London 1958.

MARWICK, M. G. "The Social Context of Cewa Witch Beliefs," in *Africa*, XXII (1952).

MAYER, P. *Witchcraft*, Inaugual Lecture to the Rhodes University, Grahamstown, South Africa (1954).

—— *Townsmen or Tribesmen.* Cape Town 1961.

MEAD, M. *Coming-of-Age in Samoa.* New York 1928.

—— *Growing-Up in New Guinea.* New York 1940.

—— *Sex and Temperament in Three Primitive Societies.* New York 1938.

—— *Male and Female.* New York 1949.

—— "Our Educational Emphasis in Primitive Perspective," in *American Journal of Sociology*, XLVIII (1945).

MERTON, R. K. *Social Theory and Social Structure.* Glencoe, Ill. 1949; new edn. 1957.

MIDDLETON, J. *Lugbara Religion.* London 1960.

MILLS, C. WRIGHT. *The Power Elite.* London 1957.

MITCHELL, J. *The Yao Village.* Manchester 1956.

—— *Tribalism and the Plural Society.* London 1960.

MURRAY, H. A., and others. *Explorations in Personality.* New York 1938.

MYRDAL, G. *An American Dilemma.* New York 1944.

NADEL, S. F. *The Foundations of Social Anthropology.* London 1951.

—— *Nupe Religion.* London 1954.

—— "Witchcraft in Four African Societies: An Essay in Comparison," in *American Anthropologist*, LIV (1952), pp. 18-79.

NEUSTETTER, M. "Demographic and other Statistical Aspects of Anglo-Jewry," in *A Minority in Britain: Social Studies of the Anglo-Jewish Community.* ed. M. Freedman, London 1955.

NUNBERG, H. *Problems of Bisexuality as Reflected in Circumcision.* London 1959.

OSBORN, R. *Freud and Marx.* London 1937.

PARSONS, T. *The Social System.* London 1952.

—— "Malinowski and the Theory of Social Systems," in *Man and Culture*, ed. R. Firth, London 1957.

PETERS, D. U. *Land Usage in Barotseland.* Rhodes-Livingstone Communication No. 19, 1960.

POLANYI, M. *Personal Knowledge.* London 1958.

POWDERMAKER, H. Unpublished report presented to the Rhodes-Livingstone Institute by the author (later published as *Copper Town*, New York 1962).

QUILLER-COUCH, A. *The Art of Writing.* Cambridge 1916.

RADCLIFFE-BROWN, A. R. *The Andaman Islanders.* Cambridge 1922.

—— *Structure and Function in Primitive Society*, London 1952.

—— *A Natural Science of Society*, Glencoe, Ill. 1957.

REDFIELD, R. *Peasant Society and Culture*, Chicago 1956.

REGISTRAR-GENERAL. *Report on Greater London and Five Other Conurbations, Census* 1951. London.

—— *Census* 1951 (*England and Wales*): *Occupation Tables.* London.

RICHARDS, A. I. *Land, Labour and Diet in Northern Rhodesia*. London 1939.

RIVERS, W. H. R. "Freud's Concept of the 'Censorship'," *The Psychoanalytic Review*, VII, No. 3 (July 1920): reprinted in *Psychology and Ethnology*. London 1926.

SACHS, W. *Black Anger*. Boston 1947; originally *Black Hamlet*. London 1937.

SCHNEIDER, D. M., and K. GOUGH (editors). *Matrilineal Kinship*. London: Berkeley and Los Angeles 1961.

SIMMEL, G. *Conflict and the Web of Group Affiliations*, tr. by K. H. Wolff and R. Bendix, Glencoe, Ill. 1955.

STEED, G. P. "Personality Formation in a Hindu Village in Gujerat," in *Village India*, ed. M. Marriott. Chicago 1955.

THOMAS, G. *Labour Mobility in Great Britain 1945-1949*. Government Social Survey. London 1950.

TRAPNELL, C. G. *The Soils, Vegetation and Agricultural Systems of North Eastern Rhodesia*. Lusaka 1943.

TRAPNELL, C. G., and J. N. CLOTHIER. *The Soils, Vegetation and Agricultural Systems of North Western Rhodesia*. Lusaka 1938.

TURNER, V. W. *Schism and Continuity in an African Society: A Study of Ndembu Village Life*. Manchester 1957.

—— "The Significance of Colour in Ndembu Circumcision Ceremonies," in *Essays on the Ritual of Social Relations*, ed. M. Gluckman. Manchester 1962.

UBEROI, J. P. SINGH. *Politics of the Kula Ring*. Manchester 1962.

WARNER, W. LLOYD, and J. O. LOW. *The Social System of the Modern Factory*. New Haven 1947.

WATSON, W. *Tribal Cohesion in a Money Economy*. Manchester 1958.

WILSON, G. *The Land Rights of Individuals among the Nyakyusa*. Rhodes-Livingstone Paper, No. 1 (1938).

—— *An Essay on the Economics of Detribalisation in Northern Rhodesia*. Rhodes-Livingstone Papers, No. 5 (1941) and No. 6 (1942).

WILSON, G. and M. *The Analysis of Social Change*. Cambridge 1945.

WILSON, M. *Rituals of Kinship among the Nyakyusa*. London 1957.

—— *Communal Rituals of the Nyakyusa*. London 1959.

—— "Witch Beliefs and Social Structure," *American Journal of Sociology*, LXI (1957).

INDEX

Abridgment: 173; and Cunnison, 183; and incorporation, 184-5; and Lupton, 183; and Nadel, 183; and race differences, 177 f.; and Richards, 184; of other scientists' work, 164; incorrect, 191; legitimate use (Turner), 176; limits of, 175.
"Abstention", duty of: 168.
Academics, as professionals: 146-7.
Adibasis: 66, 69, 78, 191.
Administration, Indian: 55-6, 57, 66, 70, 71, 73.
African Mine Workers Trade Union: 90-92; cleavages within, 96; leadership in, 94.
African Personnel Manager (Mines): 89, 91.
African Salaried Staff Association: 97-8.
Allan, W.: 164 n. 8; 184 n. 35.
Allocation of work: and informal groups, 110 f.; and labour mobility, 113; and quality of cloth, 110; machining and assembling, 107; managerial policy, 112.
Ambedkar, Dr.: 70, 76, 81; and the Congress Party, 191.
Anthropology: and economics, 203, 206; and emotions, 244; and history, 201; and micro-sociology, 254 f.; and modern societies, 258; and psychoanalysis, 257 n. 121; and race differences, 180 f.; and small-scale societies, 130; specific characteristic of, 256; subject-matter of, 158 f.
Anthropologist, circumscription of field of research: 162 f.
Azande: 244 f.

Baderi: 55-6, 62.
Bailey, F. G.: 53, 173, 187; and circumscription, 188 f.; and external variables, 187-8; separation of "in-

corporation and abridgment," 175; warranted incorporation, 169-70.
Bargaining, and joint action: 118.
Bemba: 184.
Bettelheim, B.: 36, 38, 213, 214, 232.
Biesheuvel, S., on race differences: 178-9.
Birch, A. H.: 134, 153.
Bisipara: 53-5, 62.
Brahmin: 53, 194.
Burgess, E. W.: 148.
Burgh, the: and coalminers, 136 f.; decline of fishing, 137.

Campbell, N.: 159 n. 3.
Carr-Saunders, A. M.: 146.
Caste: councils, 75; system, 64.
Circumscription: 185; Bailey, 188 f.; Epstein, 196 f.; external factors, 199, 202 f.; Hindu culture, 189 f.; limits of, 195; Lupton and Cunnison, 201; Watson, 209 f.
Civil service: 131.
Classes, in industrial societies: 210.
Clemens, R. V.: 146.
Coalminers: in the Burgh, 136 f.; and social class, 139, 141.
Collins, O.: 126.
"Community studies": 84.
Competition: effect on workers, 117; in engineering and garment industries, 123.
Compound, Mine: 86-8, 90, 95.
Compression: and Nadel, 184; technique of incorporation and abridgment, 165.
Conflict, situations of: 250 f.
Congress Party (India): 67, 77.
Costs of labour and product: 123.
Courts: 66.
Criticism, unjustified allegation of naïvety: 168.
Culture: 57-62.